Out of Order
The political imprisonment of women in Northern Ireland, 1972–98

Mary S. Corcoran

WILLA
PUBLISHI

Published by

Willan Publishing
Culmcott House
Mill Street, Uffculme
Cullompton, Devon
EX15 3AT, UK
Tel: +44(0)1884 840337
Fax: +44(0)1884 840251
e-mail: info@willanpublishing.co.uk
website: www.willanpublishing.co.uk

Published simultaneously in the USA and Canada by

Willan Publishing
c/o ISBS, 920 NE 58th Ave, Suite 300,
Portland, Oregon 97213-3786, USA
Tel: +001(0)503 287 3093
Fax: +001(0)503 280 8832
e-mail: info@isbs.com
website: www.isbs.com

First published 2006

Paperback
ISBN-13: 979-1-84392-162-2
ISBN-10: 1-84392-162-6

Hardback
ISBN-13: 979-1-84392-163-9
ISBN-10: 1-84392-163-4

British Library Cataloguing-in-Publication Data

A catalogue record for this book is available from the British Library

Project managed by Deer Park Productions, Tavistock, Devon
Typeset by GCS, Leighton Buzzard, Beds.
Printed and bound by T.J. International Ltd, Trecerus Industrial Estate, Padstow, Cornwall

Contents

List of figures and tables

Figures

Table

Dedicated to my parents: Mary Corcoran and the memory of Martin Patrick 'M.P.' Corcoran

List of organizations

ALJ	Association for Legal Justice
CAJ	Committee on the Administration of Justice
ICC	Irish Council of Churches
ICJP	Irish Commission for Justice and Peace
IIP	Irish Information Partnership
INLA	Irish National Liberation Army
NCCL	National Council for Civil Liberties
NIACRO	Northern Ireland Association for the Care and Resettlement of Offenders
NICRA	Northern Ireland Civil Rights Association
NIO	Northern Ireland Office
NIPS	Northern Ireland Prison Service
OIRA	Official Irish Republican Army
PIRA	Provisional Irish Republican Army
POA	Prison Officers' Association
RUC	Royal Ulster Constabulary
SACHRE	Standing Advisory Commission on Human Rights
SF	Sinn Féin
UDA	Ulster Defence Association
UFF	Ulster Freedom Fighters
UVF	Ulster Volunteer Force

Acknowledgements

This book could not have been completed without the generosity of others. My thanks to Liverpool John Moores University, for the teaching assistantship that helped me to do my PhD. Thanks to my former colleagues Nickianne Moody, Nicole Matthews and Jonathan Purkis. To Joe Sim for 'leaving a stain upon the silence'. I am also indebted to the following: Tim Ashplant, Mike Tomlinson, Bernie Hayes, Paddy Hillyard, Anne Worrall, Jo Phoenix, Yvonne Murphy and Kieran Crossey at the Linenhall Library, Belfast, Lin Quilty, and D.A. Tidy for her resigned good humour throughout this project.

I am indebted to the organizations which support prisoners and their families: Coiste na n-Íarchimi, the Ex-Prisoners Interpretative Centre, the Prisoner's Aid and Post-conflict Resettlement Group, the staff at the Prison Visitors' Centre at Maghaberry, Sinn Féin Prisoner of War Department, the Northern Ireland Association for the Care and Resettlement of Offenders and Tar Anall.

Many participants must remain unnamed. I extend my appreciation to the staff who co-operated with this research, to the Prison Officers' Association, the Northern Ireland Prison Service, the prison chaplains, members of the religious and voluntary organizations who support prisoners and their families, the Northern Ireland Association of Members of the Board of Governors.

I am also abidingly grateful to the former prisoners who gave me so much of their time and insights. It is hoped that this effort is an adequate witness to their experiences.

Keele University, October 2005

Introduction

Although one in twenty prisoners detained during the 'Troubles' in Northern Ireland was a woman, the nature of the regimes in which they were confined has been barely addressed in the academic literature. Despite the centrality of events in the prisons to the momentum of disorder and violence at different junctures of the conflict, most accounts have focused on the experiences of men prisoners. With few exceptions, the analysis of political imprisonment in Northern Ireland has rarely impinged on the other systematic influences that sustained it, notably the gendered organization of punishment in prison. As a consequence, the roles and experiences of women political prisoners in Armagh, and later Maghaberry, prisons have been cast as being of incidental or separate significance to the general development of political imprisonment in Northern Ireland.

This absence of women as political actors in the prisons has directly and indirectly shaped the concerns of this book. Directly, in that it addresses the 'historical' deficit in accounting for women's role in the campaign of resistance by prisoners in Northern Ireland from the internment of women in 1972 to the release of the last female prisoner under the terms of the Belfast Agreement in November 1998. Indirectly, in that women's political imprisonment was a site of converging relationships between political, penal and gendered ideologies and controls, which took the question of their resistance beyond being solely a matter of contesting the State's right to punish.

Situating women in the Northern Ireland prison campaign

Therefore, there are three separate dimensions to my task: accounting for women as political prisoners; accounting for political prisoners as women in prison; and accounting for the gendered and political dimensions of prison punishment. The first task addresses the problem whereby women were subsumed under prevailing definitions of 'political imprisonment'. The conventional analysis of political imprisonment centres on the development of specialized areas of criminal law, jurisprudence or prison administration for dealing with politically related crime. The central questions that arise from a wide variety of intellectual sources relate to the problems of reconciling the actuality of political detention with constitutional norms, or the pursuit by governments of legitimate courses of action in the face of illegal or self-authorized claims to political- or prisoner-of-war status by individuals and groups. At the same time, as Carol Smart (1992) reminds us, the law is a master discourse, concerned with establishing authoritative rulings and operating within a universalizing explanatory framework. It does not provide us with a socially differentiated explanation of the implications and practices of political detention. As this book outlines, this has significant and often negative implications for the treatment of detained women.

In one sense, the women's campaign of resistance reflected many of the defining elements of political dissent in prisons more generally, namely, an ideological opposition to the legitimacy and authority of the State, and a view of confinement as a form of political injustice. These views, in turn, supported the perception of imprisonment as the continuation of a larger struggle beyond the prison walls, and a subjective separateness from the imperatives of prison discipline within them. In this broader context, the common characteristics of prison resistance by men and women centred on their refusal to be designated as 'criminals' and, by extension, to conform to 'ordinary' prison discipline.

But whereas the previous questions have centred on a generalized, indeed dominant, understanding of political imprisonment as a set of circumstances in which women *may* be situated or which *might* allow women to be legitimized, or legitimize themselves, as equals, this study has also engaged with the ambiguities that this scenario suggests. My examination needed to take the terms of analysis beyond straightforwardly restorative concerns – that is, with reinstating women in existing definitions of the 'prison struggle' – to more fundamental questions about 'women in prison' and 'political imprisonment' as less than conclusive, taken-for-granted categories. That women's roles are contingent to dominant definitions of political struggle is not a new discovery (Elshtain 1995). At the same time, the very ambiguity of women within the terms of 'the political' summons up the argument, made frequently but not only by post-structural and feminist theorists, that institutionalized definitions of the political obscure the normative conditions of their own making. The first problem, then, is the manner in which 'political imprisonment', as a general category, is sustained by its own definitional norms and, by implication, that women political prisoners challenge them as fundamental forms of exclusion and domination.

The construction of female political prisoners: 'difficult' and 'dangerous' women

Nevertheless, in turning from the issue of 'women as political prisoners' to that of 'political prisoners as women' an equally vexatious set of questions arises. Women political prisoners are problematic within prevailing definitions of women in prison, especially with regards to the unresolved question as to whether they are ultimately treated according to their gender or their security status. Furthermore, they are viewed as presenting a particular set of challenges to prison order and discipline, especially where they have resisted being integrated into the economies of dependency and pastoral power which are embedded in prison regimes for women (Churchill and Vander Wall 1992: 388–99; Ward 1993; Anderson and O'Dwyer 1997). More broadly, the marginality of women in political and penal discourse has been paralleled by their conspicuousness as symbol bearers of 'revolution' and subversion. They have been fetishized as uniquely transgressive, as iconic radicals, and signifiers of the breakdown of the gendered and social order. Their treatment as an exceptional minority within the women's prison population demonstrates the limitations of the administrative imagination and the pernicious influence of the mythology of the 'female grotesque' in criminological discourse.

In this context, feminist penology supports the argument that political prisoners *as women* are framed by a double jeopardy in which their lawbreaking renders them 'doubly deviant and doubly damned' (Lloyd 1995) and ensnares them in a punitive bind as both high-risk and non-compliant prisoners. This predicament is captured in the title of the book. 'Out of order' is meant to convey the resilience and tactical versatility of women political prisoners' resistance to various aspects of prison rule over 26 years. However, 'out of order' also connotes the fact that they disrupted the very categories that were used to describe them – as 'offending women', as 'women in prison' and as 'political prisoners'. To borrow Carlen's (1983) phrase, they were both 'within and outwith' these descriptions. The book, therefore, traces how the control of women prisoners was shaped by the more general correctional concern with feminine 'disorder' compounded by the justifications that, as political prisoners, their 'dangerousness' positioned them as a special case. At the same time, it is not claimed that 'women as political prisoners' and 'political prisoners as women' are mutually exclusive or essentialist categories – as both conditions apply. Instead, the semantic differences in emphasis between them inform the difficulties in analysing the punishment of political women.

Resisting the gendered and political dimensions of prison punishment

The question of resistance and its relationships to broader sociological questions about prison power, political struggle and gendered subordination forms the third theme of the book. These factors established the conditions within which women political prisoners in Northern Ireland emerged as subjects of prison punishment and as resisters to it. As the correction of gender transgression and the punishment of political dissent have conventionally implied different penal objectives, I am also concerned with the circumstances which brought them together. The development of an apparatus of political imprisonment for women was rooted in the historical circumstances of the conflict, the nature of the political emergency and responses to women's political activism and violence. However, another set of conditions is relevant to analysing the punishment and resistance of political women; these are the ideological and institutional developments which ensured that the goals of containment and deterrence, which are characteristic of political imprisonment, were reinforced by a highly normative ethos of gender regulation and discipline.

Finally, if I am pointing to the dangers of laying claim to the unity of experience of political imprisonment, then I must acknowledge the differences amongst women from the opposing Loyalist and Republican factions. Republican women were the most dominant presence in prison, both statistically and in terms of political exposure. At first sight, the relatively defensive and introspective organizational style of Loyalist women appeared to confirm a 'weaker' capacity for resistance when compared to Republican women. The explanations lie in complex, external influences as well as institutional ones, and include their significantly smaller numbers both as combatants and prisoners, and their organizational marginality relative to their male peers. In addition, their 'secondariness' was intrinsically connected to the different attitudes of Loyalists to the State, and sociocultural restrictions on Loyalist women's role in the political domain. These factors contributed, in turn, to their reluctance to participate in interviews for this study (for more details refer to Appendix I). Finally, whilst I was conscious that some work with women former prisoners was being conducted by Loyalist organizations, this material has yet to appear in the public domain. Consequently, in seeking to shed some light on this most neglected aspect of women's and political imprisonment, it has also revealed the dearth of information on the prison experiences of Loyalist women.

Chapter 1

Violence, laws and commissions: preparing for the detention of women

On 29 December 1972, Elizabeth McKee, aged 19, was arrested during a house raid in Belfast on suspicion of having helped a male Provisional IRA Volunteer to escape from Lagan Valley hospital the previous week (*Irish Times* 2 January 1973). McKee was taken for interrogation to the joint policy and army holding centre at Castlereagh, along with twelve men and two other women. This first incidence of the detention of women occurred 17 months after the mass arrest and internment of 354 men in response to widespread civil disorder and the escalation of Republican and Loyalist paramilitary violence. The decision to introduce internment had been taken by the Northern Ireland Prime Minister, Brian Faulkner, with the less than wholehearted support of the British Army's senior military advisers in Northern Ireland (Lee 1993: 437). Amongst the tactical dividends that internment was meant to yield were the opportunity for the army to loosen the hold that the Provisional IRA was gaining in the Catholic working-class ghettoes, exploit the element of surprise in capturing its leadership and detain low-level suspects for intelligence-gathering purposes (Kennally and Preston 1971: 122).[1]

But if the gamble that was taken at the most senior military and political levels held out the prospect for making marginal gains, these were quickly dissipated by the subsequent activities of the army on the ground. The sweep of 9 August 1971 failed to capture the PIRA leadership, who had been forewarned by the preparatory activities of the army (MacStiofáin 1975: 169–77; Adams 1996: 188). Fewer than 60 detainees were found to have had any involvement in illegal organizations. These failures led both moderates and militants to the conclusion that internment was, in the words of one historian, a 'colossal blunder' (Lee 1993: 437), and according to Seán MacStiofáin, then PIRA Chief of Staff, 'enormously strengthened the very base [of Nationalist support] it was meant to weaken' (1975: 192). During the following six months, thousands of young men and women were caught up in a revolving door of arrest, interrogation and release (Spjut 1986: 715–16). The overwhelming majority of internees in the first three months of detention was accounted for by civil rights and community activists, students and demonstrators, most of whom ended up perceiving themselves as victims of State coercion rather than lawbreakers or deviants.

Moreover, subsequent reports of beatings, ill-treatment and torture from those who had been detained prompted an investigation into army behaviour by the Compton Committee (1971). Compton acknowledged that 'tough interrogation techniques' had been used, but the committee 'reached the thoroughly unconvincing conclusion that while many of the techniques that had been used on detainees constituted physical ill-treatment, they did not amount to brutality' (Hillyard 1978: 130). The use of 'in-depth' interrogation techniques was reconsidered by the Parker Committee (1972). The majority of that body concluded that the techniques may have been unlawful, but they were justified by the need to obtain sufficient intelligence to combat terrorism. Compton and Parker thus retrospectively sanctioned extra-judicial detention and mistreatment on the grounds of security and the need to restore the rule of law expeditiously.

The response from the streets in Catholic areas to internment and the Compton Committee was 'united and violent' (Hillyard 1978: 131), instigating demonstrations and civil disobedience campaigns. Hostilities were propelled into further violence after the events of 'Bloody Sunday', when soldiers shot dead 13 Catholic men in Derry on 30 January 1972. The subsequent toll of civilian casualties soared as the IRA turned on commercial and civil targets for its bombing campaigns. Reactive Loyalist violence against known Republicans and Catholic civilians also soared (ibid.: 130). In March 1972, the British government prorogued (discontinued) the Parliament for Northern Ireland and transferred the powers of government to Westminster, after Faulkner's cabinet refused to concede direct control for security and law and order to it (Lee 1993: 441).

Internment describes the actions of the Executive in detaining those against whom there is insufficient evidence to support a criminal charge, but who are suspected of having subversive beliefs or intentions, or allegedly aid, advocate or engage in political violence. It is distinguishable from the regular process of pre-trial detention where the suspect must be charged and brought before a court. Internment in Northern Ireland, later called 'detention without trial', was 'an extra judicial form … its essence [was] incarceration without trial or charge' (Lowry 1976: 169). A form of detention that circumvents the normal judicial process during periods of war or political emergency is also constitutionally permissible. Constitutionalists hold, however, that this should be an exceptional and temporary measure subject to rigorous legal scrutiny and review to avoid the arbitrary violation of civil liberties.

On assuming Direct Rule, the British government, now governing Northern Ireland through the Secretary of State for Northern Ireland, determined to introduce some safeguards to the internment system but also to retain powers to detain on 'security grounds' (Spjut 1986: 716). Internment was not phased out until 1976 in order to minimize the risk that released detainees would 'return' to paramilitary activity. Meanwhile, Westminster adopted a gradualist approach to replacing the blunt instrument of internment with a quasi-constitutional form of detention, which was administered through the euphemistically titled system of 'internment on remand'. Under the Detention of Terrorists (Northern Ireland) Order 1972, the Secretary of State was empowered to make an interim custody order, which allowed for the detention for 28 days of a person who was suspected of activities in pursuit of 'the purposes of terrorism', but this could be extended indefinitely on the recommendations of the Chief Constable of the Royal Ulster Constabulary (Hogan and Walker 1989: 86). These were the 'reformed' powers of detention under which Elizabeth McKee was detained. As an additional safeguard, an advisory commission was appointed to hear representations from internees (McGuffin 1973: 135–6). The new commission was limited to an advisory role, which meant that it could recommend, but not authorize, releases. Moreover, just as it lacked substantial powers, it also lacked robust judicial safeguards. Detainees had limited rights of counsel, as lawyers were only allowed to help 'respondents' to prepare written submissions, but they could not attend hearings (ibid.: 133). The hearings admitted less stringent standards of evidence than in the criminal law, being satisfied with 'a high degree of probability' as grounds for continued detention rather than requiring proof 'beyond reasonable doubt'. Prosecution evidence was submitted anonymously, and 'respondents' were often excluded from all or part of their hearings (Hogan and Walker 1989: 86–7). There were very few successful appeals against detention orders (Lowry 1976: 185).

The longer-term administration of detention was addressed in the Emergency Provisions Act (Northern Ireland) 1973, which adopted the recommendations of the Diplock Commission of the previous year. The Diplock Commission had been set up to consider 'arrangements for the administration of justice in Northern Ireland … in order to deal more effectively with terrorist organizations … otherwise than by internment by the Executive' (Diplock cited in Hogan and Walker 1989: 28). In effect, the scope of the powers embodied in the Act meant that 'terrorism' became a highly inclusive and elastic legal category which incorporated:

> the use of violence for political ends and includes any use of violence for the purpose of putting the public or any section of the public in fear; [A] 'terrorist' means a person who is or has been concerned in the commission or attempted commission of any act of terrorism or in directing, organising or training persons for the purposes of terrorism (Emergency Provisions Act (Amended) 1978, in s. 31(1) *ibid*.: 3).

Yet the very vagueness of some of these provisions, enacted to deal with the most serious violent and subversive offences, had implications for encompassing a wider range of activities within its remit. First, it converted many 'criminal' activities into 'scheduled' (terrorist) offences *per se*, but it also allowed prosecutors to 'promote' criminal charges into scheduled ones to facilitate a less convoluted passage through the judicial process (*ibid*.: 102). Secondly, it gave wider scope to the army and police to arrest and detain individuals, because the essence of the law was that the context of an arrest could be used to determine whether an offence was scheduled or not. Thus, individuals could be arrested and charged for relatively minor offences such as rioting as if for a scheduled offence, especially if they were also charged with offences such as those against the person or property or the use of petrol bombs. Throughout the 1970s and 1980s, the Act was frequently amended and extended 'to secure more convictions … long-standing and cherished safeguards for the defendants were being jettisoned as inconvenient niceties' (*ibid*.: 109). The Act also incorporated the recommendations of the Diplock Commission by establishing juryless courts, presided over by a single judge, for hearing scheduled cases.

Confessions were the principal evidence in approximately four fifths of 'Diplock' cases, and this promoted a high rate of self-incrimination and ensured greater rates of conviction (Walsh 1983: 72–8; Hogan and Walker 1989: 115).

Operation Petticoat: gendering the custodial strategy

In many senses, the detention of Elizabeth McKee, and the other 30 women who were interned between 1972 and 1975, was predictable (*Annual Report of the Northern Ireland Prison Service* (hereafter referred to as NIPS), 1977). As far as the military authorities were concerned, the newly reformed and legislatively affirmed basis of detention was a vital support for their renewed phase of counter-insurgency. This was supposed to accomplish the surgical penetration of Nationalist communities and to cut the PIRA off from its support base, whilst avoiding a repetition of previous mistakes (Kitson 1977: 296). The 'strategic detention' of women was thus initiated in order to neutralize the women's section of the PIRA, Cumann na mBan (The Women's Society), both as a reserve paramilitary force and as a supply and support network (*Telegraph* 1 February 1972). Secondly, McKee's arrest (her two female companions were interned six weeks later) was a part of a wider stratagem of thwarting the PIRA's practice of introducing 'lilywhites', or new recruits who were not as yet known to the authorities, into the field (Evelegh 1978: 62). The army command subsequently pursued a strategy of general surveillance and intelligence-gathering for the purpose of apprehending younger women involved with suspect organizations even if they were not proscribed, and as a deterrence against their future recruitment by mainstream paramilitary groups. Thirdly, the detention of women and juveniles was defended in wholly unconvincing, paternalistic terms as a necessary course of action for protecting them from the noxious influences of paramilitarism (*Irish Independent* 3 January 1973; *Belfast Telegraph* 13 September 1973). Indeed, the dangerousness of these unknowns was deemed to be confirmed by the fact that they had previously *escaped* the attention of military intelligence. In order to sustain the consistency of this position, a retrospective paramilitary 'career' was constructed for these detainees; hence, McKee was claimed to be 'a high-ranking officer of the Provisional Army' (*Irish News* 2 January 1973).

However, the belief that the PIRA was unleashing reserve divisions of operatives was not without some foundation. The significant rise in the arrests and detention of women from 1968 was directly related to mass civil disobedience and rising political violence. Initially, at least, the mobilization of Catholic women had taken the form of 'defensive' activism which was most closely associated with exercising control over their homes, streets and communities, protecting them in the process against the incursions of Loyalists determined to 'sack' their neighbourhoods, and later, against army and police squads on their way to arresting suspects. In an important sense, the visibility of women in Resistance Councils and the Women's Action Committees merged the private and personal concerns of the domestic realm with those of the public and political domain. These early expressions of 'civilian' radicalization were formative in the emergence of prisoners' relatives as a political force in organizations such as the Relatives Action Committees from 1976 and their successors, the National H-Block/Armagh Committees in 1980 and 1981.

After the initial phase of resistance on the streets, women's participation began to take various but interconnected, directions: through direct involvement in paramilitary combat, through support for PIRA 'operations' and through more general political agitation. Cumann na mBan was the women's auxiliary section of the PIRA, with a formally equivalent and separate status, but in practice was a largely domesticated and subordinated element within the Republican structure (Buckley and Lonergan 1984). After internment, some women chose a more directly military role by joining Óglaigh na h-Éireann (Irish Volunteers), which provided the substantial membership of the PIRA's active service units (ASUs). This transition in the role of women from ancillary supporters to active combatants followed the PIRA strategy of attracting recruits of a sufficient calibre to sustain a disciplined and effective paramilitary campaign, and later, of weeding out 'informers … the hot-headed, disloyal or [those] prone to break under interrogation' who had been admitted in the first intake after internment (Urban 1992: 32–3). Seán MacStiofáin (1975: 217) had broken with previous Republican orthodoxies on women's roles on the basis that British military strategists had 'failed to appreciate' the contribution of women in other colonial struggles 'because they came from societies in which women's contributions are usually underrated'. In the early 1970s:

> a selected number of suitable women were taken into the IRA and trained … on the basis of full equality with men … Some of the best shots I ever knew were women. So were the smartest intelligence officers in Belfast … [I]n support roles, the Women's Action Committees were very effective organizers of demonstrations, early warning networks, and … alarms' (*ibid.*: 218).

This was the background for the involvement of women Volunteers in robberies, the planting and detonation of roadside mines and car bombs, kidnappings and assassinations. The majority, however, remained attached to ASUs as auxiliaries involved in transporting and concealing arms and explosives, providing safe houses, monitoring army activities, acting as lookouts and couriers, and removing and disposing of weapons left on the scene by snipers. A less frequent occurrence, but one which invoked the direst anxieties about the amorality of the militant woman, involved the 'honeypot lure' where female operatives led unsuspecting soldiers to isolated spots where they were assassinated by the PIRA (*Sunday World* 6 September 1981). However, it was the PIRA's bombing campaigns against 'economic targets' which provided mainly teenaged and young women with the opportunity for 'active service' in smuggling and planting incendiary devices in various town and city-centre premises.

At the time, the security forces and newspapers publicly speculated that young women had been selected for these tasks because the PIRA had calculated that they would be relatively inconspicuous in public spaces, would not arouse suspicion at security checkpoints or would be more likely to benefit from judicial leniency if caught. However conjectural some of these observations were, they were a reflection of a society coming to terms with the apparent repudiation of conscience amongst some of its young women, which might be explained either by their essential wickedness or their exploitation or corruption by others. It is also plausible that the instrumental advantages of using young women for certain tasks entered the minds of PIRA leaders, who were no less susceptible to the attitudes and standards of the time than the security forces and the courts proved to be. Furthermore, the propaganda value of these musings provided the context for manoeuvres such as 'Operation Petticoat' in August 1977, in which nearly 100 'Catholic girls' were arrested after a number of firebomb attacks on seven towns (*Irish Independent* 8 November 1977). Operation Petticoat was one of a number of victories claimed by the security forces over the unscrupulous and desperate tactics of those who had 'no qualms about using teenage girls to ferry guns and ammunition around Belfast', or commit arson and murder on their behalf (*Daily Mirror* 13 April 1976).

Yet much of this activity was self-fulfilling, in that the inroads into the margins of paramilitarism delivered the very results that the forces of law and security had been looking for – the existence of hitherto unknown sources of subversion. For example, the tactic of apprehending potential 'low level' activists produced defendants with tenuous connections with paramilitary groups at best, and at worst relied on the legal ambiguities and prosecutorial discretion that blurred the distinction between criminal and political offending. In one illustrative case, two teenagers, aged 18 and 15 respectively, were fined for wearing 'the uniform of the Women's IRA' [sic] after an army patrol followed and stopped a van returning from a commemoration ceremony for two PIRA men who had been shot by the army. At Newry RUC (Royal Ulster Constabulary) station, they admitted to wearing the uniform of the Wolfe Tone Band after they were 'shown a photograph of twenty girls [sic] taking part in a parade on the same day'. They had also been charged, *but were not convicted*, of membership of Cumann na mBan' (*Belfast Telegraph* 7 September 1977, emphasis added). At another trial, in which a 19-year-old was sentenced to three years' imprisonment for possessing explosives and a rifle and membership of the PIRA, 'the court was told that she had been a courier for *six years*, but she had now quit the organization'. In passing sentence, the judge had remarked that the court could not overlook the fact that 'although she was an intelligent girl', she was 'easily led' and had 'a wide knowledge with arms' [sic] (*Belfast Telegraph* 26 September 1977, emphasis added).

But one of the most significant problems that confronted the army and police, the courts, and eventually the prisons, was that of isolating the 'dedicated woman terrorist' from an undifferentiated tide of female subversiveness. Far from clarifying this particular dilemma, the operation of various emergency and supplementary laws complicated the already ambiguous relationships between women's involvement in criminal and political activities. Some of this ambiguity was reflected in the custodial patterns for women. Of the 3,945 women who passed through the prison system between 1972 and 1998, approximately one half were interned or remanded (awaiting trial), a quarter were sentenced to immediate custody and another quarter was made up of 'civil offenders' and fine defaulters (Figure 1.1).

Of the 1,000 or so women who were sentenced for offences which might be most clearly identified as 'scheduled' ones, 17 per cent were imprisoned for murder, manslaughter and violence against the person, and a further 12 per cent for explosives and firearms offences (Table 1.1). The largest single category for which women were sentenced was property crimes, at 54 per cent. The remaining 17 per cent were detained for public order offences or membership of a proscribed organization as the main or sole conviction. The general pattern of the sentences handed down to women also showed two trends. First, the number of women sentenced and remanded without bail increased for all types of offences after 1972. Secondly, sentencing was bifurcated

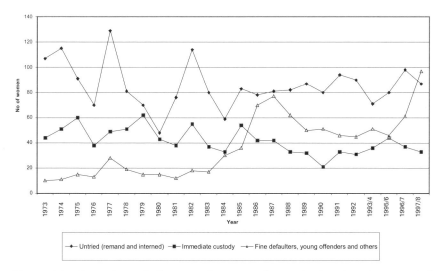

Figure 1.1 Receptions of all women by types of custody showing those untried (remanded and interned), sentenced to immediate custody and 'civil' prisoners (fine defaulters, young offenders and 'other').

Table 1.1 Types of offences of the sentenced female prisoner population in Northern Ireland, 1972–98

	Violence against the person	Explosives and firearms	Property	Other	Total offences
1972–80	45	112	229	82	468
1981–90	68	6	191	44	309
1991–98	62	0	131	48	241
Total	175	118	551	174	1,018
Percentage (n)	17	12	54	17	100

Source: Annual Reports of the Northern Ireland Prison Service, 1972–98.

between a minority serving long terms and those serving less than two years. In the 1970s, a quarter of sentenced women served over two years, and this fell to 11 per cent by the 1990s (NIPS 1972 to 1998).[2] The proportion of life prisoners was 2 per cent of the female total, compared with 20 per cent of the whole prison population. The proportion of women serving more than five years fell from 5 per cent by 1980 to 2 per cent in the 1990s, compared with 30 per cent of the general prison population.

Moreover, the implementation of emergency laws brought many of the political activities in which women played a significant part under a broader rubric of 'scheduled' offences. The expansion of the women's prison population largely reflected convictions for offences under sections of the Emergency Provisions Act concerned with breaches of the peace, the wearing of 'paramilitary-type dress', resistance to personal or property searches, and various acts of obstructing the security forces. The broad reach of s. 21 of the Act (and subsequent amendments) included membership of a proscribed organization, for which the maximum sentence was ten years. A positive intention to 'belong' was inferred from taking part in political parades, collecting money for proscribed organizations or organizing welfare for causes connected to prisoners. Furthermore, these charges could be applied retrospectively. Between 1975 and 1979, over 300 men and women were charged with membership of an illegal organization as their primary offence, of whom a half were imprisoned (*Commons Written Answers* 23 April 1980: 201), and another third fined (Hogan and Walker 1989: 141). Other sections of the Act covered more serious offences relating to the combat roles in which women predominated, such as couriering, transporting and concealing arms, and carrying and planting incendiary devices. In addition, the use of supplementary legislation such as the Public Order Act 1970 allowed greater powers of arrest and prosecution for activities such as picketing police stations or prisons, organizing roadblocks, trespassing and other acts of civil disobedience.

A third element in the criminalization of women involved the imposition by the courts of fines on householders who were involved in rent-striking and squatting. The significance of economic sanctions as a political weapon was first made clear when 18,000 householders withheld payment of rent and rates from local authorities in protest against internment. The response was the Payment for Debt (Northern Ireland) Act 1971 which allowed debts to be recovered from social welfare payments and wages. The rise of non-custodial sanctions eventually translated into custodial sentences as activists refused to pay fines for various minor offences, and were subsequently imprisoned. Between 1972 and 1977, 1,257 men and 66 women were imprisoned for fine defaulting (NIPS 1977). Fine defaulters continued to account for a substantial proportion of imprisoned women in Northern Ireland, outnumbering other categories of sentenced prisoners after the mid-1980s (NIPS 1986/87 to 1998). One incongruous effect of the use of the fine is its peculiarly gendered effects because the non-payment of debts is a persistent contributory factor to women's imprisonment more widely. Moreover, criminologists have noted the paradox of femininity which emerges from this form of criminalizing women in that they frequently commit these offences when carrying out the roles connected with their family's welfare that are usually endorsed in patriarchal relations (Mandaraka-Sheppard 1986; Carlen 1983, 1998). Whilst a directly 'political' motivation for the non-payment of fines cannot be inferred from all these cases, the judicial treatment of women in this regard gave expression to the sectarian relations, poverty and gendered deterrents that were constituents in women's offending and criminalization during the Troubles.

Normalizing emergency powers

According to Hillyard (1987) the legal reforms that were instituted under Direct Rule did not eliminate coercion, but 'reconstituted the problems of political violence' in legal-administrative terms. O'Dowd *et al.* (1980: 178–202) have also argued that the period after the mid-1970s was characterized by 'reformed repression' in which direct coercion was supplanted by a veneer of formal democracy that allowed the State to retain and embed exceptional powers in the 'normal' legislative, political and administrative functions of government. This was accomplished through three identifiable political strategies: 'Ulsterization', 'normalization' and 'criminalization'.

'Ulsterization' described the delegation of powers to indigenous police and security forces and bureaucratic structures. Ulsterization in the prison system involved placing the Northern Ireland Prison Service under the administrative structures of the Northern Ireland Office (NIO). One of its first tasks was to draft personnel from the prison services of England and Wales and Scotland to staff the rapidly expanding prison system, and to recruit local personnel, the overwhelming majority of which was drawn from the Protestant and Unionist community (NIPS 1978: 8; NIPS 1980: 11).

'Normalization' was originally conceived of as a counter-insurgent tactic for restoring civil order by utilizing various social, governmental and ideological mechanisms, rather than direct, military intervention (Kitson 1977: 281–98). However, O'Dowd *et al.* (1980), Boyle *et al.* (1980) and Hillyard (1987) have pointed to its longer-term ideological and political functions in securing a majoritarian toleration for coercion as a necessary and legitimate exercise in controlling terrorism. This analysis follows Gramsci's (1971: 57–80) argument that 'normalization' supports the rise of authoritarian State power with apparently minimal force, enables rulers to achieve ascendancy by securing the consent of subordinated groups (hegemony) and leads to the encroachment of the civil sphere by government. Hegemony, however, does not simply imply the absence or displacement of suppression, but it relies on a 'combination of force and consent, which balance each other reciprocally' (*ibid.*: 80). More concretely, 'normalization' referred to the policy of legitimizing the primacy of the rule of law by denuding violence and lawbreaking of political meanings or rationales as far as possible, and relegating the origins and causes of political violence to the status of a localized sub-war.

Criminalization extended from the strategy of normalization, and referred to the systematic redefinition of political violence as a fundamentally criminal activity (Gormally *et al.* 1993: 56–7). It followed from the reasoning that just as political violence was merely aggravated criminality, those charged with offences connected with it were engaged in aggravated crime. Accordingly, political offenders were deemed to be most appropriately dealt with in the sphere of criminal law, augmented when necessary with special powers and procedures to deal with the exceptional nature of their crimes. Criminalization was ultimately bound up with the question of upholding political legitimacy, in so far as any significant deviation from the innate criminality of political offending might concede a moral victory to perpetrators. At the same time it rested on a false dichotomy between military and 'normal' means of securing the rule of law, 'when in reality both apparatuses [were] used', and 'the dichotomy disguise[d] the political nature of legal relations' (O' Dowd *et al.* 1980: 190). Although fraught with political and practical contradictions, the issue of criminalization assumed a central place in the deliberations of a succession of inquiries into imprisonment in Northern Ireland, as the rest of the chapter discusses.

Modernizing the penal system: the Gardiner Commission

> In view of the events of the last six years and the appalling increase in the prison population, I think there is only one sensible policy … to hope for the best, but prepare for the worst (Murray 1975: 79).

Detention had posed an immediate operational problem for the penal system as the fourfold increase in the prison population (eightfold in the case of the women's population) had aggravated the congested and squalid conditions of the prisons and tested their anachronistic and inefficient regimes (NIPS 1977). Furthermore, the concentration of politically conscious prisoners focused official minds on the potential for the prisons to become inflammatory symbols of political injustice. In addition, the modernization of the penal infrastructure, which included the proposed construction of a new women's prison, was directed towards bringing the administration of prisons into line with the new counter-insurgency strategy. To this end, the Gardiner (1975) and Murray (1975) Commissions were created to report on possible alterations to the prison system to deal with the long-term effects of political violence. The Gardiner Commission was convened to discuss broader changes in the administration of criminal justice, but it quickly situated the prison system at the centre of endemic political disorder: 'The prison system in Northern Ireland has a most important role to play in the maintenance of law and order. We do not believe that it is fulfilling that role adequately at present and, to be blunt, we were appalled at certain aspects of the prison situation' (Gardiner 1975: 100).

Gardiner's analysis of legal and security reforms was bleak: tolerance and support for 'terrorism' and 'subversion' were prevalent in some sections of the community, and consequently the legitimacy of the criminal justice system had to be re-established as a matter of urgency (*ibid.*: 3). The core argument of the report was that the 'proper objective' of a penal policy was to counter political violence by isolating the volatile core of political offenders who were destabilizing the system. Gardiner is worth quoting at length, as his view of penal reform amplified the reasoning behind the criminalization policy:

> Because they are attempting to destroy Northern Ireland as a political entity, terrorists who break the law – which in Northern Ireland gives greater protection to the accused than in most disturbed communities – are not heroes but criminals; not the pioneers of political change but its direst enemies … The same is true of those who engage in subversion; who participate in attempts to undermine the authority of government or change its policy by forceful or obstructive means. Strong penalties already exist for those who devise or employ such tactics … Yet the most effective protection against development of subversion lies elsewhere; *in the recognition by government that it must act with speed to demonstrate its determination to sustain its authority* … Terrorism and subversion … can only be defeated, or guarded against, by the energetic pursuit of measures against them by the Government, and – equally important – of continued, *parallel progress in other fields of social, political and economic activity*, especially in community relations as a whole (*ibid.*: 8–12, emphasis added).

13

This account offers a comprehensive definition of the role of the prison system as a central point in a field of legitimation, in conjunction with other areas of the legal and administrative apparatus. It also concluded that if the crisis of political legitimacy could not be reversed in the prisons, it could at least be quarantined there. The most immediate problem identified by Gardiner was the obsolete prison infrastructure and its inadequacy for maintaining order and security. It must be noted that the sole focus of Gardiner's considerations was the compound camp at Long Kesh, a hastily recommissioned airbase which held male internees and sentenced prisoners, although the recommendations were intended for all prisons. Prisons of the compound type presented the greatest threat to the maintenance of security because the 'total loss of disciplinary control by the prison authorities within the compounds' meant 'rehabilitation work is impossible' (*ibid.*: 33). Furthermore, 'limited manpower' meant that 'the layout and construction of the compounds [made] close and continued supervision impossible' (*ibid.*: 104). Because there were no facilities for work or recreation, each paramilitary organization had organized inmates into a 'virtually self-contained community which keeps the premises it occupies to such standards as it finds acceptable and engages, if it so wishes, in military drills or lectures on military subjects' (*ibid.*: 103).

The most significant proposal for 'normalizing' the prison system was the removal of separate status and conditions from political detainees at 'the earliest practicable opportunity' (*ibid.*: 108). A form of separate status called special category status had operated from 1972 which entitled internees and sentenced prisoners to wear their own clothing, receive mail and parcels above the legal statutory minimum, associate with their political peers and not to do prescribed prison work. The policy had been instituted because internment had created the anomalous prisoner category of 'detainees on remand', who were nevertheless legally required to have access to resources and conditions that were not available to convicted 'criminals'. Gardiner argued that it was 'a serious mistake' as it had been quickly seized on by Republicans and Loyalists as a symbolic and practical recognition of their political status (*ibid.*: 107). The report concluded there was no justification for granting 'privileges' on the basis of a claim to 'political motivation' and cast doubts on whether the 'surprisingly liberal interpretation of Prison Rules was legal' (*ibid.*). More disturbing, according to the report, was the potential of the political factions to destabilize the prisons, as their prisoners were not as 'closely controlled as they would be in a normal cellular prison. Discipline within the compounds is in practice exercised by compound leaders, and they are more likely to emerge with an increased commitment to terrorism than as reformed citizens' (*ibid.*: 106). Gardiner presented a flexible and widely cast strategy for eliminating paramilitary influence in the prisons. The design of prison compounds was to be modified to improve internal security in the short term, whilst prisoners were to be eventually transferred to new establishments based on conventional cellular designs, with 'appropriate' levels of security, and run on the lines of 'normal' discipline. Other establishments, such as Armagh women's prison and Belfast (Crumlin Road) prison, were also to revert to 'ordinary' prison discipline and order.

The architectural technology of normalization: the Murray Commission

The Murray Commission, which also reported in 1975, took up the task of providing the architectural blueprint for Gardiner's recommendations. It considered the construction of a permanent and secure prison estate, including a new women's prison. The urgency of replacing the existing prisons was magnified by rioting at Long Kesh and Armagh women's prison in October 1974, as well as the successful escape of prisoners from Belfast prison in 1971. The Cunningham Inquiry (1972) into that escape had reported that Belfast (like Armagh) prison, which had been constructed in the nineteenth century, was 'just about as unsuitable … as could be found anywhere' for maintaining prison order, and recommended 'the construction to modern designs of a secure prison' (Cunningham cited in Murray 1975: 16). The construction of two prisons was proposed: HMP Maze, a high-security, cellular prison, was to replace the compounds on a site adjacent to Long Kesh. HMP Maghaberry was intended to replace Belfast prison for men and Armagh prison for women. The Maghaberry complex comprised two blocks of cellular accommodation for 432 males, with a separate block in its own compound for female prisoners called Mourne House.[3] Situated 25 miles outside Belfast, HMP Maghaberry was designed to provide 'an appropriate balance … between the needs of security and control and the desirability of forward-looking regimes' (NIPS 1986: 1). The complex eventually housed a range of prison populations: female prisoners, adult male prisoners and 'penitent terrorists' who could be persuaded to resign from their political structures in the other prisons and serve their sentences in an 'ordinary' regime.

One of the contentions that arose at the original Murray Inquiry centred on the proposal that Mourne House should accommodate both adult and juvenile female prisoners whether politically affiliated or not. As there was no designated prison for female young offenders in Northern Ireland up to this point, they had been accommodated in facilities run by religious orders, or occasionally sent to institutions in Scotland (NIPS 1978: 20). The Northern Ireland Association for the Care and Resettlement of Offenders (NIACRO) argued that a combined juvenile and adult prison for women 'would inevitably involve the accommodation in a maximum security prison of a substantial number of prisoners who would be perfectly well suited to a low security prison' (NIACRO cited in Murray 1975: 57), and lack the supportive environment of more personalized institutions (*Belfast Newsletter* 1 October 1975). These objections were countered by the NIO, who argued that the introduction of varied, flexible regimes would offset the debilitating influences that might arise from mixing higher and lower categories in one establishment. The Commission concluded in favour of official assurances that 'there would be no difficulty in reducing the security in a particular part or particular parts of that prison', as 'it is much easier to downgrade the security at a prison than to increase it' (Murray 1975: 57(3)). Moreover, the young offenders would be separated from the adults. The government also argued that the construction of one prison with superior facilities would be more beneficial for prisoners than a scheme which would require the duplication of staffing and running costs in different establishments (*ibid.*: 57(4)). In accepting the arguments that these potential problems would be resolved, through largely unspecified methods, the Murray Commission deferred to economic expedience and the prevailing priorities of security over the pastoral requirements of different female prisoner populations. HMP Maghaberry eventually opened on 18 March 1986, eleven years after the Murray Commission, six years after the original schedule for completion and at the cost of 32 million pounds (*Commons Debates* 17 November 1986: 551).

Mourne House: hoping for the best and preparing for the worst

On paper at least, Mourne House materialized the kinds of progressive penal thinking that underpinned penal attitudes to women's lawbreaking in the post-war period, and which placed an emphasis on welfarist intervention, rehabilitation and resocialization as the central functions of prison punishment. Mourne House was 'substantially a replica of the Scottish prison at Cornton Vale' (Home Office 1979: 149) which was the centrepiece of the new generation of prisons for women designed to simulate an intimate, domesticated and therapeutic environment:

The new prison provides facilities of a high standard including single cell accommodation with internal sanitation for up to 56 prisoners, a purpose built hospital, a gymnasium, chapel and library. Accommodation is in the form of two-storey houses which are each divided into self-contained units housing up to seven inmates. Each unit also has its own kitchen and Association Room equipped with colour television and record player and a cell equipped for accommodating a mother and child (NIPS 1986: 1).

But by the time Mourne House was completed, its prototype, Cornton Vale, had attracted considerable criticism for having recreated a disciplinarian and intrusive ethos which relied on psychiatric and behavioural controls to maintain discipline (Carlen 1983; Dobash *et al*. 1986). As with Cornton Vale, the inmates at Mourne House were organized into small 'family' groups, and subjected to an intensively disciplined regime and high levels of surveillance. The layout of individual cells along small passageways and corridors, and the positioning of glass-enclosed offices at the end of each wing for staff, intentionally 'designed out' opportunities for illicit political association, and ensured that prisoners were constantly visible. The prison complex was meant to combine extensive, if unobtrusive, physical security with 'a tolerable and constructive regime ... The idea was that relaxed regimes should be established within secure perimeter walls for all within such establishments, high-risk inmates being treated virtually the same as everyone else' (May 1979: 21).

Yet as we shall see, the priorities of secure confinement won out over the reformative promise of prison policy. From the outset, there was an obvious disjuncture between the objectives of 'rehabilitation' and 'security' both in the physical planning and function of Mourne House. This was reinforced by the underlying official fiction that the rehabilitative model of punishment, with its emphasis on the remorseful, individual offender, would be embraced *ipso facto* by those who neither regarded their offences as 'crimes', nor themselves as criminals. The language of penal 'modernization' was ultimately more assured about physical security in the new prisons than the prospects of establishing genuinely 'constructive regimes' for all women prisoners. Additionally, women political prisoners were positioned in a double bind in that the circumstances of their confinement were practically effaced by normative conceptions of offending women and official denial of the politicality of their lawbreaking. At the same time, their needs as women prisoners were subordinated to the primacy of security and counter-subversion in the prisons. However, as the following chapter discusses, although women prisoners were secondary considerations in the development of political imprisonment, they were none the less vulnerable to gender-specific interpretations of the risk they were perceived to present, and no less subject to gendered forms of mortification, constraint and discipline.

Notes

1 Throughout the book, the terms 'PIRA' or 'Provisionals' will refer to the Provisional IRA and 'Sinn Féin' to Provisional Sinn Féin, unless otherwise stated.
2 Data extrapolated from numerous reports are referenced as (NIPS 'year' to 'year').
3 HMP Maghaberry describes the entire complex, whilst Mourne House refers to the separate compound and prison for all women prisoners.

Chapter 2

Inside the carceral network, 1972–98

This chapter gives an account of women's political imprisonment from the internment of women in 1972 up to the 1990s. The outline generally follows Gormally *et al.*'s (1993) functional chronology of prison administration in Northern Ireland which reflected successive shifts in counterterrorism policy (see also Gormally and McEvoy 1995; McEvoy 2001). Briefly, these are 'reactive containment' (1969–76) which was characterized by internment, special category status for those convicted through juryless courts, military security in the prisons and massive investment in the prison estate and staffing; 'criminalization' (1976–81) which followed the removal of special category status and the implementation of an extended range of powers to persuade or coerce prisoners into accepting criminal status; and 'normalization' (early 1980s onwards) or the period of reconstruction in the prisons between the aftermath of the 1981 hunger strike and the signing of the Belfast Agreement in 1998.

Although this template provides a useful start for connecting 'actual historical events' and the 'specific relationship between government and prison management' (Gormally and McEvoy 1995: 285–7), it invariably reflects the agency of official élites and the determination of penal policy in accordance with prevailing political interests. The authors are correct to remind us of the position that prisons occupied at an interface of civil government and security policy, as well as the political priorities that were devolved to them in discharging their role. However, such accounts must also be receptive to the contradictions and lack of coherence in emerging institutional structures and practices as they responded rapidly to crises. As the previous chapter showed, for example, the administrative response to women's political offending was informed by highly uneven, partial and contradictory developments, not least of which were fundamental structural and ideological ambiguities about appropriate provision for them. Furthermore, there is no simple relationship between the grand designs of policy and the untidy evolution of prison practice on the ground. This account has, therefore, found it necessary to identify the material and discursive conditions of women's political imprisonment. It does so by exploring the emergence of prison administration from below in the context of mutual incomprehension and hostility, and developing levels of awareness and involvement, on the part of staff and prisoners alike. Additionally, the task of responding to the entry of an unfamiliar kind of woman prisoner into the system did not develop in a flux. A central concern of this account is the regressive tendencies of administrators as they fell back on institutionally embedded and paternalistic controls in response to the new kind of security and disciplinary problems that were presented after internment and special detention. Therefore, whilst Gormally *et al.*'s framework is retained, this chapter interposes an account of the constellation of structural and practical adjustments and the distinctive punitive and disciplinary assemblages that defined the political imprisonment of women in Northern Ireland.

In addition, this book is concerned with the development and consolidation of relationships of power or, more specifically, with the dynamic associations between anticipated and actual resistance on the part of prisoners and its effect on shaping administrative objectives. This dialectic is connected to the inconsistencies in prison rule which were open to exploitation by prisoners and, in turn, underpinned official efforts to recapture authority and order. Accordingly, each of the different 'eras' of prison administration is argued to have produced characteristic modes of penal re-enclosure, or practices for returning women political prisoners to conformity, which generated the conditions and contexts for further resistance.

Part one: reactive containment in Armagh women's prison, 1972–6

In an interview conducted in 1975, Bernadette McAliskey (formerly Devlin), the former civil rights activist and MP for Mid-Ulster, recalled her imprisonment in June 1970 in Armagh prison (*Belfast Telegraph* 21 March 1975). Devlin had been sentenced to six months' imprisonment for incitement to riot and disorderly behaviour. She described the austere conditions, rigid rules and petty disciplinarianism of the regime, a quasi-militaristic hierarchy amongst staff and prisoners, and an overwhelming sense of resignation and submissiveness amongst the women confined there. Association and communication between different classes of prisoners were forbidden. Although there was a compulsory uniform, Devlin was allowed to wear her own clothes, provided they conformed to the regulations and were not of a 'paramilitary type'. She had successfully lobbied the Parliamentary Privileges Committee at Westminster to allow her access to her political agents and to conduct her constituency duties whilst in custody. Devlin was released after four months having earned one-third remission for 'good behaviour'.

Two years later, as a consequence of the influx of internees and remand and sentenced prisoners, Armagh prison was 'faced with acute problems of accommodation, staffing, education, training and discipline' (NIPS 1977: 5). Prisoners were doubled up in single cells with no sanitation, so they were obliged to slop out their pots each morning. The overcrowded conditions were compounded by the fact that women prisoners had to be segregated from two male regimes comprising an overspill of internees and remands from Belfast prison, who remained until 1973, and a boys' Borstal which remained in Armagh until 1975. The needs of male prisoners prevailed over those of women in the allocation of resources and facilities. Similarly, the need to segregate male and female prisoners, and the need to separate the different categories of women prisoners, led to the *ad hoc* subdivision of the already congested wings. The Borstal was situated on the ground floor of one wing, whilst female remand prisoners occupied the ground floor of another. Sentenced female prisoners occupied the first storeys of 'A' and 'B' wings whilst internees were housed on the second levels. A third 'C' wing, with 20 places, was added in 1975 on the old breaker's yard.

The poor quality of prison food, and inadequate recreation, washing and cooking facilities, provided the first focal point for a collectively organized campaign by women prisoners. In 1972, the Republican Internees Council, which was run from the Long Kesh compounds, stated that the women in Armagh prison were 'being maltreated' (*Irish News* 18 January 1972). The presence of men prisoners in the jail meant that the recreational facilities for all the women were restricted to one small room. Their exercise yard was a 'small muddy patch of ground' and women using it reported that they were subjected to 'verbal abuse and obscenities' from soldiers patrolling the perimeters. Moreover, the 'numerous requests' which they had made to the governor for better conditions were 'unavailing' (*ibid.*).

Disciplinary assemblages: diet

Although only a handful of male prisoners in Northern Ireland were still being placed on restricted diet as a punishment by 1976 (NIPS 1977), food provision remained a direct source of conflict because the rationing of goods denies prisoners the capacity to exercise basic levels of self-provision and self-care. Penologists have also pointed to gendered relationships between food provision and the penal construction of conformity. Food acts as a catalyst for negating women prisoners' self-esteem (Carlen 1998: 92), and becomes another factor in their rejection of docile and dependent roles (Bosworth 1999: 147). The systems of reliance which centre on food also recreate distorted ideals of womanhood in an alien prison context because women are normally 'interpellated as guardians of health and home-hygiene' (Carlen 1998: 93), whilst its controlled distribution intervenes in their role as nutritional providers and decision-makers. Thus, the prison dietary system undermines the kind of productive relations of self-worth, responsibility and caring which women's prisons ostensibly nurture as their central function, whilst facilitating secondary punishments and gendered deprivations.

Women prisoners at Armagh frequently criticized the prison diet, partly on the grounds of its inadequate nutritional value, and partly because of the broader symbolic contentions and power relations connected with the distribution of basic commodities in prisons. In a 'comm' or illicit communication to a sympathetic Nationalist newspaper, the sentenced female Republican prisoners complained of 'badly cooked cabbage three or four times a week, sloppy potatoes and poor quality meat. The food is usually served cold. Milk has been reduced from one half pint per day to one eighth of a pint, this is hardly sufficient' (*Irish News* 25 September 1972). Because the allocation of food recreates the deprivations of prison in numerous direct and intangible ways, it precipitated one of the earliest and most basic forms of protest when prisoners threw food on the floors of their cells, or refused to eat it. As an example of what Foucault (1990: 101) called a reverse discourse, in which acts of reactive destruction or defilement simply invert dominant rules, the tactic failed because of the capacity of the administration to advance 'rational' solutions to the problem. The prisoners' complaints were either ignored or the matter was resolved by organizing ancillary authorities to endorse the conditions of the regime. Following the prisoners' protests, for example, the Armagh Prison Board of Visitors inspected the food, and concluded that it was of a high standard in quality and quantity, adding that 'only a few trivial complaints had been brought to the Governor's attention' (*Irish News* 14 May 1971).[1]

In the following years, the annual reports of the prison service continued to stress that 'the standard of food and the quantities offered to prisoners remained high, with daily variation of menus' (NIPS 1978: 16), and was 'of good and nutritious standard, ratified by the medical staff' (NIPS 1980: 18). Republican prisoners incorporated food protests into a broader strategy for establishing their presence as a political body through the use of short, tactical hunger strikes which were directed at a range of political grievances such as the continuation of internment or in support of the transfer ('repatriation') of prisoners from British prisons (*Irish News* 21 September 1971; *Irish News* 26 November 1974). Five women participated in the 35-day hunger strike initiated by male PIRA prisoners in 1972 which eventually won special category status. Female prisoners staged hunger strikes every Friday during 1975 in support of the transfer of Dolours and Marion Price from H.M.P. Durham, England, to Northern Ireland (*Irish Independent* 28 March 1975).

Medical provision

Unlike the England and Wales prison system, there was no separate medical service for prisons in Northern Ireland. Medical care for prisoners was the responsibility of the Senior Medical Officer for the Department of Health and Social Services and the Director of Regimes of the Prison Service (Home Office 1979: 58). A male doctor was assigned from a local practice on a part-time basis to Armagh prison, and a full-time nurse was assisted by medical orderlies, who were prison officers trained in basic medical care (*ibid.*: 60–1). According to Sim (1990: 12), the distribution of health facilities in prisons reflects the utilitarian principle of 'less eligibility', where care is provided 'in a way which [does] not better or indeed equal the care that those beyond the walls receive'. Sim's larger point is that this fulfils the prerogatives of classed and criminal discipline by instilling the values of austerity and fixing the standards in prisons to those available to the most deprived sections of the public. Certainly, the cheaper option of providing medical care on 'an agency basis' was at the forefront of official considerations (NIPS 1977: 13). Sim (1990: 9) has also argued that positive medical relationships are militated against in prison because the values of care and treatment become subordinated to the prison's punitive and regulatory functions. In a letter to the press, Republican women prisoners argued that:

23

medical conditions are, to say the least, inadequate. Medicine is handed out by one medical officer, from the top of the stairs. If a prisoner cannot go down to receive treatment, then she does not get any. Some prisoners have refused treatment because of the attitude taken by this particular officer (*Irish News* 25 September 1972).

Other reasons for the inaccessibility of basic medical care to political, and women, prisoners can be discerned from the background of staff. For example, in defending its recruitment of medical orderlies from the ranks of discipline officers, the prison service argued that 'these *men* have statutory nursing qualifications prior to entering the prison service, and a great majority had nursing experience *in the army* (NIPS 1977: 12, emphasis added).

As with other instances where prisoners protest against poor conditions, their complaints were treated as ill-founded and vexatious. Assurances were issued in the minimalist language of officialdom:

From the earliest period inmates were medically interviewed and clinically examined within 24 hours of remand ... The ratio of medical officers to inmates in any one establishment compares favourably with the ratio of general practitioners to the population in Northern Ireland, as does the response time to sudden illness or injury both during normal working hours and silent hours (*ibid.*: 12, 13).

This initial 'medical interview' and 'clinical examination' referred to in the report above occurred at reception to prison, a process which has been connected by Goffman (1991: 27) with the 'mortifying' rites of passage into confinement, described by Carlen (1998: 43) as the exposure of prisoners' bodies as sites of the 'State's power to punish', and by Sim (1990) as an example of the subordination of prisoners to multilateral disciplinary, medical, psychiatric and surveillant powers. The deficiencies in medical care were persistently criticized by civil liberties and prison welfare organisations, and as prisoners increasingly resorted to strategies of publicly exposing their conditions, official sensitivities were increasingly heightened towards 'persistent, unfounded allegations of brutality and neglect' in the provision of medical services (NIPS 1980: 16).

Education and training

Educational provision in Armagh was shaped by paternalistic perceptions about appropriate provision for women prisoners. The educational service had initially provided training and prison work in cooking, needlecrafts and laundry in line with the prevailing rehabilitative aspirations which aimed to prepare women for domesticated social roles after release (Dobash *et al.* 1986: 160–6). A very small number of sentenced prisoners were involved in the available work of tailoring, laundry and cleaning because internees and prisoners with political status were not obliged to do prison work (NIPS 1977). The prison system was not required to provide work or education for remand prisoners unless they were minors. Academic tuition was introduced after representations by various prison welfare organizations because a significant number of juvenile prisoners had been incarcerated whilst still at school. Sentenced adult prisoners campaigned for appropriate prison education and alternatives to prison work as a right which corresponded with their political status. By the mid-1970s, the educational programme in Armagh consisted of 'remedial subjects', physical recreation, shorthand and typing, dressmaking, handicrafts, Irish Gaelic, and politics and history classes (*ibid.*: 15). In the late 1970s, prison education reverted to a primarily vocational programme because of a 'steady diminution in the number of special category prisoners and the introduction of the young offenders centre within the prison' (NIPS 1979: 31). The 'young offenders centre' was a nominal provision as it simply involved allocating separate space for juvenile females in the main prison. Academic courses for public examinations were 'largely replaced' with remedial subjects in numeracy and literacy 'to combat the educational retardation which was seen as a direct result of the truancy and behavioural problems' of young offenders (*ibid.*). However, the real reason for the decline in academic provision was 'the activities of protesting prisoners who … withdrew from all educational programmes' in protest at the removal of special category status (NIPS 1980: 19). From 1977, most educational programmes were 'non-effective'.

Political status and counter-disciplinary formations

Special category status (called 'political status' by prisoners) was introduced in 1972 as a well timed gesture towards the Republican hunger strikers in the context of a PIRA ceasefire. The official designation 'special category' intentionally retained the meaning that it fell short of full political status and was, rather, an exceptional concession which was revocable should the legal or political context of detention alter. The new arrangement was viewed by the government to be a pragmatic settlement that allowed prison administrators a degree of flexibility and respite from outright confrontation with both Loyalists and Republicans, whilst practically addressing the problems of maintaining discipline given the inadequacy of the prison facilities.

With the introduction of political status, Republican women prisoners formalized their structures into the Provisional IRA 'A' Company (Armagh) in 1974. 'A' Company was divided into three sections named after women Volunteers who had been killed on 'active service': Ethel Lynch from Derry (1974); Vivienne Fitzsimmons, Downpatrick (1973); and Julie Dougan, Portadown (1972) (*Irish News* 23 November 1974).[2] It was recognized as the primary structure through which political prisoners formally mediated with prison management. Their commanding officer (OC) interceded in disputes with staff, negotiated with the governor on behalf of prisoners, and maintained an ethos of internal discipline and community by allocating work to the company, conducting roll calls, wing inspections and holding political meetings.

A prisoner wishing to claim political status applied to the paramilitary organization of her choice and either satisfied the requirement that she was acting under orders, or that her terms of sentence qualified her for consideration as a member. The political structures produced what Sykes (1958) identified as 'rank-and-file specialists' who played formative roles in consolidating the identity and cohesion of the group. Internees initially took these specialist roles because they were the most visible group in the public consciousness, having been represented as victims of State harassment by their own organizations which were 'opposed to [the] internment without charge or trial of *our* women' (*Irish Republican Bureau press release*, 19 January 1973, emphasis added).

The first women internees installed systems for identifying incoming peers and making contact with them. As internees had relatively greater access to visits and postal communication, they corresponded with their constituency of supporters outside through a series of communiqués or 'comms' which outlined the central contention of Republican prisoners, namely, that they 'refused to recognize the attitude of the authorities, as they had not been charged or put on trial' (*Irish Independent* 23 June 1973). Convicted prisoners played a more formal role in organization and recruitment in accordance with the standing orders and directives of their respective paramilitary organizations. Republican OCs tended to be drawn from the sentenced prisoners, and were normally appointed from the outside by the PIRA Army Council. They in turn appointed a second-in-command, welfare officer, quartermaster and education officer (D'arcy 1981: 59). Loyalist OCs belonging to the Ulster Defence Association (UDA) were directly elected by their members in prisons, or selected by their external command if members of the Ulster Volunteer Force (UVF) (Crawford 1999: 30).

Modes of re-enclosure: mundane discipline and punishment

Republican historiography asserts that 'the system was effectively railroaded into working along with the prison structure' in Armagh prison (*Iris* 1984: 1, 4, 17). In reality, the women's political formations tended to develop more tacitly, and in accordance with the quality of reciprocal relationships that could be established with senior staff. Their development as a political force was impeded by attitudinal and structural constraints. The implementation of special category status relied on governors' discretion as to what conditions or modifications to the regime were consistent within the terms of 'political status', and which of the prisoners' demands exceeded them. Of equal importance was the extent to which a governor's authority held sway over prison staff averse to relinquishing their positions of influence over prisoners. The Prison Officers' Association (POA) had vigorously opposed the introduction of special category status on the grounds that it endangered their members and undermined discipline in the prisons. As the decade progressed, an increasingly militant POA expressed its opposition to the policy through a variety of practical and symbolic actions such as temporary work stoppages, which led to the closure of recreational facilities and the suspension of prison visits. Other activities included the refusal of members to handle letters in Gaelic as a 'security precaution' (*Irish News* 8 September 1973) and the intensive searching of visitors and the seizure of documents. Whilst the POA justified these actions as reasonable responses to breaches of security and the failure of management to curtail the traffic of illegal communications and personal letters across the different prisons (*Daily Telegraph* 12 December 1972), they were also signally directed towards prisoners as a deterrent against using violence or intimidation against staff.

The province of distribution is a complex matrix of other penal powers such as domination and discipline. After mortification, it is 'largely the privileges system that provides a framework for personal reorganisation' (Goffman 1991: 51). In this context, the distributive and disciplinary realms of penal authority merge in subtle, but significant ways. In particular, they open up prisoners' resistance to everyday deprivation to the realm of penal control in which minor, 'vexatious' or 'irrational' infractions become privileged sites of discipline and punishment. Yet even the prison regulations do not fully codify the arbitrary and opportunistic use of punishment for actual or suspected infringements in women's prisons (Mandaraka-Sheppard 1986). The incidence of very serious offences like assault, murder or escaping is rare in women's prisons, whereas the areas of greatest concern lie with

27

the looser categories of 'minor' offences connected with 'misbehaviour' and 'bad' attitudes (Quinn 1995). Women in prison are charged more frequently, and given proportionately higher punishments for lesser infractions against the prison regulations than men prisoners (Home Office 1995). In this context, observers have pointed to the ideological supports that are used to justify the gratuitous punishment of women in prison which arise from the equally loosely defined standards of behaviour that are applied to them.

These analyses suggest that punishment in women's prisons is vested in the routine and commonplace policing of prisoners' behaviour, and tie together the discretionary authority held by discipline and senior staff, pre-emptive interception of 'minor' infractions and preconceptions about the nature of 'disorderly' women. They also point to the unrecorded incidences of conflict between staff and prisoners that largely occur on the margins of formal disciplinary mechanisms. In this context, the very low levels of punishments awarded for offences against the prison rules in Armagh when special category status was in operation seem to suggest that women political prisoners were largely exempt from the kind of close regulation and punishment that is applied to women's behaviour in prisons more generally (Figure 2.1).

Certainly, the relatively low levels of recorded punishments at this time appeared to confirm the conclusions drawn by senior prison administrators that special category status placed excessive constraints on detecting trouble and intervening in substantial, underlying levels of disorder. An alternative explanation suggests that the low levels may have reflected the relative success of the prisoners tactic of disengaging from staff, who had fewer opportunities to monitor individuals, detect infractions, recruit informants or exercise other kinds of influence over them (Mandaraka-Sheppard 1986; Marquart 1986). As McKeown (2001: 27–48) has argued in relation to Republican male prisoners, and Crawford (1999: 35–52) with respect to Loyalists, organized political prisoners had recourse to a self-regulatory code which acted as a surrogate authoritative structure. Whilst the relevance of theories of counter-authoritarian inmate structures to women prisoners is problematized in the next chapter, it is noted here that the formalities of special category status did not exempt women from punitive intervention. Rather, their regulation and control evolved from a continuum of formal punishment and discretionary regulation, the privileges system and, as the next section discusses, the use of explicit institutional violence.

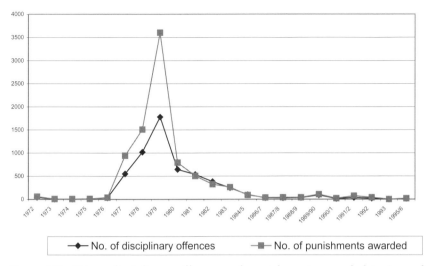

Figure 2.1 Prison disciplinary offences and punishments awarded in Armagh prison and Mourne House HMP Maghaberry, 1972–96

Modes of re-enclosure: punitive responses to resistance

There was at least one major disturbance each year between 1973 and 1975 where a number of women prisoners in Armagh were injured. In the meantime, other allegations of assaults and the mistreatment of individual prisoners regularly filtered through to the public domain. In 1973, a failed escape attempt by three women was followed by a punitive and violent response against the escapees and other prisoners (*Irish News* 5 March 1973). The escape had been collectively organized and took place whilst prisoners on 'A1' wing set up a diversion. Prison staff were joined by joint army and police units in restoring order by violently returning all prisoners to their cells and imposing a general lockdown. The disturbance continued into the night as word spread through the prison that the recaptured prisoners had been badly assaulted. Later accounts also revealed the extent to which the authority of the governor, Hugh Cunningham, had been overruled by the army command in directing searches and retaking control of the prison. Cunningham later claimed that he had been unable to prevent the assaults on prisoners. As with later disturbances, the events were obscured by the minimal information available from the Northern Ireland Office (NIO), who stated that 'efforts were made to persuade [the prisoners] with *normal prison discipline* and it was subsequently necessary for prison officers to use a minimum amount of force' (*Irish News* 6 March 1973, emphasis added).

29

A number of allegations emerged in the ensuing public controversy, notably about the random and excessive use of force against a large number of uninvolved prisoners, and the role of male police, prison and army officers in violent assaults against women prisoners. Paddy Devlin, then an MP from the Social and Democratic Labour Party (SDLP), alleged that the governor of the prison had failed to restrain army personnel and staff, claiming that he 'had the situation under control after the escape attempt was stopped, yet he continued to direct severe punitive measures against the prisoners' (*Irish News* 8 March 1973). Devlin's requests for immediate visits to the prison by a team of doctors and solicitors and for disciplinary action against staff responsible for 'excessive violence' were turned down by the NIO (*ibid.*).

On 16 October 1974, a series of co-ordinated disturbances by Republican prisoners occurred at Long Kesh, Magilligan and Armagh prisons. The governor and three female officers at Armagh were taken hostage by Republican (and one Loyalist) prisoners, but were released unharmed after 14 hours. During the subsequent lockdown, which lasted three days, military personnel moved into the prison and cut off the electricity and water supplies (*Iris* 1984: 1, 4, 17). The disturbance started after Republican prisoners in Long Kesh burned their compound down. The women's request to hear reports about the male prisoners, some of whom were relatives, from a Sinn Féin representative was refused, and at a company meeting they decided to 'cause as much damage as possible to the jail' (*ibid.*: 18).

Young male and female adult prisoners were treated in Armagh prison according to perceptions that they were equally disruptive, immature and lacking in full adult status. Republican women prisoners had previously drawn public attention to the mistreatment of the Borstal inmates, and were considered by staff to have encouraged them to stage protests over their conditions. In September 1975, the women intervened when the young men were subjected to intensive drilling in the exercise yard as punishment for fighting (*Newsletter* 29 September 1975). In the ensuing disturbance, three young offenders and four prison officers were injured, whilst a woman prisoner was reported by the NIO to have acquired 'self-inflicted injuries' (*Irish Times* 29 September 1975). The civil liberties group, the Association for Legal Justice (ALJ), later said that the injured woman 'had been left on her cell floor bleeding for two hours and her wound required 30 stitches'. The official statement from the NIO 'did not state these facts', nor disclose an official reason for the disturbances (ALJ press release 30 September 1975).

Adams (1992) argues that a military approach to suppressing prison disturbances tends to predominate over more historically tenuous innovations such as mediation or negotiation. The strategies for controlling disturbances at Armagh prison followed the more widely applied principles of riot control in Northern Ireland, which emphasized 'aggressive containment', isolation of the 'principal perpetrators' and dispersal (*The Times* 12 March 1975). After this disturbance, the prison was placed on a full lockdown for at least three days, pastoral representatives were denied access to prisoners, prisoners were confined to their cells, and visits and mail cancelled. What had by now become the ritualized request from prisoners for independent medical examiners and scrutineers to investigate the incident was also, predictably, turned down. Scraton *et al.* (1991) have argued that official responses in the aftermath of disturbances follow characteristic patterns of official denial, justification and the reassignment of liability to prisoners themselves. In these instances, significant details about the origins of violence are obscured by the closure of channels of communication, and explanations other than official ones about the severity of measures taken to restore order are subject to intense official rebuttal (*ibid.*: 114–24). The testimonies of prisoners are subjected to official counterclaims that they are, at best, tainted by self-interest and, at worst, motivated by subversiveness. Finally, the degree of violence used to quell disturbances is justified on the basis that the 'minimum use of force' is necessary, and legitimized by a broader consensus over the 'volatility' and 'dangerousness' of the prisoners involved (*ibid.*: 63).

Gendered aspects of reactive containment, 1972–76

The patterns of maintaining prison order in the Armagh prison during the period of 'reactive containment' alternated between coercion and concession. This reflected the fundamental confusion of direction in penal policy with respect to women's imprisonment, and was reinforced by the absence of clear operational principles for implementing special category status. These ambiguities were tellingly reflected in the view that, deprived of a 'middle ground' of conventional penal controls, prison administrators were compelled to resort to severe remedies to restore order. Nor were these inconsistencies reducible to the argument advanced by 'modernizers' such as Gardiner (1975) that a combined lack of appropriate security measures in the prisons, and the existence of exceptional and privileged variations in prison regimes, contributed in the long term to an unnecessarily punitive climate.

Rather, even these positions understate the gendered particularities of the construction of 'disorderly' political women prisoners, which were inferred as much from their disengagement from correctional influences and withdrawal from dependency on staff, as from their political or organizational capabilities. The development by women of their structures was shaped as much by the need for self-preservation as by ideological commitment or political opportunism in furthering their goals.

Whilst the disarray and uncertainty within the prisons during this time opened up opportunities for women to develop political, symbolic and cultural resources for resistance, there were persistent constraints on their capacity to operate collectively or politically. Whatever levels of recognition or legitimacy that might have existed for women's political structures, they were bounded within entrenched ideologies of gender conformity, as well as being subject to the discretionary powers of respective governors and staff. Special category status was implemented in a much more uneven and tenuous form in the women's regime; many of the relevant conditions were introduced later than in the men's prisons; and the thresholds of toleration for the women's structure were conditional on the expectation that their conduct remained intelligible within deep-rooted and narrow standards of gender-appropriate behaviour. Where these values were breached, the motives of women political prisoners were reinscribed within familiar, deprecatory frames of reference where their demands were treated as excessive or irrational, their political objectives trivialized and their relationships circumscribed within ideological, behavioural and physical deterrents.

In this sense, the contingency of special category status was underpinned by the calculated manageability of the relatively small group of women prisoners, and the corresponding assumption that potential disorder could be forestalled by exercising gender-specific controls. For these reasons, the women's strategy of political preservation was based on the exigencies of managing various domains of penal controls through fluid, multifaceted tactics of negotiation or confrontation. As a consequence, a great deal of their political work was practically displaced into managing interpersonal relationships with successive governors and other authorities. However, when women prisoners collectively confronted prison rule, the use of force was officially endorsed as an appropriate, legitimate and efficient method of restoring order.

Part two: criminalization, 1976–81

The phase of 'criminalization' commenced with the removal of special category status in 1976 and lasted at least until the ending of the 1981 hunger strike at the Maze, in which ten Republican male prisoners died. Prison relations were marked by outright confrontation between Republican prisoners and the administration, institutional violence and the use of extreme forms of resistance including naked protests, non-cooperation and no-wash strikes, and hunger strikes in 1980 and 1981. The 'criminalization' policy was enacted in the Treatment of Offenders Act (Northern Ireland) 1976, which formally ended internment, and revoked special category status for incoming prisoners sentenced after 1 March 1976. The maximum rate of remission was raised from a third to a half of sentences served, as an additional incentive for sentenced prisoners, except lifers, to conform, and applied uniquely in Northern Ireland. The removal of special category status had been held back for the duration of the Constitutional Convention, which ended in March 1976, having failed to find a political settlement to the conflict. Merlyn Rees (1985: 127), then Secretary of State for Northern Ireland, had previously indicated his intentions to implement the recommendations of the Gardiner Report for 'phasing out detention consistent with the requirements of the security situation' and, more tellingly, 'to show that detention could be ended if there was a response from the paramilitaries'. Rees also revealed that the programme of prison building brought about the opportunity to turn Gardiner's recommendation into a reality, although, as shown in Chapter 1, the situation of women prisoners was clearly not a part of these deliberations:

> We were simply unable to act without having prison cell accommodation and it was only when I decided to take the short cut of building the H-Blocks at the Maze that we could begin to plan the ending of special category status in earnest. *The new Maghaberry prison planned for 1984 did not enter into my short-term considerations'* (*ibid.*: 275, emphasis added).

The non-cooperation protest, 1976–82

A month after political status was revoked, Republican women prisoners indicated their intention to withdraw from welfare, educational and work programmes and 'any of the State-introduced activities in the prison' (*Irish News* 3 April 1976). The non-cooperation strike entailed:

[A] policy of non-participation with the governor in the running of the jail. By this course of action [we] will show our disgust at the British government in trying to class anyone charged with a political offence committed after March 1st as a criminal. We will support those affected by the removal of political status until they get what is rightfully theirs. The only way open to us is to make the system within the jail unworkable. They can imprison our bodies, but not our spirits (*Irish News* 21 April 1976).

On 13 October 1976, male Republican prisoners at the Maze initiated the first challenge to criminalization when the first prisoner to be sentenced after 1 March, Kieran Nugent, refused to wear the prison uniform, and was placed in solitary confinement wearing only a blanket. The Republicans' objectives were formulated in their 'Five Demands', which were free peer association; the right not to do prison work and to organize their own recreational and educational pursuits; one visit, letter and parcel weekly; the right not to wear prison uniform; and the full restoration of remission lost through protest. As the Blanket protests and hunger strikes in the men's prisons are the most extensively chronicled aspects of imprisonment during the Troubles (see Coogan 1980; O'Malley 1990; Feldman 1991; Campbell *et al.* 1994), the following account focuses on the women's prison protests during the period.

In December 1976, the first woman to be sentenced for a scheduled offence and denied political status, Brenda Murray, was reported to be in 'solitary confinement' in Armagh prison (*Irish News* 3 December 1976). She was joined within a month by Mairéad Farrell and Elizabeth Morgan in the 'fight for the retention of political status' (*Irish News* 31 December 1976).[3] Within a year, all sentenced prisoners had withdrawn from work and education, and were refusing to interact with staff or follow orders that were not transmitted through their OC (*Irish Times* 12 September 1977; *Irish Times* 11 October 1978). By 1979, 34 sentenced and four remand prisoners were on the protest, in addition to four 'status' prisoners, sentenced before criminalization came into effect, who 'morally supported' the strikers (H-Block Information Bureau n.d. (circa 1979)). The issue of prison clothing did not directly affect women prisoners, as the requirements to wear a prison uniform had been lifted since women were interned in 1972, 'following a similar move in Great Britain several years before' (NIO 1981: 11). In the first few months of the non-cooperation strike, Republican women prisoners noted that their protests had not significantly inconvenienced the prison administration: 'In Armagh Jail there has been nothing like the degree of tension [as in the Maze]. Interference and communication between staff and prisoners has been kept to a minimum by *mutual consent*. [However] it was doubtful ... that these relations would continue' (*Irish News* 11 October 1976, emphasis added).

Modes of re-enclosure: discipline and punishment

The revocation of special category status allowed the full application of the prison rules and the reintroduction of normal disciplinary procedures. Although the obligation to adhere to the prison rules had formally stood between 1972 and 1976, it had been rendered almost ineffectual by special category status. The effects of the return of formal adjudication against the non-cooperating prisoners were dramatic and contentious. After the first year of the non-cooperation strikes in Armagh prison alone, the number of recorded disciplinary infractions rose 16-fold, from 33 to 550, whilst the number of punishments awarded increased 23-fold from the previous year (Figure 2.1). The rates of recorded offences doubled again in 1978, to just over 1,000, and increased by a further 70 per cent in 1979 (Figure 2.1). Furthermore, the small number of women who were punished evidenced the concentration of the punishment system against those involved in the political campaign. In 1977, the number of women disciplined totalled 45 for 550 infringements and 944 awards of punishments, or a ratio of 21 punishments for every prisoner convicted (Figure 2.1). This increased to 57 awards per prisoner convicted in 1979. In addition, new, specified offences were created as the protest continued. In 1977, a new category of 'refusing to work or wear a prison uniform' was introduced (NIPS 1978) whilst in 1979, the offence of 'non-conformity' was implemented (NIPS 1980).

The conspicuously enlarged role of the adjudication system against the protesters prompted the authorities to distance themselves from any instrumental political motives that could be inferred from it: 'For the duration of their sentences [prisoners] are members of small, enclosed communities, confined within clearly defined physical perimeters. In such circumstances, if firm control were lacking, the weak would be at the mercy of the strong and life would become unbearable for many prisoners' (NIPS 1979: 15). As indiscipline increased and internal judicial mechanisms failed to curtail the non-cooperation strike, the authorities sought to further downplay the political character of the protesters' motivations: 'At Armagh, some 30 women continued to refuse to work but otherwise did not actively seek confrontation with the prison authorities' (*ibid.*: 16). The official tactic of equating the women's protest with mere indiscipline was outlined in a special pamphlet issued by the NIO, *Day to Day Life in Northern Ireland Prisons* (1981: 11, emphasis added) which asserted that, as there had been 'much less overt confrontation' in Armagh than in the Maze:

> The punishments awarded *were correspondingly less* – letters were not restricted and association was not lost *to the same extent.* Despite the protest and the deliberate attempt to bring about a deterioration of the regime, there has been *no increase in the punishments given* … With the exception of association, which could no longer be free, owing to the prisoners' aggressive behaviour, there has been no change in the regime other than that *self-imposed by the prisoners.*

The pamphlet thus issued the disingenuous claim that the number, as opposed to the rate, of punishments awarded in Armagh was lower than that in the considerably larger male population. Furthermore, it disregarded the extraordinary rise in offending recorded at Armagh between 1976 and 1980. The NIO's main concern was to emphasize the normal functioning and unchanged nature of the regime at Armagh, and to restate the position that regular conditions 'were available' to prisoners who nevertheless stubbornly persisted in depriving themselves of normal privileges (*ibid.*: 15). Yet in contradiction, the Northern Ireland Prison Service defended the:

> large numbers of offences listed under 'other breaches of regulations' and punishments under 'loss of privileges' [which reflected] the groups of prisoners engaged in the various prison protests … In Northern Ireland the system is faced with cohesive groups of prisoners, many convicted or held on remand for the most serious of offences, who seek to challenge the conditions of their imprisonment and the very legitimacy of the State which imprisons them (NIPS 1981: 13).

In 1980, the number of infringements dropped by two thirds, and remained constant, although relatively high, until 1984. Although it is difficult to establish one predominant reason, a number of external and internal influences contributed to the apparent decrease in indiscipline. From 1980, the NIO had altered their system of recording punishments, so that the number of repeat offenders and the ratio of multiple punishments borne by individual prisoners could not be so clearly established. These changes in calculation may have reflected an increased political sensitivity to public criticisms of conditions in the prisons. An alternative view is that the character of confrontation in the prison had shifted to informal violence and an escalating culture of retaliation between prisoners and staff (Faul 1978: 135–7). The decline in formal punishment from 1980 was also related to changes in the direction taken by Republican prisoners, who shifted their protest to more extreme forms. As discussed below, Republican prisoners at Armagh were engaged in a 'no-wash' protest for much of 1980. Republicans also suspended elements of their non-cooperation protest to coincide with two hunger strikes, in 1980 and 1981, respectively, although they were still refusing to participate in compulsory work well into 1982 (McKeown 2001: 122). With the escalation of the prison protests to a far more serious and politically contentious scale, the authorities turned to more directly repressive measures to quarantine the disruptive effects of the protest. In this context, the fall in recorded punishments from 1980 does not conclusively establish a break from the cycle of conflict that had developed in Armagh prison. Rather, the methods for establishing control reflected a shift in focus from individual punishment to suppressing the protesters as a group.

The 'no-wash' protest, 1980[4]

The precise origins of the 'no-wash' protest are obscured in the debates and counterclaims of prisoners, civil libertarians, Republican prisoner welfare organizations and the Northern Ireland Office. An early indication that women Republicans were preparing for an additional form of protest appeared in February 1980, when the Republican prisoners' welfare organization, the H-Block Information Centre, reported that the occupants of 'B' wing of Armagh prison, which housed the protesting prisoners, were being 'denied proper facilities to keep their cells clean' (*Irish News* 7 February 1980). As prisoners were refusing to engage in routine prison work, including cleaning, and as there was an outbreak of scabies on the wing, they concluded that the authorities had taken the decision not to maintain 'B' wing so as to 'force them … into a no-wash strike' (*ibid.*).

The events that precipitated the no-wash strike were reported accordingly. On 7 February 1980, a Republican prisoner told the prison chaplain and her MP that she had been assaulted after being prevented by staff from leaving her cell to go to the toilet when she was ill. The following day, the NIO issued a statement that a number of women had been confined to their cells and deprived of toilet facilities, except for their 'slop-pots' [*sic*] (*Irish News* 8 February 1980). The day after, the prison service confirmed that a lockdown was implemented after 'paramilitary clothing and flags' were discovered during a search of the Republican wing (*Irish Press* 9 February 1980). That morning, a separate disturbance had broken out when five Republicans had to be carried by staff to the fortnightly adjudication to account for charges of indiscipline accrued in their non-cooperation protest (*Irish Times* 9 February 1980). The NIO later said that there had been no incidents until midday, when the sentenced prisoners were collecting their meal whilst the other prisoners were locked up: 'The governor then had the (sentenced) prisoners lined up at the hot plate on the ground floor and … announced a general search', with which the prisoners refused to co-operate (*ibid.*). Male officers from the Maze had been called in to 'assist' in the search, and it further emerged that male 'trade officers' or maintenance staff 'went to the aid of women warders when trouble broke out' (*Irish News* 9 February 1980). Prisoners' relatives said that 33 Republican and three Loyalist prisoners were involved, and that most had been beaten by prison staff (*Irish Press* 9 February 1980). The Republicans were moved to 'A' wing over the weekend, whilst the Loyalists were confined to their cells. On 12 February, the Republican women started to throw the contents of their slop buckets out of cell windows into the exercise yard below them. When cell doors were opened for meals and evening recreation the women scattered excrement and urine across the landings. The prison department at the NIO later stated that by the following Monday 'most of the women' in the whole prison were washing themselves and that the claims that prisoners were 'forced into a "no-wash" protest were a fabrication'. 'They were being allowed to leave their cells and eat meals, take daily exercise and visit the washrooms each morning. But they were refusing to work, hand over their sheets for cleaning or read books from the library, *although facilities were still open to them*' (*Belfast Telegraph* 14 February 1980, emphasis added).

From the official perspective, access to sanitary, recreational and other facilities was available to prisoners once they agreed to end the non-cooperation protest and abide by the prison regulations. For ten months, 34 women (which later fell to 26) were confined to their cells for 23 hours a day, refusing access to sanitary and other facilities on the basis that it was subject to conforming to the criminal regime. Prisoners eventually took to smearing the walls and ceilings of their cells with excrement and menstrual blood, and draining urine underneath their cell doors (D'arcy 1981: 51). They damaged the fittings and furniture in their cells, with the result that the governor ordered the removal of cell furniture, except for one iron bedstead, one mattress and one pillow. The fetid condition of the cells was compounded by the accumulation of excrement and leftover food, and because the circulation of air and natural light was blocked when cell windows were boarded up by staff to prevent prisoners from pouring out their waste. The grim conditions on the strike emerged through 'comms' written on sheets of toilet paper and smuggled out of Armagh:

> We have been here on 'A' wing since the 15th of February, and conditions have rapidly deteriorated. We are on a 23 hour lock up and are living in cells completely covered with excreta … After three months of living under inhuman conditions, surrounded by our own excreta and denied basic human rights, we are suffering considerably. Our bodies are encrusted with dirt[,] our hair is matted and greasy to the touch, and the smell emanating from our bodies is really disgusting. To lie in a cell smeared with excreta is a hideous experience, but we have to endure it. It is either this or accept the label 'criminal' and none of us here on this protest are criminals. We are prisoners of war, gaoled for political acts and firm in the knowledge that what we are fighting for is just.
>
> Our cells are dark and dreary and the fact that there are boards on the windows does not help. As a result of this, no daylight enters our cells and we have to keep the electric lights on. Very little air gets in either, so there is no way to dissapate [sic] the stench that assails us. We have one hour of exercise each day, one hour of fresh air, a chance to stretch our legs and to see the sky. This may not sound like much, but to us it is the high point of our day. Not only do we get out of our cell but we also see nine of our comrades. The same nine girls each time, but at least we have some contact with each other (original 'comm', signed Anna Freil, 'A' wing Armagh prison, May 1980).

Hunger strike, December 1980

The 'no-wash' strike lasted until 1 December 1980, when three women prisoners, Mairéad Farrell, Mary Doyle and Mairéad Nugent, joined a Republican hunger strike that had been in progress in the Maze since 27 October. The decision to escalate their protests to a hunger strike occurred after Republican prisoners rejected a series of concessions on clothing and limited association as inadequate and unrelated to the question of political recognition. In an interview after her release, Farrell said that the women's decision was prompted partly by the need to 'create an additional source of pressure on the prison authorities', and also because of a 'calculated risk' that the deaths of women in prison would place 'additional moral pressure' on the government to come to an agreement with Republican prisoners (*Magill* October 1986: 4–5).[5] Farrell was initially separated from the other two strikers, but soon all three were moved to a separate wing. They refused all food, but drank water and took salt tablets. By the eleventh day, they were moved to the prison hospital, by which time Farrell was experiencing difficulty in swallowing.

Farrell, Doyle and Nugent had joined the 1980 hunger strike in the face of contrary advice from the PIRA leadership outside, having earlier laid plans with the Maze prisoners for their possible entry on to a cross-prison strike a month before the men commenced theirs. Farrell had written to the acting commanding officer in the Maze, Bobby Sands, arguing that they had already drawn the conclusion that the 'no-wash' protest was insufficient, and that the participation of women on a hunger strike would introduce additional practical and symbolic dimensions to the whole prison protest:

> As was generally expected here the Cardinal/Atkins talks were a failure.[6] We have been making a general assessment of the no-wash protest here to see if there is any way in which we could step up the protest for status. We all believe that something else, some other form of action is needed to ram it home to the Brits. So discussion at present is heavy (Original comm, signed
>   M. Farrell, Armagh prison, 29 September 1980).

If the government did consider the implications of women's involvement in a hunger strike, it did not openly demonstrate any deviation from its position when Humphrey Atkins, Secretary of State for Northern Ireland, told the House of Commons, 'we shall not be coerced by threats, whether the blackmail of a hunger strike or other forms of protest inside or outside the prisons, into recognising that the alleged motive for a crime justifies some form of preferential treatment in prison' (*Commons Written Answers* 12 December 1980: 489). At the same time, the government made a formal gesture of recognizing the separate status of the women when it sent its proposals to end the hunger strikes to the Maze and Armagh simultaneously (*Commons Written Answers* 19 December 1980: 358). However, Farrell did not record her involvement in any negotiations, nor any influence the Armagh prisoners had on the course of subsequent decisions. This is hardly surprising, given the confused accounts of the events leading to the ending of the first hunger strike on 18 December 1980, amid Republican recriminations that the government had reneged on the agreed terms, and counter-claims from the government that they had substantially acceded to the 'humanitarian' aspects of the five demands, without conceding the moral principle of non-recognition.

What is evident, however, is that whilst Sands, who was not a participant in the 1980 strike, was able to mediate with official negotiators and the outside leadership, Farrell had been separated from 'A' company whilst leading the hunger strike from the prison hospital. She was informed by her acting OC, Sheila Darragh, that the NIO had come to an agreement with the prisoners at the Maze, and the strike was called off. A second hunger strike commenced on 1 March 1981, which involved men prisoners in the Maze only, and ended with the death by starvation of ten Republicans before it was halted on 3 October 1981. This time the will of the Provisional Army Council had prevailed, as Farrell's request for permission for the women in Armagh to go on hunger strike was vetoed. Loyalists in the men's prisons had also started a hunger strike in February 1981, but it was characteristically short lived (*Commons Written Answers* 5 February 1981: 161). The second strike also ended with some acrimony but with the prisoners having achieved some of their demands – wearing their own clothing, the restoration of half the remission lost through protests, freedom of association, a 'review' of prison work, extra facilities – but not the reinstatement of special category status.

Gendered aspects of prison struggle

The significance of the women's protests in advancing their status within the broader Republican prison campaign was shaped in the context of, even despite, contradictory ideological and strategic constraints. From the outset, the official strategy had been to marginalize the protests at Armagh by understating the severity of their conditions during the protest, and by claiming that it amounted to a relatively inconsequential disciplinary problem. Similarly, the initial ambivalence of the Republican leadership towards their involvement in the first hunger strike had left them at risk of remaining on the margins of the prison campaign. The decision by women prisoners to embark on hunger strike had been opposed by the Provisional Army Council, which had already 'faced the prospect of a revolt against its authority' by the Maze prisoners on the issue (Taylor 1997: 230). More concretely, by 1980, there were concerns that any escalation in the protests in Armagh would divert attention from the Maze and over-extend the capacity of the Republican movement to manage any external political fallout caused by the death of a prisoner (Coogan 1980: 118). In addition, the leadership feared that the women's campaign was more susceptible to defeat, which would jeopardize morale and dissipate the political support that had been gained by the Blanket strikes. The Armagh women were sensitive to being represented as the 'weak link in Republican resistance' both within their own organization and by the prison administration (*H-Block/Armagh Committee press release*, 2 March 1981). By contrast, they held that the legitimacy of their protests arose less from motives of 'solidarity with the ... H-Block prisoners', and more in self-defining terms as an 'uncompromising refusal to be intimidated ... into abandoning their fight for political status' (*Armagh Protest Committee press release*, 27 February 1980). The attitude of the Army Council must also be seen in the context of their view that it was precisely the potent effects of a possible propaganda coup which could be gained from women dying on hunger strike, as Farrell had advocated, that could equally become its undoing. Furthermore, they were damaged by charges, deployed so effectively by their critics, that the Republican movement was a forcing house of martyrdom wherein susceptible young and female Volunteers were compelled or deluded on to starvation strikes.

However, the strikes had succeeded in placing the conditions and demands of women prisoners in the public domain, and legitimizing their role in the Republican prisoner structure. More practically, by 1980 there were sufficient numbers of prisoners sentenced without political status to sustain a viable campaign. Similarly, Doyle's, Farrell's and Nugent's hunger strike was influenced by the need to sustain morale, as some prisoners had elected to came off the no-wash strike and conform to the regular regime. In this context, the role of the post-criminalization leadership, including Mary Doyle and Ellen McGuigan, commanding and second officers respectively from 1976 to 1978, offers evidence of tighter internal discipline and tactical perspicacity on the part of the women's prison structures, compared to the relative incoherence and factionalism of the early 1970s. Farrell, who assumed command in 1979, and Nugent, who had mediated with external negotiators during the no-wash strike, had meticulously consolidated the objectives and momentum of the Armagh protests with those in the Maze. Crucially, too, the women's decision to escalate their protests had been driven by a number of precipitating stresses including the intense antagonism and distrust between prisoners and administrators that had developed over the preceding years, the neutralization of the non-cooperation campaign and the additional certainty of defeat and dispersal of 'A' Company if the wider political impasse over the criminalization policy continued. For this reason, their break with the external leadership was taken on the balance of preventing their exposure to official retaliation and the necessity of not breaking ranks with the other prisons.

Modes of re-enclosure: the medical management of prison protests

The hunger strike is a long-standing and relatively common form of prison resistance which has a political genealogy that embraces nationalist and colonial struggles, as well as being a powerful symbolic route of individual protest (Ludwig 1981). The legislative grounds in the UK for intervening to end a starvation strike against the will of the prisoner were originally embodied in the Prisoners Temporary Discharge for Ill-health Act 1913, enacted to deal with hunger-striking suffragists, which ordained that prison officials had a duty to preserve the life of prisoners. Subsequently, prisoners who refused to eat were placed under the authority of prison medical officers as patients, and fed against their will, on the basis that their willingness to undergo 'self-inflicted' harm established their mental incapacitation. Alternatively, the infamous 'cat and mouse clauses' of the Act allowed prisoners to be temporarily released, subject to recall by order after they recovered. The last instance in England and Wales where forced feeding was used under these terms was during the strike by Dolours and Marion Price. The Prices, who had been imprisoned in 1973 with five other PIRA members for bombing the Old Bailey, commenced a hunger strike in Holloway prison in pursuit of their demand to be treated as political prisoners and to be 'repatriated' to Northern Ireland. The longevity of their hunger strike, which lasted for over 200 days (from 12 November 1973 to 3 June 1974), was due to the fact that they were forcibly fed, with intermittent respite whilst they brought injunctions against the prison authorities to prevent medical intervention. Following intense public pressure after the death by starvation of another Republican, Michael Gaughan, the Home Secretary agreed to their transfer to Armagh prison on 18 March 1975. From 1974, medical interventions were guided by the 'Jenkins protocols', formulated by the then Home Secretary for England and Wales, Roy Jenkins. These confirmed the powers of attorney held by prison medical officers to determine the competence of prisoners to make a rational decision to refuse medical treatment. Whilst the rules did not permit a doctor to treat a patient forcibly, intervention was permitted if 'individual prisoners cause an unacceptable health hazard to other inmates, staff or the community, such measures as may be necessary will be taken to counter the risk' (*Commons Written Answers* 19 December 1980: 342).

Ludwig (1981: 169) points out that the State 'has no affirmative obligation to intercede to preserve a life', but considerable legal and political problems arise when it assumes responsibility for the life of a hunger striker in deciding 'whether [to] let the inmate or patient run the risk of dying from hunger strike or compel them to take sustenance'. Despite the existence of legal precedents, medical intervention in hunger strikes in the UK was significantly informed by political calculations on the part of successive government ministers when applying the guidelines for intervention. In Northern Ireland, there had been no intervention in the 1972 hunger strikes that led to special category status being granted. In Britain, the decision to intervene in the case of the Price sisters two years later was prompted by the potential consequences of allowing women to die in custody, as well as creating a deterrent effect against such a protest being embarked on in the future (Coogan 1980: 120).

During the hunger strikes of 1980–1, the government maintained its position that the decision to intervene was guided exclusively by the professional competence and authority of doctors and lawyers, with which the State interfered with the greatest reluctance. As Humphrey Atkins told the House of Commons:

> prisoners will continue to be kept under close medical surveillance and will be offered any medical treatment that may be necessary. *This will be on the judgement of the doctors in charge,* acting in accordance with the ethics of their profession. Medical treatment is not forced on a prisoner who refuses it (*Commons Debates* 27 November 1980, 556–7, emphasis added).

At the same time, this posture of scrupulous disinterest was vested in larger moral, political and ideological struggles over the legitimacy of the government's position. A consistent strand in the government's public utterances against special category status was that it had institutionalized 'privileged, differential treatment' which was 'greatly resented by the ordinary criminals' (*Irish News* 30 July 1975). Thus, further significant concessions could only be forthcoming after these unfair advantages were eradicated and the system reverted to a common set of standards 'applicable to all prisoners and designed to produce a fair and humane prison system' (NIPS 1978: 2). This rhetorical concern with 'privileges' was a crucial persuasive tactic: it sought to isolate the mercenary and divisive demands of Republicans from the higher causes of equity, justice and prisoner's rights more generally; it allowed the government to recover the moral momentum by being seen to resist illegitimate demands on any grounds; it positioned the striking prisoners as opponents of enlightened penal policy; and it connoted the restoration of just deserts to prisoners who had previously escaped the full rigours of punishment because of special category status. Yet as O'Malley (1990: 206–7) has pointed out, the representation of the prison strikes in these terms reflected 'the form the propaganda war took' on both sides, and was one of the reasons why Republicans steered away from the term political status, 'referring only to the five demands of prison reform'. Finally, the focus on 'privileges' was a method of driving a wedge between those who openly endorsed the 'political' basis of the prisoners' demands and the wavering unease of public opinion. It largely succeeded in directing the debate away from objectionable arguments about political status and towards more morally justifiable incentives to prisoners to serve their time in relative conformity.

In this context, the official language of the government's duty of care was redolent with magnanimity in the face of the prisoners' refusal to abandon their 'bizarre campaign of self-imposed squalor' (*Irish News* 7 March 1980). 'Medical supervision of the protesters continues, as far as they themselves allow it. There have been no cases of illness attributable to the conditions, which the prisoners concerned have created for themselves' (*Commons Debates* 12 November 1980, 245–6). The position was affirmed by the European Commission on Human Rights which ruled in June 1980 that the conditions in the prisons were indeed self-inflicted and politically motivated, and thus did not constitute a violation of the prisoners' human rights. The government was thus vindicated: 'this decision clears away the carefully fostered belief that the human rights of the prisoners engaged in the protest have been interfered with. The conditions in which protesting prisoners live ... are caused by their own actions. The Commission has recognized this fact' (*Commons Debates* 18 June 1980: 587–8).

Hystericization, medicalization and clemency: pathologizing women's protests

Considerable critical attention has been paid to the reciprocal relationships between medical practice, gendered governance, and discipline and punishment in prisons (Ignatieff 1978; Porter 1990; Sim 1990). Historically, this relationship developed out of separate developments in correctional and medical interventions which sought to create 'the well-adjusted individual out of an undifferentiated mass of criminals' (Sim 1990: Preface), but which eventually allowed the prisons to become flourishing laboratories in 'which the advice and expertise of the medical profession, both physicians and psychiatrists, were geared to reintegrating the confined back to normality' (*ibid.*: 9). Furthermore, the history of scientific progress attests to the objectification of women as the material and metaphorical 'other' of Enlightenment thought and, from the end of the nineteenth century, as distinctive subjects of criminal pathologization in psychiatric and eugenicist narratives (Martin 1989). Feminist scholarship has pointed to the history of innovation in the clinical and correctional sciences which has centred on the morbidity of women's 'hystericized', immoral and 'disordered' selves (Sim 1990: 129–76; Russell 1995). 'Deciphering that inscription is usually seen as a matter of determining the "cause" of the disorder … But always the process requires a trained – that is to say a highly specialized – professional whose expertise alone can unlock the secrets of the disordered body' (Bordo 1993: 67). Professional power and knowledge in prisons have thus constructed women's penal identity through intersecting practices of correction, 'cure', moral discipline and experimentation. Furthermore, the medicalization of female prisoners cements the association between penal categories of the 'dangerous' and 'disturbed' woman and novel forms of therapeutic intervention. As Mandaraka-Sheppard (1986: 208) notes, this has continued to support the use of 'psychiatric methods and psychotropic drugs of therapy' against 'hard core troublemakers' in the contemporary prison system for women.

Whilst acknowledging the considerable critical contribution which this literature makes to recognizing how women prisoners are positioned in a matrix of professional scrutiny, institutional discipline and social reconstruction, the State tends to figure as a relatively distant entity which licenses medical practice and provides, through the prison welfare and therapeutic services, the domains of specialist intervention. However, the interventionist interests of governmental and medico-juridical spheres in Northern Ireland conspicuously combined at the most serious points of crisis during the prison protests to bring them to an end (O'Malley 1990: 117–28; Campbell *et al.* 1994: 242–56). As Sim (1990: 181) has pointed out, the oppressive relations that converge around prison medicine do not simply arise from the appropriation of clinical expertise to the disciplinary ethos of prisons, although that does occur, but also through the intricate convergence of professional, ideological and 'individualized understandings of deviance'. However, Sim has also argued that this relationship 'becomes complete in a political sense' as prisons acquire a complex interventionist-punitive function, supported by the professional authority and discretion of various 'organic intellectuals' in the prison therapeutic network (*ibid.*: 180).

Just as pertinently, prison medicine played a part in deterring the continuation of the prison strikes in Northern Ireland. The physical condition of women prisoners on the no-wash strike deteriorated noticeably, with prisoners reporting that they were suffering from eye infections, scabies and dermatitis, bleeding gums, cystitis, diarrhoea, and weight and hair loss (D'arcy 1981: 79–83). The prison authorities maintained that 'no mental or physical illnesses [were] attributable to the conditions which the prisoners concerned have created for themselves' (*Commons Written Answers* 12 November 1980: 245–6), although 'vigilant steps' were taken 'by medical and other clinical staff to counteract the environmental health aspects of the "dirty protest"' (NIPS 1980: 18). The clinical supervision of the prisoners was deemed to be adequate as 'a medical officer visit[ed] the cells at least once a week to monitor and observe the internal conditions, personal hygiene standards and inmates' health, so far as this [was] practicable' as 'prisoners do not in general cooperate with ... clinical staff' (*Commons Written Answers* 19 December 1980: 341–2). D'arcy (1981: 86), however, noted the infantilizing attitude of the prison doctor in Armagh prison, who was alleged to have referred to their conditions as 'honeymoon disease', caused by 'nerves', and issued advice to them to 'get pregnant to clear up your skin'. 'The implication of the comments was that women are physically and mentally too weak to defy the government, and therefore they should give in ... and avail themselves of the selection of tranquillisers ... always ready in surgery' (*ibid.*).

There was a significant occurrence of eating disorders amongst women prisoners during the late 1970s, partly as a result of the prison protests, and in the case of remand and special category prisoners, because they could not eat prison food (*Commons Written Answers* 22 January 1981: 235–7). The NIO was prompted to repudiate allegations that Largactyl, a sedative used in the treatment of schizophrenia and depression, and known for its use in prisons as a 'chemical straightjacket', was being prescribed for 'experimental or disciplinary purposes' (*Irish News* 24 November 1978). Prison doctors, the NIO continued, had 'complete freedom of judgement in prescribing them'. Some incidents of self-mutilation by remand prisoners were also reported (*Irish Press* 29 April 1980). Between 1978 and 1981, eight female prisoners were released on licence or pardoned on medical or compassionate grounds, of whom seven were serving sentences for politically related offences. In two of the four cases of release on medical grounds, 'anorexia nervosa' was cited as the principal or only illness (NIPS 1978: 15). One prisoner subsequently died after her release from prison (*Commons Written Answers* 22 January 1981: 235–7). Two more prisoners resigned from the no-wash strike on the grounds of ill-health related to 'severe weight loss' and various 'nervous conditions' and were transferred to the 'ordinary' wings. The medical grounds for releasing a prisoner on licence were stringently applied in cases where it was 'reasonably clear that a person was suffering from a terminal illness and that death was likely to occur soon', where a prisoner was bedridden and totally incapacitated, and where it appeared that 'further imprisonment would of itself endanger life or reason, or shorten life expectancy' (*ibid.*).

A small number of prisoners who were not on the protest were released in 1980, in response to civil libertarian and political campaigns on their behalf. These included Marion Price, who was released at the end of April 1980 (*Guardian* 1 May 1980). Price's health was acknowledged by the NIO to have deteriorated to a point where she 'was in imminent danger of sudden collapse and death if she remained in custody' (*Daily Express* 1 May 1980). Edith Mullen, a Loyalist, was released with full remission one year before her sentence expired (*Craigavon Times* 27 June 1980). The releases, and especially that of Price, aroused Unionist outrage. The following year, Dolours Price was released to condemnations of the 'deliberate use of the ploy of this so-called slimmer's disease to secure their release from prison', and criticisms of the 'weakness of the Secretary of State for engaging in a trade with the Republican movement', by using releases to encourage the cessation of the hunger strike at the Maze (*Belfast Telegraph* 22 April 1981).

Although the early releases were granted on the basis of substantive medical and humanitarian grounds, their timing, and the justification of the case for clemency within a matrix of legal, political and medical discourses, had wider implications for constructing the women's protests in pathological terms. The recourse to clinical and psychiatric authority (in anticipation of the political outcry that would inevitably follow their releases) subsumed their motives and political agency into the domain of clinical discourse. For example, the references in official bulletins to anorexia and other 'hysterical' disorders harnessed contemporary discourses of wilful and 'self-inflicted' deprivation to historical, penal constructions of women's irrationality and frailty. In a broader sense, the period of prison conflict was defined by the contradictory effects of the women's resistance. It reinscribed them in denser networks of therapeutic and punitive intervention, enhanced the authority of judicial and psychiatric decision-making, and reinforced the legitimacy of clinical and correctional intrusions into their bodies and minds.

Part three: 'normalization', 1982–98

At this point it is useful to clarify the terms of reference of 'normalization' as conceived of by Gormally and McEvoy (1995), as theirs is a functional model of administrative priorities which differs from our concerns in the first chapter with normalization as an element of a 'militaristic technocracy ... inscribed within legal and bureaucratic practices' (O'Dowd *et al.* 1980: 20). Gormally and McEvoy's (1995: 295) version of normalization refers to the period after 1981 which, they argue, saw 'an explicit abandonment of the policy of criminalisation' at least in its pure form, a growing recognition of the prison system as 'a mechanism for managing some of [the] human consequences of political violence' and an acknowledgement of the 'normality of division and violence'. The authors' concern is with characterizing new styles of prison management and relating them to administrative concepts of normalised penal treatment, under which prisoners have the same rights to legal protection and access to care and welfare services as other citizens. At the same time, neither the objectives of normalizing prison administration nor establishing uniform standards for all offenders could be dissociated from previous ideological struggles over criminalization, nor from the implications of the new approach for further levelling out the vestiges of separate status that remained after 1981. As Tomlinson (1995: 218, emphasis added) succinctly put it: 'the generally more tender-minded managerial approach [of the post hunger-strikes era] ... *was* the direct outcome of that conflict.'

The period between the aftermath of the 1981 hunger strike and the release of prisoners under the terms of the Belfast Agreement (1998), then, is understood in this analysis as one of tentative, and highly contested, penal experimentation which rested on the anomalous precept that the abnormalities of political imprisonment could be smoothed over by bureaucratic normalcy. The new departure in prison administration proceeded from a range of initiatives for making 'constructive progress' in establishing working relationships with the political factions in the prisons and to enabling the prison administration to 'put behind them the disruptions and tensions created by the hunger strikes of 1980 and 1981' (NIPS 1982: 1–2). 'Normalization' had two interconnected objectives. Politically, it referred to an ostensible shift away from the orthodoxies of 'defeating terrorism' that had prevailed since 1976 towards an official adaptation to the realities of paramilitary influence in the prisons. This appeared to signal the tacit moderation of the

49

criminalization policy in favour of 'flexible' approaches and 'pragmatic' strategies for minimizing conflict by engaging political prisoners in common grounds of interest. The criminalization policy itself, however, was never formally revoked, although senior prison managers were allowed a degree of discretion in engaging with prisoners on a narrow range of concerns whilst excluding as far as possible from this remit any 'grand questions of political status' (McEvoy 2001: 251).

From the administrative perspective, normalization fostered a range of managerial approaches for reconfiguring the problems of dealing with political prisoners as merely bureaucratic concerns that were comparable to those arising in other, more 'normal' prison systems. This particular variant of normalization supported the tactic of heading off potential conflict over political status and conditions by stripping these issues of their political symbolism and treating them as neutral technical or operational problems. At the same time, there were considerable overlaps between the administrative and political dimensions of prison management, especially in the concern with identifying and containing the influence of prisoners as the main source of instability in the prison system. The new technocratic ethos thus facilitated the more acute management of the public face of the prison system, whilst internal prison governance was conspicuously directed towards quietly containing paramilitary influence in the prisons.

In practice, 'normalization' covered almost two decades of advances and retreats over a series of issues connected with the central question of political recognition in the prisons. As such, the policy evolved in two phases, the first of which saw a continuation of conflict between 1981 and 1987 centring on changes to regimes that largely resembled earlier stratagems for imposing criminalization. Specifically, these were the introduction of an 'integration' policy which attempted to complete the unfinished business of disbanding the paramilitary structures and dispersing Loyalist and Republican prisoners into the general prison population. The second area of contention arose as a consequence of enhancing prison security, which was viewed by prisoners as an encroachment on the rights of autonomous association and self-management that had been gained by the hunger strikes (McKeown 2001: 81–6). More broadly, political prisoners rejected the 'rehabilitative' and incentive-based ethos of the new approach as being tied to modes of governance which required individual conformity and self-reform, which implied in turn that they relinquish their political subjectivity and disband their structures.

The integration policy

Political prisoners assert that segregation, or the claimed 'right' to be held with those of similar political allegiance and apart from other prisoners, is a central practical and symbolic condition of their detention. The broader penal context in which the review of segregation in Northern Ireland took place followed a series of major security breaches. The Pearce Inquiry (1981) into the escape of eight Republicans from Belfast prison recommended the immediate implementation of substantial improvements to security. In 1983, the escape of 38 Republicans from the Maze instigated a more radical review of security. The subsequent Hennessey Report (1984) concluded that, as well as 'considerable shortfalls' in security procedures, there had been widespread failures on the part of staff which had led to the suborning of individual officers by the escapees (*ibid.*: 3.05–3.08). Significantly, Hennessey reasoned that the continuance of 'segregat[ed] paramilitary factions' had 'made it easier for groups of prisoners to plan and conduct escapes or disturbances'. 'We have little doubt that prisoners in segregated Blocks are generally better able to plan and execute subversive activities of all kinds. Except on those rare occasions when opposing factions are prepared to act together in pursuance of a common objective, integrated Blocks are easier to control' (*ibid.*: 9.29).

Eight years later, the Colville Inquiry (1992) was conducted into the death of a Loyalist prisoner in Belfast prison, following violent Loyalist and Republican resistance to integration. Colville placed the continuance of segregated association at the centre of endemic disorder in the prisons, over 60 foiled escape attempts, violence against staff, and between Loyalist and Republican prisoners. As with all other aspects of prison discipline, Colville reasoned, political prisoners inevitably and adroitly reshaped the prison rules for the 'evidently political ends' of subverting prison order (*ibid.*: 3.1.1). Furthermore, the 'long-standing commitment' to treatment and rehabilitation was negated in segregated conditions because the prisoners were shielded from professional intervention by their command structures, and consequently posed a fundamental obstacle to prison reform (*ibid.*: 7.2.3).

Segregation and enhanced security at Armagh prison, 1982–86

The implementation of the integration policy at Armagh prison produced few comparable levels of disorder, in part because the predominance of Republican women practically ensured that they had segregated use of facilities, and in part because confrontations with the authorities were treated in terms of orchestrated disorder to be dealt with through the disciplinary process: 'For a short time, some [Loyalist and Republican] women prisoners in Armagh attempted to secure segregation by staging fights and intimidating other prisoners. The governor dispersed the prisoners involved throughout the prison, and the protest ended' (NIPS 1983: 10). However, enhanced security in Armagh prison was primarily defined by the significantly increased reliance on cell and body searches between 1982 and 1986. Strip searching had been in use in Northern Ireland since 1949, although its practice was generally confined to 'reception' strips and on some occasions when prisoners entered or left the establishment. This policy was reviewed in November 1982 following the discovery of keys in the possession of two young remand prisoners after a court hearing (*Commons Written Answers* 15 March 1983: 120). The number of strip searches rose significantly when the procedure was systematically applied at all times of reception and discharge, before and after visits, attendance at court, entry and exit from temporary and compassionate leave, inter-prison visits and attendance at outside hospitals. The incidence of strip searching on prisoners subsequently fell in 1984, following a second review in 1983, when the prison department reformulated the guidelines for its use on a 'random basis only' (NIO 1985: 4). Nevertheless, the circumstances and frequency with which random strip searching was used continued to draw widespread criticism from humanitarian, political, professional, religious and academic sources. In this context, the NIO moved to allay their 'well meaning' concerns about prison conditions: 'It is regrettable that many grossly inaccurate, and often malicious accounts of the procedures have been and still are in circulation. The government is satisfied that it is necessary to have recourse to this form of searching in the interests of security, including the safety of the prisoners themselves' (NIPS 1983: 10).

In the pamphlet, *Armagh Prison Strip Searching: The Facts* (1985), the NIO outlined its defence of the procedure in response to specific points of disquiet that were raised by a succession of unofficial investigations into strip searching.[7] The document noted the widespread normality and common acceptance of the procedure in various countries, as well as its soundness as a method for ensuring prisoners' safety and security (*ibid.*: 1). Every prisoner was legally required to be searched on reception, 'and at such subsequent times as the governor may order' (NIO 1982: 9 (1)). Prisoners were to be searched in 'as seemly a manner as is consistent with discovering anything concealed' (*ibid.*: 9 (3)), were not to be stripped in the sight of another prisoner and were to be searched only by, and only in the presence of, officers of the same sex (*ibid.*: 9 (4, 5). The use of the procedure was argued to be 'broadly the same' in Britain and Northern Ireland, although the type of search and occasion for use depended 'primarily on operational and security considerations', which could 'differ not only between the two jurisdictions, but also from institution to institution' (*Commons Written Answers* 5 July 1983: 79–80).

Having sought to defend the legitimacy of strip searching, the authorities then turned to narrowing humanitarian concerns to specific security and technical considerations. In response to criticisms raised by the British Medical Association that there were insufficient medical safeguards in place, the NIO countered that 'search procedures [were] a security requirement [and] not a medical one' (SACHRE 1986: 34). Furthermore, it was claimed that strip searching was not invasive, in so far as searches initially constituted a bodily 'rub-down' and the use of a metal detector whilst the prisoner was clothed, and only extended to a visual inspection of the naked body 'should any further intervention be considered appropriate by the searching officer' (NIO 1985: 3).

Yet other guidelines for dealing with non-cooperative prisoners suggest that it was doubtful that the procedure was devoid of physical contact. The procedural specifications that were eventually submitted by the NIO at the request of the Standing Advisory Commission on Human Rights (SACHRE) contained sufficient ambiguities to substantiate prisoners' allegations about intimidation, the forceful removal of their clothing and the presence of up to six staff, including male officers, at a search. It was, for example, an 'administrative practice, (*but not statutory requirement*) that only two female prison officers [were] *normally* present during the searches' (SACHRE 1986: 21). Whilst the official documentation eluded the question as to what occurred if a prisoner did not co-operate, it did concede that a search was enforced 'if a prisoner refused to lift her hair or her feet or to turn over her hands' (*ibid.*: 8). When prisoners who were menstruating refused to remove their sanitary protection, officers had 'the right to remove a sanitary towel, but not a tampon', adding that 'there has been no occasion … *when any refusal to meet such a request has been maintained*' (*ibid.*: 21, emphasis added). Moreover, the extensive testimonies collated by civil liberties groups shows a marked disparity between officials' and prisoners' perceptions, with the NIO suggesting that the process was discreet, perfunctory and impersonal, whilst prisoners and campaigners argued that it was degrading, often protracted and enforced.

The shift in policy from 'routine' to 'random' strip searching in 1983 implied, at least in theory, that well defined criteria were put in place for identifying the grounds for authorizing and carrying them out. In practice, according to an inquiry conducted by the National Council for Civil Liberties (NCCL), the decision to conduct a search adhered less to the principles of 'random' selection 'to avoid unfair bias', than to arbitrary risk assessments, based on the discretion of senior officers, in which the 'element of bias remain[ed]' (NCCL 1986: 15). The NIO repeatedly justified the necessity for high levels of staff vigilance because of the prisoners' 'dangerousness' (*ibid.*: 21), claiming that 'three quarters of the women prisoners in Armagh prison are charged or convicted of terrorist-related [*sic*] offences, including murder, attempted murder and possession of explosives and firearms' (NIO 1985: 4). At the same time, the yield of contraband that was found over four years, which might have silenced the critics, amounted to some tranquillizers, perfume, money and a 'comm'. These were discovered in prisoners' clothing and cells rather than on their bodies (SACHRE 1986: 23). Alternatively, it was officially argued that the number of complainants had increased because of the 'schooling and coercion' of incoming prisoners, 'as part of an orchestrated campaign' against the integration policy (*ibid.*: 34). The NIO thus summarized the circularity of its logic when it stated that 'in practice it is those prisoners who do not cooperate (i.e. in refusing to use the sheet, or lift the hair, etc.) who complain' (*ibid.*: 15).

In the long term, the implementation of 'random' strip searching was a serious political miscalculation on the part of the prison administration, as it brought events in Armagh prison to the political foreground, and mobilized a wider range of political, trade union, voluntary and civil liberties groups than might otherwise have been willing to lend support to a campaign connected with paramilitarism. Although the conclusion was widely drawn that the context and manner in which it was implemented indicated disturbing levels of conflict and the loss of order in Armagh prison, there were other factors which supported the view that the ramifications of strip searching were greater than simply augmenting internal security. The rise in the women's prison population after 1981, largely as a consequence of the civil disorder and increased recruitment to the PIRA during the hunger strikes, created the potential for women Republican prisoners to present a more formidable challenge to the integration policy.

Similarly, the escapes from Belfast and Maze prisons underlined the urgency of staunching the traffic of 'comms' or intelligence to other prisons and external sources. Remand prisoners, who made up the largest group of newcomers to the women's prison population, were most likely to be searched because of the risk of 'their acquiring, possibly under pressure, some dangerous or prohibited article while away from the prisons' (NIPS 1985: 6). The frequency of searches conducted on remand prisoners was also compounded by the comparatively long periods of remand, averaging two years for prisoners charged with scheduled offences (NCCL 1986: 22), and the longer sentences served by prisoners in Northern Ireland. An additional aspect of the allegations of partiality in implementing the practice was the protracted strip searching of prisoners remanded on 'supergrass' evidence.[8] The case of Catherine Moore illustrates the structural and administrative contexts which made the issue so politically charged. Moore was widely reported to have been strip searched over 120 times between 1982 and 1984 (IIP 1985: 4; NCCL 1986: 12). She was one of the influx of remand prisoners into Armagh in the early 1980s, having been charged with 92 offences on supergrass evidence. Given the frequency with which remand prisoners such as Moore made court appearances or received legal visits, even the application of 'routine' searches on exit and re-entry to their wings invariably supported perceptions that the implementation of security policy at Armagh was rudimentary, excessive, non-essential and retributive.

Enhanced security and reform: Mourne House, HMP Maghaberry, 1986–onwards

Prison reform in Northern Ireland was implemented in three strands arising from a series of reviews of the prison service between 1987 and 1991. The closure of Armagh prison and the transfer of female prisoners to the new prison in Mourne House also presented the authorities with a fresh opportunity to implement measures consistent with the 'normalization' policy. The first review, in 1987, which embodied the main tenets of the new penal thinking, placed an emphasis on providing 'a secure and high standard of accommodation' and the provision of training, education, welfare and probation services (NIPS 1988: 1). Secondly, the plan sought to restore the principle of rehabilitation and personal reform to the centre of the function of prisons by introducing progressive incentives for prisoners who co-operated with the regime, and encouraging prisoners to take full advantage of the opportunities offered during their confinement (ibid.). Crucially, the attainment of these objectives was tied to treating prisoners 'as individuals regardless of their religious beliefs or political opinions', and, 'as far as possible, [offering] them the opportunity to serve their sentences free from paramilitary influence' (ibid.). The third element of prison reform entailed constructing partnerships between the community and the prison service, and enhancing the public accountability and transparency of its procedures. The document, Serving the Community (NIPS 1991a), outlined a series of recommendations arising from consultations with 'stakeholders' in the prison system, including representatives of statutory welfare and probation agencies, voluntary agencies working with prisoners and their families, and after an initial boycott, representatives of political prisoner organizations. The main objectives of *Serving the Community* were improving relations between prisoners' communities and the prison service, enabling prisoners to retain links with their families, managing resources 'efficiently, effectively and economically', and making 'a contribution to the achievement of peace and stability' in Northern Ireland (*ibid.*: 10, 18).

By the mid-1980s, the improvements in conditions appears to have successfully addressed the causes of organized resistance to the extent that 'there was no apparent general sense of crisis' in the prisons (Rolston and Tomlinson 1988: 167). However, Republican women prisoners in Mourne House alleged that they were being discriminated against in terms of access to rights of association and recreation, visits, education and medical care, compared with the men in the rest of Maghaberry prison:

> The fact that the majority of the women in Maghaberry are Republican POWs made the Northern Ireland Office even more reluctant to treat them equally with men. Unlike the male prisoners [in Maghaberry], the Republican women did not change their political beliefs on being imprisoned, so they do not receive the rewards given to the non-political male prisoners (statement from Republican Women Prisoners in Opsahl *et al.* 1993: 285).

A second area of contention between Republican women prisoners and the prison administration arose over strip searching in Mourne House. Although the government had been forced to retreat from its policy of implementing 'random' strip searching in Armagh prison, routine strip searches were resumed for remand prisoners after the transfer to Maghaberry prison. By the 1990s, the distinction between 'random' and 'routine' usage of the procedure appears to have been largely semantic, as the decision to implement the procedure in Mourne House was largely guided by general security assessments and responses to incidents of arson and drugs smuggling in the *men's* prison.[9]

On 2 March 1992, a mass strip search was conducted on all 21 political and 13 of the 14 'ordinary' prisoners in Mourne House, with the exception of one woman who was recovering from a hysterectomy. Whilst there has been considerable dispute about the precise course of events, the following facts emerge from the available evidence.[10] Whilst awaiting their morning unlock, prisoners were informed that a search of the wings, including full body searches, was to take place. Although the non-politicals complied with the order, Republican prisoners refused to co-operate, and barricaded themselves into their cells. At approximately 9.30 am the search commenced in the non-political wing. An hour later a number of female officers in full protective clothing and helmets, supported by male special incident officers, entered the first of the three landings where Republican prisoners were housed. The men proceeded to remove the barricades and force their way into the cells. The searches appear to have been conducted with military efficiency. On gaining entrance to each cell, male officers pinioned each prisoner to a wall or floor with their shields, whilst up to six female officers moved her into a disabling position. The bottom half of the prisoner's body was then fully stripped, and her body and clothing visually examined. A sheet was placed on each prisoner before the process was repeated on the upper parts of her body. Prisoners later testified that they were sat or stood on as they struggled against the search, and many sustained extensive bruising and sprains. Each prisoner was then escorted or dragged down the corridor and locked into the Association Room whilst their cells were searched. The process involved a heightened element of psychological and emotional tension as prisoners heard the distress of women in adjacent cells undergoing strips, and because officers selected cells on a random basis. The search of the three sentenced wings continued for over ten hours, until 8 pm. Officers broke the search for lunch at approximately 2 pm. Prisoners who were still barricaded in their cells reported that male officers patrolled the yard, shouting obscenities and making sexual gestures at them. Others testified that the officers had entered the wing to start the search singing 'Happy Days Are Here Again', and alleged that some smelt of alcohol.

All 21 prisoners were charged with the disciplinary offences of refusing an order and making a barricade, receiving punishments ranging from 14 days' loss of exercise and association to 14 days' remission and three days of confinement to their cells. Five prisoners were also convicted for assault. No member of staff was disciplined. An additional dimension to these events was the presence of the Chairwoman of the Board of Visitors at one search. The decision to invite medical staff or official visitors to be present as eyewitnesses followed guidelines issued by prison headquarters in the mid-1980s, purportedly as an additional procedural safeguard, but also to avoid the disputes and claims that had previously followed searches in Armagh. Two official visitors subsequently praised the professionalism of the officers' conduct at an unofficial inquiry into the incident conducted by an inter-church commission (CRSS 1993: 4.3.2). According to that report, the members 'understood that the decision to conduct the search had been taken at the level of Prison Headquarters', and that the safeguards and guidelines for security had been followed (*ibid.*).

There are informative parallels between the incident at Maghaberry and comparable events in the Canadian Federal Prison for Women (P4W) in April 1994, when male emergency response personnel were called in to conduct a 'cell extraction and strip search' of eight women, using similar tactics of enforcement as those at Maghaberry two years previously. The controversy generated by events in Canada prompted the establishment of the Arbour Commission (1996) which concluded that extensive violations of prisoners' legal and civil rights had taken place, and condemned the 'absence of the rule of law' and institutional negation of a 'culture of rights' in the Canadian correctional system (*ibid.*: 180, 249–60). The contrasts in the political and administrative responses to these respective events are equally illuminating. The absence of similar published inquiries and the lack of disclosure of any internal investigations which might have been conducted by the prison administration in Northern Ireland meant that the source of authorization and reasons for the search in Mourne House remain obscured. Furthermore, the tactic of collective body searches which were conducted in the prisoners' cells were of a different character from those conducted in Armagh, but, as with the previous use of strip searching, no item which might have constituted a security hazard was found.

The suddenness and violence of the incident were also connected by various witnesses with the deployment of male officers who were accustomed to a more 'vigorous' style of dealing with prisoners on the men's side of the prison, and as a broader expression of staff discontent with proposed changes in working conditions and other cost efficiencies which were being implemented in line with the normalization policy. The incident may also have been connected to the determination of lower ranking officers to deliver a politically embarrassing message to the authorities, as it took place two days before the publication of the Colville Report, amidst rumours that it might retain some form of paramilitary segregation in the prisons. Although the subsequent criticism of the prison service meant that a similar search was not conducted in Mourne House again, new guidelines concerning the use of the practice were not disclosed, if any were established, nor were the details of any internal inquiry published, if one was held. Indeed, the following year 'more rigorous searching procedures for professional visitors' were introduced in response to Colville's recommendations (NIPS 1992: 2).

Ironically, these respective incidents occurred when both prison systems were ostensibly undergoing comprehensive reforms. The events in P4W occurred four years after a review of the federal prison system for women in Canada, which had produced what was then claimed to be a radical shift in penal thinking towards a 'woman-centred' model of penal reform, with appropriate security levels and specialist support units for the needs of different prisoners (Task Force on Federally Sentenced Women 1990). Similarly, the modernization of women's imprisonment in Northern Ireland was founded on the assumption that enhanced technical security would reduce dependence on excessively intrusive personal searches, whilst the 'prisoner-centred' ethos was meant to facilitate a consensual approach to discipline and conflict. Whilst there are differences in the contexts of reform in both jurisdictions, there are germane points of comparison, notably the conflicts that arose as a consequence of implementing 'progressive' regimes and practices against the greater reality of institutionalized assumptions about unco-operative, high-risk and ungovernable prisoners. As noted by Canadian commentators, the outcome of such reform programmes was that prison governance acquired a 'dual character' of extended security alongside 'prisoner-centred regimes', which rendered penal reform 'a contradiction in terms, simply changing the content of a penal regime … [left the] wider institutional framework unchallenged' (Hannah-Moffat 2001: 197). Similarly, the signal failure of prison reforms to introduce any substantive improvements to women's regimes or conditions in Northern Ireland cast doubt on whether the new approach represented much more than an instrumental mechanism for containing the critical mass of male paramilitary prisoners, to the detriment of women, juveniles and 'ordinary' men prisoners.

Conclusion: women's imprisonment and the failures of 'normalization'

In their analysis of prison governance in Northern Ireland, Gormally *et al.* (1993: 124–5) argued that the principle of normalization was 'a sophisticated and sensible model', both for 'point[ing] the way to at least limited [political] progress' outside the prisons, and for developing a working framework with the political factions in prison without either side 'appearing to concede substantial ideological terrain'. The introduction of penal reforms, they continued, made some progress in directing some of the more sensitive, soluble issues away from the old conflictual agendas, and imparting a technicist approach and language to prison administration which were consistent with a broader counter-terrorist strategy of managing political violence: 'What normalisation has done in Northern Ireland is to use parts of the criminal justice system, in particular the prison system, as a managerial tool to contain what is seen essentially as a managerial problem' (*ibid.*: 125). However, they continue, the danger of approaching political violence on the same terms as 'the economy, the health service, or transport policy' is that it 'either ignores or designates [as] insoluble the political and structural reasons that create the problem ... [and] the cost in human terms is subsumed in the language and actions of the ostensible moral neutrality of management' (*ibid.*). McEvoy (2001: 250) subsequently qualified the original hypothesis, stating that such initiatives provided 'a set of discourses and working practices within which prison managers could frame [this] changed relationship' (*ibid.*: 263).

An alternative perspective is that the policy was as much directed towards allaying wider criticisms of the prison system, emanating from various political quarters, as to its cost and inefficiency, outdated practices, violations of prisoners' rights, cumbersome administrative structures and systems, and paucity of custodial programmes for women and juvenile prisoners, as with redressing its substantial legitimacy deficit in the community. Moreover, the timing of the introduction of reforms on life sentence reviews, prisoner transfers, eligibility for pre-release programmes or other benefits has been likened to a calculated political tactic for ensuring some degree of consensus from the prisoners' organizations (Rolston and Tomlinson 1988). Whether 'normalization' was a progressive and far-reaching strategy which laid the basis for constructive political engagement, or a hegemonic tactic for drawing political prisoners into a collaborative mindset, the fact remains that changes to the women's regime were delayed, inconsistent and qualified by external considerations that had little to do with their specific conditions. The shortcomings of normalization were also related to the glaring exclusion of women's imprisonment from definitions of penal change, even in the midst of 'radical' reforms or the establishment of a managed framework for minimizing conflict. At the same time, these contradictions can only be explained in the context of previous institutional practices, ideologies and correctional reflexes in relation to controlling women political prisoners. The more far-reaching consequence of the shortcomings of the normalization policy was that many of the underlying causes of contention were still largely in place in Mourne House up to and beyond the signing of the Belfast Agreement in 1998.

Notes

1 Under the terms of the Prison Act (Northern Ireland) 1954, the Secretary of State was obliged to appoint a Board of Visitors to every prison to oversee its workings and participate in adjudications (i.e. punishment proceedings).

2 Lynch (22) died in an explosion at a flat in Derry in what the army described as a 'bomb-making factory', Fitzsimmons (17) was killed whilst preparing a device (McKittrick *et al.* 1999: 330, 505). Dougan is not listed in McKittrick *et al.'s* encyclopaedic account of those killed in the Troubles. The involvement of young women in incendiary campaigns declined towards the end of the 1970s partly as a consequence of these 'own goals', as the security forces grimly called them.

3 Most accounts state that Farrell was the first woman to be sentenced after criminalization. However, she was not sentenced (for 14 years) until 12 December 1976 (*Daily Mirror* 12 December 1976). Murray was the first woman to be sentenced (for 15 years) in April 1976 (*Irish News* 2 December 1976).

4 The 'Blanket protest' refers to the protest against criminalization in the Maze. Women protesters disliked the term 'dirty protest' that was applied to their strike, preferring to call it the 'no-wash protest'.

5 Farrell was the PIRA commanding officer in Armagh prison from December 1979 until her release in 1986. She was one of the three PIRA members, along with Daniel McCann and Seán Savage, who were killed by the SAS in Gibraltar in March 1988.

6 Cardinal Tomás O'Fiach had met the Secretary of State, Humphrey Atkins, on a number of occasions to mediate a settlement.

7 For independent inquiries by non-governmental agencies, see Irish Information Partnership (IIP) (1985); National Labour Women's Committee (1985); National Council for Civil Liberties (NCCL) (1986); Standing Advisory Commission on Human Rights (SACHRE) (1986); A Christian Response to Strip-searching (CRSS) (1986); Committee on the Administration of Justice (CAJ) 1987; London Strategic Policy Unit (1988); United Campaign against Strip Searching (UCASS) (1989). Despite their highly publicized recommendations, the NIO remained publicly impervious to them, dismissing them as the work of agitators or misguided interference by professional do-gooders.

8 The 'supergrass' trials arose from the use by the Royal Ulster Constabulary and Crown Prosecution Service of accomplice evidence from 30 Loyalist and Republican 'converted terrorists' between 1981 and 1986. Over 300 people were prosecuted before the system was finally overturned at the Court of Appeal in 1986.

9 Correspondence from the Office of the Minister of State, Northern Ireland Office, to the Commission on the Administration of Justice (CAJ), 18 April 1988.

10 This includes evidence from inquiries conducted by A Christian Response to Strip Searching (CRSS) (1993), press statements from the Prison Service Headquarters, prisoners' legal statements and interviews with two of the prisoners involved, a prison chaplain and the governor who issued the order.

Chapter 3

Paradoxes of women's political imprisonment: sociological narratives and closures

> Precisely because of their anomalous and subversive character within established definitions of the political, the politics of nationalist women has been eclipsed in the accounts of [the] Northern Ireland conflict. Women have been left out not because analysts have recognised their subversive potential but because, by not fitting existing discourses, they have not been recognised at all as socially relevant (Aretxaga 1997: 4).

Women 'terrorists' or political offenders are inescapably represented through discourses of deviance, transgression and dangerousness. They are conceived of as uniquely dangerous individuals, or what Elshtain (1995: 163) has called 'the ferocious few', and as exceptions to normative womanhood – 'the non-combatant many'. This chapter examines the anomalous figure of the female political prisoner. It argues that they pose an epistemological 'problem' in three analytical fields. These are, first, in accounts of the role of women in the commission of political crime; secondly, in analyses of resistance in prison; and, thirdly, in contemporary accounts of women's lawbreaking and imprisonment. In bringing these domains together, one is presented with the critical problem whereby existing analyses of political crime and punishment rarely intersect with the body of academic research on women and imprisonment. Not only have women been obscured in analyses of political crime and punishment but the confinement of women for crimes against the State is rarely considered in debates about women in prison. The question of their marginality, in either case, is not just their minoritarian position within the women's and political prisoner populations, although this contributes to the relative scarcity of criminological literature on female political prisoners (Zwerman 1988; di Giovanni 1990; Churchill and Vander Wall 1992). Rather, the problem of women political prisoners is that their difference within 'political imprisonment' and 'women in prison' interrogates and reshapes both these categories. The chapter, therefore, makes three arguments.

First, criminology has produced ways of talking about women who engage in armed struggle as defying rationality. Positivist explanations of women's involvement in political crime are founded on assumptions about their biological predispositions towards crime and violence. However, social constructionist correctives to this view have tended towards culturally essentialist explanations for women's 'attraction' to risky and dangerous behaviour as a sign of the breakdown of the gendered social order. Each of these approaches denies the agency and rationality of women involved in political crime.

Secondly, prisoner subcultural theories, which are germane to the analysis of political solidarity amongst prisoners, do not extend coherently to women's social organization in prison. Classical 'inmate subcultural' theory either explicitly refers to fraternal prisoner societies, or assumes that women in prison are anomic. Accordingly, women are denied full status as political actors in prison.

Thirdly, women sentenced for political offences are implicitly conceived of as different from other women in prison. Contemporary penology rightly focuses on the social and material marginalities that surround women's offending and imprisonment. However, these discussions defer the problem of addressing the additional marginality of long-term sentenced or seriously offending women in the prison system. In addition, the problem is compounded in the penal construction of a binary distinction between 'difficult' and 'dangerous' women prisoners. These distinctions obscure both the impact of prison punishment on all women prisoners and the specific controls that are targeted towards 'dangerous' women prisoners.

The Lombrosian effect and the pathology of the female political offender

The 'violent woman' of criminology is constructed out of intersecting, historically produced discourses of political terror, and positivist influences on theorizing crime and deviance from the late nineteenth century.[1] The work of Cesare Lombroso in *Criminal Man*, first published in 1876 (Gina Lombroso-Ferrero 1972), and *The Female Offender* (1895) (with Guglielmo Ferrero) was influential in advancing the principles and methods by which 'the aetiology and nature of crime' could be discerned from biological abnormalities which supposedly predisposed individuals to criminality and other social aberrations. Proceeding from these objectives, Lombroso and Ferrero devised experimental procedures for measuring the physical characteristics of inmates of prisons, asylums and other correctional institutions, and systematically classifying them into categories such as 'born criminals', 'insane criminals' and 'occasional criminals'. By meticulously recording and classifying the skull measurements, facial features and proportions, and the nervous system, height and weight of their subjects, they concluded that the confined exhibited congenital signs of atavism, or evolutionary regression. These full degenerate tendencies, however, were deemed to be less pronounced in male political prisoners because they possessed the 'genius of the revolutionary spirit' which elevated them beyond the atavistic 'born criminal' (Lombroso, cited in Schafer 1974: 134–5). Political offenders were 'criminals by passion', who were characterized by a high degree of 'affectability', and led to crimes of violence 'under the stress of unusual circumstances'. Hence, 'while not all criminals by passion [were] political criminals, all political criminals [were] criminals by passion' (*ibid.*: 135). The 'passion' of the political prisoner meant that he [*sic*] retained some of his 'moral equipment' and thus was classified as an 'occasional criminal'. However, their confinement was necessary because of their inability to adapt to 'the governmental and social environment' (*ibid.*).

By the time Lombroso and Ferrero published *The Female Offender* (1895), they were confronted with the additional difficulty of reconciling their theory about women's degeneracy with the fact that women were convicted of fewer and lesser crimes than men. Thus, Lombroso 'assigned himself the very difficult task of arguing that women were less criminal than men because of their inferiority to men' (Hahn-Rafter and Gibson 2004: 9). They did this by constructing an elaborate system for distinguishing the 'normal' female from the 'normal' male in the evolutionary hierarchy as a prelude to examining the differences between normal and 'criminal' women. They concluded that women's reproductive role meant that they had a tendency to 'perpetuation' rather than 'development' and as such their maternal functions produced superior powers of endurance, primitive intelligence and resistance to mental and physical pain, whilst men surpassed them because of their active drive ('passion') in evolutionary competition (Lombroso and Ferrero 1895: 110). Whilst the physiological and psychological immobility of women accounted for their limited moral and intellectual range, it also accounted for their organically conservative and passive traits. The authors asserted that women criminals were markedly degenerate because the biological restraints of 'piety, maternity, want of passion, sexual coldness and an undeveloped intelligence' (viewed as beneficial characteristics in women) had failed in them (*ibid.*: 151): 'What we look for in the female is femininity, and when we find the opposite in her we must conclude as a rule that there must be some anomaly' (*ibid.*: 112).

The 'true' type of female criminal was found amongst women who had been imprisoned for serious offences including homicide, arson ('incendiaries'), murder in the domestic environment and prostitution. In some instances mitigating social influences such as ill-treatment, domestic violence, forced marriages or male coercion were admitted to reclassify serious women offenders as 'demi-types'. No such ameliorative reasons were admitted in the cases of women who 'denied [their] guilt persistently', selfishly profited from a robbery connected with homicide, failed to confess to their crimes or explain their motives (*ibid.*: 89–90). One 'female brigand' of the 'true type', who 'was the companion in arms of a band of brigands, one of whom was her lover', exhibited prominent and asymmetrical facial features ('a congenital division of the palate') and a 'virile physiognomy' (*ibid.*: 93). Female political criminals were, accordingly, 'born' criminals, distinguishable by their promiscuity and 'moral dissipation'. Moreover, 'the moral physiognomy of the born female criminal approximates strongly to that of the male … When by an unfortunate chance muscular strength and intellectual force meet in the same individual, we have a female delinquent of a terrible type indeed' (*ibid.*: 187–8). Even in Lombroso and Ferrero's theory, the links between female 'criminality' and 'political crime' were rarely viewed together. Where this did occur, they deviated from male political offenders, who were partly exempted from the basest criminal categories by their 'revolutionary passion', whilst the motives of women political offenders were incontrovertibly rooted in their inferior biological and moral disposition (*ibid.*: 244–68).

These early criminological theories played a significant, if ambiguous, role in encoding gendered difference in the analysis of political offending. It must be noted that Lombroso's influence on the treatment of political offenders in Britain was tangential rather than direct, as his theories were received sceptically there (Sim 1990: 130) and failed to persuade legislators and jurists to abandon the legal convention whereby political outrages were defined by the criminality of the acts, as opposed to admitting of the exceptional character of perpetrators (Radzinowicz and Hood 1979: 1422). Nevertheless, as Sim (1990: 131, emphasis added) points out, this is less because biological determinism failed to take root in the criminal justice system, and more because an indigenous positivist tradition had 'already set the parameters for and responses to *women's* deviance'. Thus, the medical professions in Britain were already 'exerting an influence in the courts well before the advent of Lombroso's work on the female offender and, indeed, long after' (Edwards cited in *ibid.*). It might also be added that the influences of legal positivism and patriarchy on the practical workings of the courts and criminal administration meant that they formed at least part of the explanation for the treatment of female political offenders. Nevertheless, the standing of such women remained ambiguously defined by their lack of intelligibility within categories of political criminality. Indeed, the determination of their treatment as a social and pathological phenomenon was informed by the relative rarity of women's appearance before the courts as political offenders, their exceptional standing within existing and developing categories of female offending, and their apparent sociocultural and behavioural 'aberration'. The genealogy of women political offenders as emotionally and psychologically flawed was given additional weight in later theories of the socially and sexually maladjusted female 'delinquent' (Pollock 1978; Klein 1979; Widom 1981).

'Terrorism' theory: placing women in pathologies of violence

'Terrorism' and 'security' studies emerged as academic disciplines in the larger context of Cold War politics in response to the counter-cultural, civil rights and radical popular movements in Western liberal democracies of the 1960s, and the rise of liberation insurgency in the colonized world. From this point, the study of political violence has been largely institutionally and epistemologically embedded in developing counter-insurgent policies alongside intelligence, military and security agencies (Schmid and Jongman 1988), and is characterized by an 'easy identification' with neo-conservative and 'right-wing' frames of reference (Krause and Williams 1997: xiv). Accordingly, security studies depict political violence, or 'terrorism', in terms of a catastrophic threat to liberal democracy (Wilkinson 2001), and endorse the State's monopoly of force, the accommodation of emergency measures within civil laws (normalization) and the criminalization of 'perpetrators of violence' (Corrado 1979; Alexander and O'Day 1984, 1986).

Violent 'extremism' in post-1968 Europe emerged from the two distinctive strands of nationalist separatism in the Basque region of Spain and in Northern Ireland, and radical Marxist revolutionary groups such as the Red Army Factions (RAF) and Baader–Meinhof groups in Italy and Germany. Whilst both were held by governments to be deeply illegitimate, the violence of the former groups was at least comprehensible to security thinking as a consequence of unresolved historical grievances, committed by tough and disciplined cadres, and as having some popular support. By contrast, the 'nihilistic' terrorism of the RAF was viewed to be the product of the misconceived revolutionary ennui of the bourgeois, post-war generation (Georges-Abeyie 1983), and perpetrated by 'the spoilt children' of the affluent society (Wilkinson 1977: 93). The emergence of a few women as leaders in these organizations gave rise to speculative 'analysis' from academic and popular or mass media sources which was disproportionate to their actual roles, and went beyond security or political commentary (Becker 1977; MacDonald 1991). Amongst the more 'serious' theories included Reef's view that the influence of women in 'quality and number' was explained by the 'feminization' of insurgency movements. This was manifest in the fact that paramilitary organizations of the Left had actively engaged women by addressing 'issues important to [them]' and eliminating 'inhospitable or sexist internal relations and barriers to women's recruitment' (Reef cited in Vetter and Perlstein 1991: 118).

Notwithstanding the latter's emphasis on *social* degeneracy as a causal factor, the positivist legacy remained remarkably intact in these accounts of women's role in political crime. Wilkinson's account of the 'characteristics and typology of political violence' exemplified the position. 'Terrorist violence', he argued, was 'inherently indiscriminate in its effects [and] essentially arbitrary and unpredictable' (Wilkinson 1977: 52). Moreover, the terrorist's disregard for 'all rules and conventions of war' was a reflection of his [*sic*] 'rejection of all moral constraints', and his recourse to 'barbarous cruelties and weapons in pursuit of his goals' (*ibid*.: 53). Georges-Abeyie's (1983: 81–3) 'theory of women as terrorists' argued that although women, 'except for a few notable exceptions', had conventionally played a relatively minor role in terrorist violence:

> female participation both as freelance and members of terrorist organizations is set to increase dramatically in the future … Their input in terrorist acts is tied in part to feminist demands and

practices ... Contemporary female terrorists are likely to exhibit male personality or physical traits. Terrorist acts by females are more instrumental and less expressive.

Oliverio (1997: 51) has noted that, whilst the influence of these theories is largely 'ineffective' in providing useful approaches for understanding political conflict, they continue to have a central purchase in 'terrorism' studies. Without revisiting the enormous body of research on colonial 'insurgency', 'global' and urban terrorism or civil disorder since the Cold War, this discussion notes the positivist influence in 'terrorism' studies as evidenced in methodological precepts which support a 'scientific' approach to taxonomies of violence (Wilkinson 1977), and the delineation of the characteristics and morphology of 'the terrorist' (Alexander and O'Day 1984: 88–95; Schmid and Jongman 1988). The concern here, however, is to evaluate the construction of 'political crime' in ways which have understood and positioned women as the objects of academic analyses within positivist, sociopathic and essentialist discourses.

The 'feminist turn' in 'terrorism': sex-role theory and women's criminality

The contemporary 'discovery' of the 'female terrorist' occurred at a juncture of revisionism within counter-insurgency studies and the emergence of 'emancipatory' or 'liberationist' theories in criminology. These focused on the emergence of a 'new breed' of criminal women who were engaged in 'violent and militant' crime (Adler 1975: 3; Burton 1979; Vetter and Perlstein 1991). From the late 1960s, criminological discourse was concerned with an apparent rise in women's conviction for crimes of violence, and was allied to the proposition that 'the trend in violence by women ... may be accelerated as women become emancipated from traditional female role requirements' (Ward *et al.* 1979: 137–8). These trends, furthermore, required that 'female criminality' be explained as 'a separate and distinct order of criminal behaviour in which *cultural* factors relating to sex roles in our society are of critical importance ... because crimes of violence by women directly contradict the role women in our society are supposed to play' (*ibid.*: 136–7, emphasis added).

The authoritative basis for the shift in emphasis from biological to social factors was Adler's *Sisters in Crime* (1975), in which she claimed that the blurring of traditional 'feminine' and 'masculine' social roles had created the conditions for the 'upward equalization of women's violence' with that of men: 'these crimes involve a greater degree of violence and even in prison this new breed exhibits a hitherto unmatched pugnacity' (*ibid.*: 3). According to Adler, the 'militant' female criminal emerged from the 'zeitgeist of liberation' (*ibid.*: 101) which converged with a 'new broad-based awareness of women's place and potential [and] developed side-by-side with the civil rights and antiwar movements' (*ibid.*: 25). Consequently, women's roles in radical political movements altered from the 'traditional functions' of routine support to leadership and 'active, vociferous and sometimes violent' participation (*ibid.*: 101).

Adler's causal analysis of the role of women in political crime resonated with that of security 'traditionalists' in that she claimed that, whilst post-war economic and social changes had created unprecedented social mobility for women, they had also created destabilizing effects caused by 'the growing emphasis on competition and individual rights', the 'increased stress on affluent goals', the 'growth of nonproductive leisure' and 'greater dependency on peers' rather than family (*ibid.*: 108). The pressures of greater social aspiration, equal rights, prolonged education, altered job opportunities, urbanization and 'family fragmentation' encouraged women, 'especially those who are socially disadvantaged, toward deviant means to achieve socially approved goals' (*ibid.*: 105). Paradoxically, the post-war social revolutions, which 'virilized its previously … docile female segments', were ultimately adverse for women. In the first instance, Adler claimed that in abandoning their conventional roles, women had 'comparatively few opportunities within the system to find others', and thus were compelled to emulate 'aggressive, masculine' drives (*ibid.*: 87). Secondly, the resulting fluidity of male and female sex roles made 'an anomic contribution to female delinquency by eroding the structures which have historically protected and restrained girls' (*ibid.*: 103). Consequently, where previously the historical benefits of such 'chivalry' had ostensibly created for women a customary respite from the full rigours of judicial punishment (Pollak 1979), this was rapidly depleting for them as traditional protective biases were eroded. The inevitable consequence was that the social sanctions and punishment applied to women would match those that already applied to men, especially where they had appropriated 'masculine' criminal roles (Adler 1975: 89).

A revisionist strand within terrorism studies similarly rejected 'the masculinization of female behaviour [which] can be traced back to Lombroso', and turned to 'role convergence between the sexes' and the influence of 'female emancipation' on the 'emergence of women in

69

increased numbers and influence' in 'guerrilla combat, and serious and violent crime' (Wiener and Eubank cited in Vetter and Perlstein 1991: 114). Moreover, the social conditions that were conducive to terrorism were compounded by:

> the addition of feminist demands, both logical and irrational ... Understanding the role of women in terrorism implies the recognition that women comprise a self-conscious, dynamic sector of society that often perceives itself to be an oppressed majority – a majority oppressed not only because of religion, ethnicity or national origin but also because of gender (Vetter and Perlstein 1991: 115).

Accordingly, women were attracted to militancy and violence as a means of 'fostering and reinforcing demands for socio-cultural change of both a socialist and feminist nature' (*ibid.*: 116). Two conclusions arose from these assertions. First, that 'gender-consciousness' had emerged as one of the ideologies of discontent underpinning political violence in addition to more 'traditional ... terroristic' motives. It is notable, of course, that the view of 'feminism' espoused here did not refer to a coherent political analysis of patriarchy, nor the (then-existing) Women's Liberation Movement, but was defined as a mass expression by women of sex-role frustration. Secondly, the inequalities which inhered in male-dominated radical movements would inevitably undermine women's expectations of 'sharing the risks ... and profits' of terrorism: 'disillusionment comes when this process does not go far enough' (Cooper 1979: 153). Thus, women were precipitated into further violence, becoming 'more ferocious and more intractable in these acts than their male counterparts. [They] have been inspired to enter into terrorism for its own sake, moving rapidly into positions of responsibility for these heinous activities by using their own fatal proclivities and ability' (*ibid.*: 151–2).

These revisionists did not radically depart from previous explanations of women's role in political violence, but placed some familiar positivist concepts – their 'fatal proclivities' – alongside the altered social conditions and opportunities that allegedly enabled women to exercise their newly discovered 'abilities' in the field. Sex-role rebellion as a 'social theory of political conflict' was in effect overlaid on earlier theories of the socio-biological signs of abnormality in 'militant' women who:

> assert markedly radical demands for structural-functional change in regard to role sets assigned to women or to any oppressed

majority or minority [which] may be viewed as masculine in character. [They] may seek success in some non-feminine realm by displaying aggression, unadorned faces and bodies, toughness or other masculine qualities (Vetter and Perlstein 1991: 116).

The recurrent themes of the new cultural essentialism of 'terrorology', then, were that women who engaged in political violence were motivated by a psychological and erotic attraction to risk and danger, eschewed feminine empathy and strove to compensate for their feminine 'weaknesses'. Indeed, the 'terrorist woman' was bound by an 'obsessive' and 'pathological … erotomania' in her dependency on insurgent men and 'seemed unable to escape male influence in this sphere' (Cooper 1979: 154). Similarly, and without contradiction, women insurgents were driven by ruthless drives that placed them beyond the control of the male leadership of their own organizations. From this paradox arose the predicament of revolutionary women, whose unique 'dangerousness' was vaguely mitigated by their biological and social dysfunctionalism, yet who were none the less deprived of liberation because of their sexual subordination and complicity with violent men. The analysis now turns to the use of these themes of sexual dependency and adaptive 'weakness' in criminological accounts of women's agency in prison.

The gendered limits of prison sociation theories

This section explores a third analytical approach which has conventionally been used to theorize collective and political resistance and agency in prison. Whereas the political structures in the women's prisons in Northern Ireland might be viewed as resembling those elements of instrumental affiliation with which 'inmate sociation' and subcultural theory are concerned, it is argued that these theories have limited relevance to the formation of collectivist and self-defining alliances amongst women prisoners. First, 'sociation' and 'subcultural' analyses lack a gendered analysis, that is a consciously critical view of formations of masculinities or femininities within 'inmate structures', or their relationships with 'official' prison culture. Secondly, some correctives to the androcentrism of prisonization theory resort to equally problematic, essentialist explanations of women's 'needs' to convey the fragility of women's alliances in prisons. The final section, however, examines how women's relations with other prisoners are persistently incapacitated by pre-emptive monitoring and punishment, or discouraged as sources of suspicion, staff resentment and pathologization.

Prison sociation theory gives an account of imprisonment which emphasises 'survival' through 'making out' in the 'underlife' of carceral institutions (Goffman 1991). Prisoner 'subcultural' theory, as put forward by Clemmer (1965), Sykes (1958) and Goffman (1991), was largely concerned with identifying the use of personalized rituals as a 'way out' of the pains of imprisonment and its resulting anomie. Whilst 'prisoner subcultural' analyses contested the concept of total institutional rule and sought to identify its 'discrepancies' (Bowker 1977), these accounts commonly proceeded from the basis that agency was already framed by the anterior powers of carceral institutions which, at best, allowed inmates minor or temporary escapes from institutional rule. The most conspicuous expression of prisoner agency, in subcultural theory, was 'inmate councils' which mandated 'natural' leaders and 'rank-and-file specialists' from the informal prisoner structure to act on their behalf and manage relationships with authority (Sykes 1958). Mathiesen (1965) held that inmate councils had an ambivalent relationship with penal order in that they afforded inmate cohesion, but ultimately worked to supplement the legitimacy and stability of the institution by providing an additional layer of control, albeit one legitimated by prisoners' 'consent'. Sykes also concluded that inmate councils were 'counter-intuitive', because the solidarity acquired by prisoners in the totalizing environment of prison consolidated reciprocal relationships between the official and unofficial prison systems.

Crawford's (1999) study of Loyalist prisoners in Northern Ireland, largely influenced by sociation theory, considered the parallel relationships between these dual lines of internal and external discipline. He concluded that Loyalist groups comprised 'consensus communities' in which inmates accepted the authority of their own leaders, and 'consequently, the alienation experienced in conventional regimes was almost completely avoided' (ibid.: 34). However, this account reverts to a social contractarian explanation which reconciles the 'consensual, liberal, and permissive' regime in Long Kesh with 'comparatively negligible incidents of rule-breaking' and conflict with the administration (ibid.: 33–4). Whilst Crawford usefully raised the preservationary function of prisoner structures, his analysis overstated the extent to which they amounted to discrete social systems. Crawford did not address the dynamics of convergence with the formal regime or the lack of equilibrium between them observed by Sykes, and there is little scope for analysing the instances where discretionary realms of autonomy were revoked to a significant degree *because* of the perceived threat posed by prisoner collectives. Neither did he explain the realignment of prisoner structures in Northern Ireland as a form of resistance to the removal of special category status. More specifically, as described in Chapter 2, the legal recognition of special category status did not enable women's political structures to operate discretely. Rather, their structures practically resembled a 'regime-within-a-regime' which was susceptible to myriad forms of official penetration and discretionary contingencies.

The 'prisonization' of women and the 'feminized' limits of agency

The application of 'inmate socialization' theories to women's prisons sought to establish whether or not the rituals of initiation, 'doing time' and 'making out' had specific meanings, or indeed existed, in female establishments. Women's prisonization theory proceeded from the observation that female inmate structures were similarly constrained within the limits of reciprocity by serving both the prisoners and 'custodial ends for the staff as well' (Ward and Kassebaum 1966: 30). Ward and Kassebaum held that inmate structures in women's prisons were maintained through 'a system of friendships, mutual obligations, statuses, reciprocal relations, loyalties, intimidation, deception and violence', and other forms of 'self-policing' which rendered official prison controls 'negligible compared to control by prisoners themselves' (*ibid.*). Heffernan (1972: 74) found that the 'supplementary inmate system of production and exchange' in women's prisons functioned through an elaborate division of labour which created a 'sense of counter-power [within the] organized inmate system'. However, whilst Heffernan concluded that 'the code' operated through the distribution of goods and favours in women's prisons, the relationship between social stratification and power in inmate systems was not reducible to economic activity (*ibid.*: 151). Rather, she emphasized its interplay with 'the development of a family unit', which provided 'a rationale for a multiplicity of close relationships … as well as legitimating dependency and dominance roles' (*ibid.*: 88).

Although Heffernan noted the interdependence of material and personal transactional 'subsystems' (*ibid.*: 160), Giallombardo (1966) and Ward and Kassebaum (1966) focused on subaltern 'family' units and domesticated arrangements as the nexus of economic, social and emotional ties amongst confined women. Starting with the hypothesis that 'homosexuality [in prisons] is either not mentioned or disguised under terms such as "relationships"', Ward and Kassebaum contended that 'butch' and 'femme' lesbian roles, or other quasi-marital relationships, were central to women's identification and structures.

The 'conjugal' character of women's relationships in prison was prompted by 'the need for stable patterns or expectations and frames of reference' (*ibid.*: 31). Similarly, female 'subcultural patterns' were grounded in ineluctably passive and conventional drives borne out by the necessity to construct 'pseudo-family' units as an outcome of 'women's psychological needs ... psycho-sexual needs and symbiotic needs' (*ibid.*: 73).

In dispensing with the motives of self-interest or rational, contract-based adaptations noted by Heffernan, Ward and Kassebaum proposed that individualism was the greatest threat to making and retaining strategic alliances in women's prisons. They measured the 'stability' of women's inmate cohesion by investigating adherence to, or deviation from, principles of 'the [male] code' on informing, theft, involuntary disclosure of information to staff, and the ability to conceal information or suffer punishment at the expense of the self, and compared their data against the strength of male prisoner codes. Unsurprisingly, they 'found' that women 'broke the rules' of the inmate code more frequently on all counts, and that they turned 'snitch' more extensively than was generally acknowledged (*ibid.*: 32–5). Accordingly, women's adherence to 'the code' was weaker than that of men, as they did 'not feel bound to maintain group solidarity by no-ratting rules' (*ibid.*: 53). As female codification was susceptible to such selfish interests, their structures were accordingly unreliable and more prone to fragmentation than those of men. Women's failure to uphold 'the code' (or their rejection of it) thus corresponded with their underdeveloped 'criminal maturity', and reflected lower levels of cohesion amongst women lawbreakers more generally, where 'women in our society are not prepared to "play it cool"', 'take it like a man' (*sic*), refrain from 'copping out' or 'use force to fight for one's rights' (*ibid.*: 67–8).

Although Mandaraka-Sheppard's (1986: 8) study of the dynamics of conflict in women's prisons appeared two decades after prisonization theory, her analysis consciously addressed the predominant belief 'that male inmates are ... more collectively organized in its opposition to staff compared with their female counterparts' by arguing that obstacles to women's agency were ingrained in prison regimes themselves. She proposed that differential role expectations and gendered controls in women's prisons created structurally determined differences in the development of extensive and lasting alliances amongst prisoners. Mandaraka-Sheppard thus focused on the institutional role in the 'escalation of friction' and consequent 'spiralling effects of punishment on inmate violence' (*ibid.*: 84). The dynamics of conflict in women's prisons were 'frequently' caused by, and extenuated through, 'overzealous rule imposition', based on 'preconceived ideas of a troublemaking prisoner', assumptions about the guilt of the offending prisoner, 'failure to question the veracity of staff' and 'disproportionately severe punishments', which aggravated 'already poor relationships' in women's prisons (*ibid*.: 83–8). Additionally, the specifically 'feminine losses' caused to women in prison, such as isolation from family and children and the invasion of their personal privacy, led to either withdrawal and ritualistic compliance, or defiance and individualistic rebellion (*ibid*.: 121–2):

> [D]ue to [the] mistrust which prevailed among the women prisoners, it was not easy for them to form a group which could stick together in their common grievance against the authorities ... The women prisoners lack group identification and comradeship. One can observe anomie in their formal system, in that the inmates are confused as to what rules to abide by (*ibid*.: 136).

Accordingly, because women were inclined to individual self-interest or more susceptible to alienation, their alliances were more tenuous and unreliable. Furthermore, they were unable to engage with disciplinary or complaints systems as 'men prisoners have more resources than women prisoners to cope and play the bureaucratic-instrumental roles already learned outside' (*ibid*.: 140). Hence, women's exclusion from even legitimate opportunities to remedy grievances caused them to resolve their problems by haphazard and individual means, which exposed them to the risk of further punishment (*ibid*.: 140–1). The importance of Mandaraka-Sheppard's analysis is the attention she draws to the official disruption of alliances and friendships because women in prison are enmeshed in punitive, surveillant and deterrent mechanisms. As a consequence, their 'resistance' is limited in scope and style to individualistic and petty forms of rule-breaking. Women in prison cannot or do not effectively exercise collaborative agency because of institutionally determined forces, rather than innate failures on their part, she concludes. Rather, women's alliances are constantly exposed to co-option, dispersal, punishment and control. This alignment between gendered correction and the formation of penal constraints has been explored in other analyses of women's prison punishment, which are now discussed.

Women's political imprisonment: feminist perspectives

This section considers how the female political prisoner avoids easy categorization in the analysis of women's imprisonment. The conditions of confinement for long-term, serious or political women prisoners have not informed general analyses of women's imprisonment to a significant degree (with some notable exceptions; see Genders and Player 1988; Carlen 1988, 1998). This absence does not simply reflect an empirical oversight, but amplifies ongoing debates about the social function of women's punishment, the shifting nature of control in women's prisons, and the deferral of their needs within wider concerns about women's incarceration. It must be noted that long-term serious and political categories are not interchangeable. However, I argue that they are collectively constituted as a problem group in the prison system by a combination of unsystematic practices, that is, random and reactive attitudes and arrangements which marginalize them in the women's prison population.

Since the 1980s, feminist penology has retained as a central analytical paradigm the primacy of poverty, profound social marginality and exposure to gendered violence and controls as explanations for women's 'pathways' to crime and punishment (Heidensohn 1985; Faith 1993; Carlen 1983, 1988, 1998). Carlen has consistently argued that the 'meaning of women's imprisonment' originates in pervasive gendered controls and forms of social exclusion which precede the confinement of women and which are reproduced in prison regimes. Accordingly, the significance of women's imprisonment as a social institution references 'both penal discourses' and 'discursive forms and practices which are conventionally considered to be quite unrelated to penology' (Carlen 1983: 15). 'Offending women' suffer multiple burdens of social marginalization, being seen as 'outwith family, sociability, femininity and adulthood ... they are often seen as being outwith "real" criminality too' (ibid.: 155). Hence, imprisonment extends a very specific form of social control 'especially tailored' for disciplining women who are 'deemed not only to have broken the law' but to have transgressed their roles as 'women, mothers and wives' (ibid.: 59).

In arguing that any analysis of 'women's conformity, law-breaking, and punishment' must engage with the 'ideological and material circumstances' within which they are criminalized, Carlen holds that women lawbreakers exercise volition in a sociopolitical sense, 'not only because they "find themselves" outwith conventional classes and gender controls, but also they *choose* criminal means in attempts to apply individualistic remedies to the social inequities stemming from class exploitation, sexism and racism' (1988: 17, emphasis in original). Accordingly, women's recourse to crime must be seen as responses to the magnitude of social conditions which produce offending. The appropriate objects of penological analysis, therefore, are the material relationships of classed, gendered, cultural and racial domination, 'which are [neither] reducible to each other', nor separable from the multifaceted realities of women's punishment (*ibid.*). The signature of 'the extremes of social exclusion', such as poverty, substance abuse and sexual and domestic terror are constituents in the lives of women who go to prison (Prison Reform Trust 2000: xv). The disturbing increases in women's incarceration from the 1990s has compelled critics of the prison to renew their emphasis on the aggregate social harm caused to imprisoned women, relative to the social harm caused by their crimes. Considerable emphasis has been placed on the fact that women in prison are infrequently serious or violent offenders, that the majority are imprisoned for property or drugs offences, or prostitution, and 'that women are less likely to commit crimes than men, they are less likely to commit serious crimes and their offending careers are shorter' (*ibid.*: 8).

Furthermore, the rising rates of women's imprisonment cast into relief the extensive social costs of confining them, on the basis that their 'patterns of offending remain very different from that of men' and pose 'lower levels of risk to the public' (*ibid.*: xii). As nearly half of all women in custody are separated from their children, the cost of women's imprisonment 'has wider and longer term social repercussions' than individual deterrence (*ibid.*: xiii). Women, moreover, are victimized in criminal justice and prison systems that are 'designed for men, rather than women' (*ibid.*: xv). In the course of committal, they are constructed 'within the discourses of domesticity, sexuality and pathology … [as] needy, greedy and sick' (Worrall 1995: 85). Within such constructions of social inadequacy, dependency and subordination, they are portrayed as 'victims' with 'generally chaotic lives' or as serially offending individuals who 'must undergo a further transformation' by being imprisoned 'for their own, rather than the public, good' (Carlen 1983: 86). The observation that 'instead of harming others they harm themselves' has, therefore, been generally linked to the argument that 'on none of its possible definitions would the majority of women [in prison] be seen as dangerous' (*ibid.*: 115). The relative 'harmlessness' of offending women, furthermore, underlines the case for reducing their committal to custody or changing the nature and function of prisoner regimes:

> a greater proportion of women could be held without physical security restrictions as … the majority of women entering the prison system do so without having committed a serious offence and without being a risk to the safety of the public … However, none of this is to deny that there are some women in prison who

have committed serious offences and have caused harm to their victims, [but] *these women represent a small proportion of all those entering the prison system* (Prison Reform Trust 2000: 8).

Despite the limited efficacy of social harm arguments (in so far as they have generated a plethora of concerned official initiatives) their tenets remain prescribed within paradigms of social victimization and balance-of-harm arguments. Much of this is empirically defensible, and the objections to social harm advocacy as a simply reductive defence of the 'victimhood' of women offenders, which denies them agency and subjective complexity, remain unconvincing (see Daly and Maher 1998: 10; Bosworth 1999: 5 and for the counter-argument, Hannah-Moffat 2001; Carlen 1983, 1994, 1998, 2002a, 2002b).

Neither can it be said that these factors (racism, poverty, State and 'private' violence) necessarily *preclude* the circumstances of women convicted for violent, serious crimes, including political prisoners. It is all the more surprising, then, that the conditions and treatment of the minority of women who have been deemed risks to public safety continue to constitute the most problematic category for progressives and radicals. Much of the analysis of imprisoned women has focused on low-security regimes and those serving short or medium terms of imprisonment (Howard League for Penal Reform 1999). As a consequence, the specific hardships and institutional adjustments by women serving life or long-term sentences, or those confined in high-security regimes, are not only secondary concerns. Rather, existing reform discourse does 'not begin to address the existential features which constitute women's experience of life imprisonment', such as the losses of liberty for life or lengthy periods, their fertility, family relationships and 'what she has come to view as her being' (Walker and Worrall 2000: 28).

This omission reflects, in part, the political urgency of giving prominence to the materialities of women's offending as a counter-argument to the upward cycle of women's imprisonment. Similarly, the lack of an obvious, socially ameliorative reason for reducing the harshness of sentences or regimes for serious women offenders is not simply the outcome of prudent, gradualist campaigning. Rather, the issue reflects the crux of harnessing the case for change to arguments based on an offender's socially victimized status, whilst having to avoid becoming mired in populist discourses of danger and public harm attached to 'dangerous' women. A shared tactic of penal reform (Prison Reform Trust 2000), and reductionist or abolitionist positions (Carlen 1998: 134), then, has been to emphasize that the standards of risk assessment, deterrence and retribution that have been the predominant political response to the apparent rise in women's criminality have not been based on the general *'realities* of women's lawbreaking' (*ibid.*, emphasis in original). Nevertheless, these arguments introduce obvious impediments to positioning female serious or violent offenders within either the 'facts' of women's pathways to imprisonment, or the norms of an aggressively punitive law and order discourse, other than as unique and exceptional cases (MacDonald 1991; Lloyd 1995).

The rest of this chapter takes three elements of the previous observations: the oversight of serious female offenders in certain penal analyses, the continuing segregation of women into 'difficult' or 'dangerous' categories, and the possibilities for analysing continuities and differences between these two categories, to argue that:

• Women political prisoners are susceptible to the behavioural scrutiny and gender discipline that are deployed against the majority of 'difficult' women of penal discourse.

• There are transitional points between 'regular' discipline and specialized forms of enhanced security that are justified by the existence of the 'dangerous' women of penal discourse.

• The punishment of women political prisoners creates significant areas of continuity and overlap with that of 'ordinary' women prisoners *and* also leads to specialized regimes of control and security.

Governing 'difficult' women in prison: the domestication of penal control

Women's prison punishment has largely been shaped in relation to conventional constructions of the 'difficult' woman of penal discourse, who is deemed to be replete with personal inadequacies, emotionally demanding or self-destructive, has pernicious behavioural problems and lacks the capacity to reform herself. She is thus primarily defined as needy and socially dependent, and requiring intensive professional involvement to render her suitable for reform. A central function of the reformative discipline of women's prisons, therefore, has involved deconstructing or rearranging their undesirable social habits and attitudes. In this context, women's prison regimes have conventionally assimilated and reproduced a range of social imperatives for restraining them from straying from docile femininity, at least whilst they are confined, whilst the need for additional behavioural vigilance against rule-breaking has been harnessed to the broader logic of 'rehabilitating' them, that is, restoring them to normative womanhood.

Consequently, the principles of compulsory domestication and the exposure of women to the beneficial influence of exemplary 'family' relationships have been central to the ideology of women's rehabilitation since the inception of the penitentiary (Zedner 1998; Dodge 1999). Carlen (1983) and Dobash *et al.* (1986) critically observed that the 'new' women's prisons which opened in the 1970s, and were modelled on 'house' or 'cottage-style' residential units, were purposefully designed to integrate prisoners into an elaborated system of behavioural deterrence and surveillance, petty discipline and emotional and psychosocial dependency on staff. Furthermore, the simulation of 'family-type' regimes in Cornton Vale prison, Scotland, which was the prototype for Mourne House, Northern Ireland, had deeply 'repressive' effects, in that the physical division of prisoners into small groups 'made for easy physical and social control' (Dobash *et al.* 1986: 186). Carlen (1983: 111) further argued that the 'familiness' of 'progressive' regimes combined 'the denial to prisoners of sociability and adult womanhood with the organization of the women into small family units, to ensure a mental and bodily surveillance which denudes the prisoners' daily life of all dignity and independence'. In this context, domestication effectively created a more pliable surrogate for the less desirable kinds of association which prisoners were deemed likely to engage in if left to their own devices, not least because the culture of personal intervention was so 'successful' that it took 'extraordinary strength to resist the degree of control, surveillance and manipulation directed at preventing the foundation of such bonds or at breaking them once formed' (Dobash *et al.* 1986: 186).

From domestication to dynamic security

Since the 1990s, however, this critical concern with stultifying domestication has given way to urgent objections to excessive and punitive security, the lack of safety in prisons evidenced by the soaring rates of suicides and self-harm, overcrowding, and stresses on the prison system which have become normalized across all categories in women's prisons (Carlen and Tchaikovsky 1996; Carlen 1998; Walker and Worrall 2000; Hannah-Moffat 2001). In England and Wales, this security drift has been driven by the resurgence of a new punitiveness, which is associated with a paradigm shift in criminal justice and penal policies from 'therapeutic' and rehabilitative goals to austere, retributive and deterrent regimes. The security drift originated with the reviews to prison security in response to escapes from Whitemoor (1994) and Parkhurst (1995) prisons. In historical mirroring of developments in Northern Ireland, the restructuring of prison security in England and Wales following the Learmont Inquiry (1995) was based on assessments of physical risks in men's prisons, but led to the wholesale application of enhanced security in women's prisons without an assessment of their suitability or impact (Carlen 1998: 132–5). Furthermore, the problems with securitization do not only derive from the monolithic application of security policy, but also from the deployment of 'dynamic' security which supposedly involves the precise, surgical use of procedures on the basis of individual risk assessment. Yet, as Carlen (*ibid*.: 123) observed, 'the main problem with dynamic security … is that attempts to put it into practice have been either nullified or swamped by straightforwardly repressive changes'. To Carlen's cogent evaluation of the misapplication of security practices in prison systems where women prisoners are already systematically marginalized can be added the further observation that security in women's prisons is dynamic because it works in tandem with, and reinforces, other structural imbalances and normalizing practices: 'This combination of high-level security, great distance from family and communities, and few choices for daily activity or movement, together with individual reasons for despair, results in lethargy, claustrophobia, depression, self-injurious behaviour and suicide' (Faith 1993: 139).

Further complications occur with the downward percolation of security practices when higher-category remand women are confined in low-category women's prisons. With the exception of the small group of sentenced women in Britain who were classified as the highest security risk and housed in 'H' wing, HMP Durham, the provision of facilities for serious women offenders has been applied in an *ad hoc* fashion, alternating between the adaptation of units in existing male high-security prisons or quarantining prisoners remanded for serious offences in lower-category women's prisons. The conditions in Durham, which held women PIRA prisoners from 1974, and was at the time of writing the only Category A facility for women prisoners in Britain, exemplify the problems with the former strategy. In their inquiry into Durham women's prison commissioned by prison reform groups, Lester and Taylor (1989: 10) reported the 'depressive appearance' and cramped environment of the wing, the 'manifestly insufficient' provision of exercise facilities, restrictions on access to educational and workshop activities and the unnecessarily high use of strip searching. They concluded that women in 'H' wing were 'being treated less favourably in important respects than … if they were male … and it is strongly arguable that their unequal treatment is unlawful' (*ibid*.: 5).

Conditions had deteriorated even further by the time the first and only official inquiry into 'H' wing was conducted 15 years later (Her Majesty's Inspectorate of Prisons 2004). In a highly critical report, the prisons inspectorate condemned the 'extremely oppressive' environment which was 'scarcely likely to enhance the mental state of women … who may spend years in this environment' (*ibid*.: 3). In addition, the report criticized the presence of vulnerable prisoners who were 'subject to a level of security which they did not require', the curtailment of activities because of protracted searching procedures (*ibid*.: 89), the disturbing record of six 'self-inflicted' fatalities in the previous two years and the regular use of the punishment strip-cell and disciplinary procedures against those at risk of suicide. The severe shortcomings that were identified in every area of provision and safety were essentially attributed to 'the lack of separate policies for women' largely because the unit was 'out of the line of sight of the overall management' of Durham and 'on the periphery of the women's estate' (*ibid*.: 3). Yet, the report was as significant in its timing as its content. The state of 'H' wing by the time the inspection was conducted epitomized the longstanding crisis in the provision of gender-appropriate and security-appropriate detention for women. This was evident from the confusion of purpose of the unit, which had been increasingly obliged to house lower-security prisoners contrary to its original function (*ibid*.: Appendix ii). The report concluded that 'Durham prison is not an appropriate environment for women prisoners serving long sentences. Alternative locations for the women there should be found' (*ibid*.: 20). Shortly after the inspection, the Home Office scheduled the closure of Durham's female wing within one year and the transfer of the remaining 76 women to new, privately run Bronzefield and Peterborough prisons (*Guardian* 27 May 2004). The fate of the seven 'high-risk' prisoners there, however, remained conditional on the availability of 'spare capacity elsewhere' (*ibid*.).

The alternative and more 'humane' option of housing women on remand or awaiting trial in lower-security, women-only institutions, has been equally problematic. The presence of Republican remand prisoners in HMP Holloway women's prison in the 1980s and 1990s, for example, had previously led to the blanket application of maximum security regimes to the detriment of lower-category prisoners (Irish Council of Churches 1990). Furthermore, their confinement in either male high-security facilities, or low-category women's prisons, led to further isolation and marginalization, as the testaments of Irish women prisoners have shown (O'Dwyer 1986a, 1986b, 1986c; Ward 1993). In either case, the treatment of high-security women prisoners reveals the anomalies of transferring them across the prison estate because assessments of the security risk they pose, or the need to be near family or legal advisers are subordinated to the availability of suitable facilities. The case of Róisín McAliskey, an Irish prisoner who was remanded in custody for 15 months, illustrates that these problems underpin an informal system of 'ghosting' (being moved without forewarning or on short notice to another prison). McAliskey was arrested in Belfast in November 1996 on the basis of an extradition warrant connected to the PIRA bombing of British army bases in Germany and transferred to Holloway prison in London, which had no designated facilities for housing Category A prisoners (British/Irish Rights Watch *et al.* 1997). She was, accordingly, transferred to a special secure unit in the men's prison of Belmarsh. As she was pregnant when arrested, and her health deteriorated in Belmarsh, she was returned to Holloway, where she was held in isolation. McAliskey was strip searched 75 times in the first three months of her remand, and although the governor of Holloway petitioned for her to be allowed access to exercise facilities, the request was turned down by the Home Office. She was released without any extradition hearing taking place in March 1998. The general security drift and *ad hoc* arrangements for 'high-risk' prisoners have thus generated significant points of conversion between gender controls and enhanced security which cross and re-cross different regimes for women prisoners.

Controlling 'dangerous' women in prison: the ecology of special incapacitation

The 'dangerous woman' of penal discourse is at the opposite end of the discursive spectrum from that of the 'difficult' woman prisoner. Because of the nature of their convictions, and their construction as exceptional to criminal and gendered norms, women political prisoners are not readily identifiable as the passive or victimized subjects of penal subordination more commonly found on the literature on women's confinement. Rather, it is precisely their social competence, highly developed organizational skills, critical consciousness and, most of all, their resistance to self-abnegating collaboration with authority which confirm their subversiveness in official eyes. The construction of such women as deliberately placing themselves out of reach of rehabilitative or benevolent influences both reinforces perceptions of their irreformability, and provides the justification for organizing security and control around the principles of containment. 'Containment' is applied here in the general criminological sense that a question of crime or disorder is deemed to be so extensive in scope or intractable in character as to be irresoluble, so that the principal approach has been to manage the problem by containing or minimizing its criminogenic effects (Feeley and Simon 1994). In prisons, it is characterized by special regimes for maximizing control and surveillance, calculating the behavioural responses and dangers posed by 'high-risk' groups, and isolating 'unstable prisoners'. The precepts of containment additionally imply the 'pragmatic' construction of political prisoners as being impervious to conventional correctional and normalizing interventions. This in turn makes securitization the primary penal objective.

Consequently, the institutional designation of women as 'high-risk' prisoners is supported by four material and explanatory frameworks which set them apart for repressive penal treatment. First, the dangerous woman of penal discourse is ontologically differentiated from other women prisoners as inherently disruptive and high-risk, prone to violence or escaping from custody. Such risk assessments are grounded in 'descriptions and inferences about the terrorist's mind [which] are unequivocal in assuming incurable pathology, and emphatic in warning about the futility of social or rehabilitative approaches to their incarceration, especially for women' (Zwerman 1988: 36). Therefore, 'traditional forms of rehabilitation, e.g. work, training programmes, recreation and therapy' are not perceived to 'have any positive impact on the political terrorist, in that s/he will not use these as avenues for personal growth, but rather as opportunities to criticise the prison and its authorities' (*ibid.*: 37).

Secondly, as conventional standards of punishment and rehabilitation are considered to be ineffectual, administrators have turned to methods of 'special incapacitation' as a primary strategy for ensuring internal security and limiting their contaminating influence. These strategies have involved isolating prisoners in secure units (or in segregated cells or wings where there are no specialized facilities) and introducing intelligence-gathering, surveillance and other counter-insurgency methods for the purpose of 'containing and monitoring primarily (though not exclusively) women political prisoners' (*ibid.*: 32). At the same time, the decision either to disperse individuals across the prison system, or to concentrate them in one institution, is as much a political as a security decision, 'because of the risk of association and politicization of non-political prisoners' which extends 'the "prisoner-terrorist" link' (Flynn cited in *ibid.* 36).

Thirdly, political prisoners, like other women sentenced for long terms of imprisonment, are institutionally segregated as logistical peculiarities, being both a minority of women prisoners and a neglected few within the Category A prison population. Historically, the lack of separate high-security facilities for women has led to the establishment of 'female annexes' (Dodge 1999) in men's prisons, with the consequence that the needs of long-term sentenced women have been submerged beneath the greater weight and importance of the main male prison. Their marginal position in the prison system has also led to the arbitrary application of security practices, the shuttling of individuals from one unit or institution to another and the *ad hoc* improvization of security controls to supplement deficiencies in the design or policies of establishments.

Fourthly, none of the arrangements have precluded the use of gender controls, but rather they have established the context within which the close governance of women is adapted to special security measures until 'the authoritarian element … is heightened' (Zwerman 1988: 37). In this context, the 'special incapacitation' of women has evolved into an ecology of small-group containment which combines an unremittingly 'secure' physical environment with the kinds of behavioural enclosure that resemble a perverse variant of the 'familiness' that is to be found more generally in women's units. This hybrid facilitates the closer monitoring of the group's activities as well as the greater scrutiny of an individual prisoner's conversations and correspondence, and justifies pre-emptive and invasive security procedures such as strip searching (Churchill and Vander Wall 1992). Female political prisoners are thus doubly contained as 'women' for the purposes of regulation and deterrence, and as 'political' for the purposes of security and control.

Conclusion: women political prisoners as difficult *and* dangerous women

In her analysis of trial proceedings against women who have been charged with serious, violent crimes, Allen has argued that the meanings attributed to the offences and defendants are 'typically manipulated, modified and reconstructed' to 'neutralise … the assertion of the woman's guilt, responsibility or dangerousness' (1998: 55). Accordingly, they undergo a series of elaborate transformations which systematically delete 'all that would mark [their] action [as being] by an intentional and culpable subject' (*ibid.*: 56). Female defendants in these circumstances are discursively 'tamed, sanitized, and rendered harmless' through the deployment of psychiatric, medical and social assessments which are entered as mitigating defences in ways that 'alter the material and moral significance' of their offences, and which are 'either absent or untypical in cases involving males' (*ibid.*: 55–6). Rather than seeking to confirm the 'chivalrous' disposition of the criminal justice system, Allen identifies the subtler, prejudicial processes which reinforce the abnormality of the violent women, and cumulatively contribute to 'a simple denial of the woman's mental engagement with her behaviour, as if such an unreasoning and unreasonable condition were a quite natural state of womankind' (*ibid.*: 57).

The suppression of women's agency in the commission of political crime takes a similar, if more convoluted, trajectory in successive sociological narratives. Nevertheless, these are equally involved in displacing offenders' motives into the realms of pathology, irrationality, overwhelmingly emotional responses to social or political injustices, or psychological or social maladjustment. However, a curious bifurcation occurs in accounts of the 'causes' of women's political violence. In the first instance, the figure of the exceptional individual who singularly embodies a range of psychosocial deviations is invoked so that alternative causal explanations, political rationales, social experiences or other plausible interpretations are suppressed. Positivist approaches construct women political offenders as pathological exceptions, or rare social and physiological phenomena who elude easy categorization either as women or as criminal types, and therefore embody the most 'degenerative' examples of both. The putatively corrective successor to this tradition applies rigidly normative categories of social or 'sex-role' adaptive theory to reify the 'sociopathic' attributes of the maladjusted or rejectionist woman.

At the same time, these analyses admit some qualifications which seek, if not to exonerate these offenders, to at least enter mitigating, 'victimizing' explanations, such as their subordination within their political organizations, or the relegation of their political protests in prisons to the marginal and gestural realm. In either case, women's rationality is rendered inadmissible, either by outright denial, or because they are differently admitted to the economy of, if not legitimized, at least intelligible 'terrorist' violence. What is also clear, however, is that explanations of their 'victimization' are still harnessed to sociological accounts which require the signifier of a readily identifiable, highly culpable offender. As Allen notes, '[a]t the very moment where these narratives seem most to require a definitive moral subject, as the responsible author of the crime, these women's status as [victimized] subjects is emphatically revoked' (*ibid.*: 57).

In turning from the 'causes' of women's involvement in political violence to analyses of their potential agency in prison, we similarly see that they disrupt the conceptual unity of political agency and gendered subjectivity in prison. Part three of the chapter explored the limited relevance of prison subcultural theory to analysing the collective agency of either women, or political women, in prison. With the exception of Mandaraka-Sheppard (1986), the application of sociation theory to women's prisons turned on essentialist accounts of women's inherent passivity and lack of solidarity, which undermined the sustainability and coherence of their prison communities. The fourth section argued that the emphasis in feminist penology on social harm, victimization and social oppression, whilst relevant to women political prisoners, nevertheless could not be a primary explanatory framework. However, feminist critical analyses of the social organization of punishment, and its relationship to the prescriptive norms of prison discipline for women, created an analytical bridge for positioning political offenders within criminological analysis. This occurs especially where the fluid networks of security and gendered controls blur distinctions between regimes for the 'difficult' and 'dangerous' women of penal discourse. However, some outstanding questions remain to be explored in relation to the formations of agency and subjectivity amongst women political prisoners in Northern Ireland, which is discussed in the next chapter.

Note

1   The overall analysis in this book does not view women who commit violent offences against the person, and discourses of the 'lethal' woman and the 'female militant' as interchangeable phenomena, but these have often been conflated in the literatures discussed here. Feminist criminological analyses have taken up the task of critically unravelling these constructions by arguing that they can only be rendered intelligible by reference to a grid of related discourses in legal and social thinking with respect to the 'abnormality' and aberration of 'violent' women (see Smart 1992; Cain 1994; Lloyd 1995; Worrall 1995; Ballinger 2000).

Chapter 4

The dynamics of punishment and resistance in Northern Ireland's prisons

This chapter accounts for the continuities and discontinuities in the cycle of punishment and resistance in Northern Ireland's prisons for women. It follows from the arguments in the previous chapters which indicate that the resistance of women political prisoners was imbricated in power relations that reflected, and were constituted within, an alignment of the State, the prison, and political and gendered punishment. Political imprisonment also cast into sharper relief the interrelationship between institutional power, ideology and the criminalization of women prisoners. In the first instance, the State's investment in the political and discursive integrity of the prison system was harnessed to restoring the legitimacy of the rule of law, and confirming that the 'normal' functioning of the legal and security apparatus was generally viable. Secondly, in order for the project of political imprisonment to function smoothly, the prison system utilized a number of systems of closure which involved political demonization, enhanced powers for punishment and containment, and justificatory principles for the exceptional measures taken to counter crises. Thirdly, women political prisoners were more explicitly involved in resistance than has been usually observed in prison studies. In these circumstances, conflict in the prisons took on a conspicuously dialectical character. However, whilst the *cause* of the prisoners' campaign was ostensibly grounded in the fundamental contention over criminalization, the dynamics of the *women's* struggle meant that it developed, in practice, into a wider resistance to multifaceted penal controls. Consequently, the dialectical nature of the women's prison campaign took on additional characteristics. It is therefore argued that:

Events in Armagh and Mourne House revealed the fluid, contingent and relatively unpredictable course of prison conflict. Thus, prison resistance can be seen in terms of Foucault's concept of *productive power*, with its emphasis on the agency of the suppressed, the dispersal of conflict across different points of a social field, the subversion of institutional closure and the subsequent disruption of historically determined outcomes.

At the same time, there is a deep tension between the freedom of manoeuvre implied by Foucault and the repressive forces the prisoners confronted. This meant that women prisoners resisted within circumscribed boundaries that were drawn by the institutionalized contexts of the State apparatus and gender.

Similarly, there were *relational* and *situational* dimensions to the cycle of punishment and resistance. *Relational*, in that the countermeasures that were taken against women prisoners can be seen as responses to the gendered and political abnormalities their rebellion was deemed to represent. *Situated*, because women prisoners' resistance was directly shaped by the conditions of punishment they experienced. In short, the trajectory of prison conflict was dialectical, productive, relational and situated.

The dialectics of prison struggle

The starting point of the analysis is the crisis of legitimacy in the prisons that followed the implementation of criminal status. Republican women and men prisoners were involved in a continuous and dynamic prison struggle for the reinstatement of the conditions that were commensurate with political status.[1] The *continuity* of their campaign derived from its longevity, versatility and relative coherence. Its *dynamism* was related to the formation and reformation of prison policies through successive phases of coercion and 'accommodation', and the prisoners' own strategic renegotiation of these realignments. As McKeown (2001: 225) observed, the longer-term Republican strategy was focused on precipitating 'ongoing change within the continuity of the prison struggle', in which prisoners 'switched tactics according to what suited the particular issue, period or objective'. Thus, they alternated between collective self-management during the period of internment, physical protest and direct confrontation during the 'criminalization' era, and at other times involved 'subversion of the prison rules as displayed in the segregation and prison work issues', in the 'dramatic flouting of prison's "security" as in the mass escape in 1983' from the Maze, the use of litigation 'and, in the 1990s, primarily through dialogue and engagement with the prison authorities' (*ibid.*: 222).

The dialectics of struggle occurred along a range of potential points of conflict between the prison administration and prisoners. As Sparks *et al.* (1996: 34) noted, the maintenance of control and order in prisons is achieved through versatile mechanisms that include violence and coercion and 'countervailing impulses towards accommodation, co-operation and sociability'. In this way, to 'speak about the problems of order and control in prisons today raises questions of power, of unintended consequences, of the impact of modern managerial techniques, and the relationship between social structure and personal agency that prison studies has yet to confront adequately but which are the very stuff of modern social theory' (*ibid.*: 62).

Viewed like this, prison regimes constitute a complex set of interests that are involved in the construction, and reconstruction, of penal 'order'. Penal punishment does not have a unitary meaning but creates in practice 'a shifting patchwork of compromises and arbitrary decisions' (Duff and Garland 1994: 5). Furthermore, this mutability and contingency undermine the apparent seamlessness of penal sanctions and powers. As Sparks *et al.* (1996: 35) have noted, an 'emphasis on the imposition of order by relentless force glosses over many important complexities of prison life and effaces some significant variations in the social organization of different prisons'. Because order and control do not occur 'equally, always and everywhere' (Bottoms and Sparks 1995: 51), penal power is thought to be a normalizing force that seeks out pathways of least resistance rather than taking the form of unreconstructed coercion.

In following the logic that prison relationships are characterized less by confrontation than by conformity (of either a consensual or hegemonic nature), writers such as Bottoms (1983), Bottoms and Sparks (1995) and Sparks *et al.* (1996) have sought to re-engage the admissibility of 'legitimacy' as a principle of penal order and justice. As Bottoms and Sparks (1995: 53) inquire, '[a]re there, indeed, any conditions under which prison management could reliably call upon a recognition of legitimacy by prisoners (in the sense of being "justified" in terms of their beliefs …), as distinct from mere acquiescence or dull compulsion?' The authors were referring here to the problems that are incurred when good order is disconnected from consensus and legitimacy in penal practice. Their analysis is ultimately concerned with the conditions in which these discrepancies have been addressed, most notably through reforms that attempt to establish a strategic consensus with the confined (Sparks *et al.* 1996). The approach is rooted, in part, in the revival of the social contract as the basis of reformed prison governance in the Woolf Report (1991) on disturbances in the England and Wales prison system in 1990. Woolf (*ibid.*: 14.437) concluded that prison conflict could be minimized by means of substituting the language and rules of discretionary privileges with those of prisoners' 'rights', fostering procedural transparency and fairness, and acknowledging the mutual rights and responsibilities of administrators and prisoners alike. Such measures were fundamental to the stability of the system. Although not uncritical of Woolf's instrumental adjustment of the principles of legitimacy to the maintenance of order in prisons, Sparks *et al.* (1996: 87) retained as a central aspect of their case the argument that 'many of the dimensions of prison life … are unintelligible without reference to implicit (albeit not necessarily consensually shared) conceptions of legitimacy amongst prisoners and staff'. Nevertheless, whilst justice and legitimacy were part of the purview of liberalizing prison regimes, these standards also extended the moral threshold of consensus in such a way as to identify and isolate detractors from the new contractarian order. 'The achievement of justice will itself enhance security and control' (Woolf 1991: 14.437). 'While not preventing all disruptions, they would marginalize those who claim they must resort to deeply damaging and costly disturbances on the grounds that there is no other way to have their voices heard' (*ibid.*: 14.438).

Normalization and its discontents: the [il]legitimacy of consensus in Northern Ireland's prisons

The pursuit of legitimacy on similar terms was also at the forefront of the 'normalization' policy of the Northern Ireland Prison Service. Its consultation document, *Serving the Community* (NIPS 1991a), had set out, in impeccably contractarian terms, the prison service's objectives for fostering stability and order in prison regimes, by implementing:

> positive and constructive regimes which will encourage prisoners to exercise self-discipline and to act in a manner conducive to good order for their own benefit, the benefit of everyone working in prisons and ultimately the benefit of society on their release … We shall enable prisoners to retain their dignity and self respect

> ... by working to create a climate which will assist prisoners in developing a sense of personal responsibility ... [and] by giving reasons, where possible, for our actions (*ibid.*: 9–11).

Nevertheless, the obvious impediment to restoring the authority of prison regimes in Northern Ireland was that these commitments reignited the ongoing conflict over the legitimacy of the State's right to punish. The question of legitimacy in the context of political detention does not just impinge on the abstract realms of political theory or ideological conflict *per se*. It is also relevant to the wider politicization of criminal justice administration, in which governments play a significant role. A number of problems arise for governments when they make contentious policies into ideological standard-bearers or objects of essential political principle. This was especially applicable to criminalization, as the Gardiner Report (1975) had insisted upon merging the separate questions of restoring the legitimacy of government and the rule of law, with the exceptional, but not historically new, problem of detaining prisoners who would challenge the political and correctional viability of imprisonment. The problem became even more crucial, as successive administrations found, when resistance to either political or correctional legitimacy brought about the possibility that *both* objectives could be undermined. It took a further decade before the separation of the more 'political' resonances of the legitimacy question from some of its more achievable goals was attempted again in Northern Ireland, and even then the more ideological dimensions of the strategy were not eluded (McEvoy 2001).

An additional problem with uniting the issues of prison conformity and political legitimacy was that it paved the way for creating an almost limitless field of confrontation out of commonplace interactions between the prison authorities and prisoners. The Gardiner Report had redefined the question of 'good order' in official discourse as an essentially political matter. On a more practical level, criminalization invested the various mechanisms of prison discipline with charged political meanings that had been masked by special category status. For political prisoners, accepting criminal status was not just a matter of yielding to the larger symbolism of conforming to the prison regime. Rather, the most minor engagement with the system acted as a continuous reminder of their obligation to discover and give expression to the many different ways in which they did not see themselves as criminals. In Foucauldian terms (1979), criminalization was a quintessential expression of governmentality in its evolution from a political discourse to a pervasive correctional technology for inculcating stigma and discipline. In response, political prisoners adopted tactics for countering the prolific repressive, regulatory and voluntaristic imperatives that were implied by the penal social contract. It is difficult to avoid the conclusion, then, that the policy lent a defining clarity to both the ideology and praxis of resistance, and eventually became an unwieldy, contradictory instrument which, rather than minimizing conflict, multiplied it.

Productive power and prison struggle: a Foucauldian perspective

In the course of nearly three decades of prison protest, the prison regimes in Northern Ireland underwent 'ever-innovative, ever-revisionist and ever-transformative' adaptations to 'the effects that changing political and social conditions have on the penal system' (Carlen 1998: 42). These contingencies significantly influenced the material contexts in which women prisoners converted their position from that of subjectification to agency. The following discussion traces the emergence of prisoners as resisters through the linkage that Foucault (1990: 92–102) makes between power and resistance, and the claim that institutional power is altered by struggles against it. This occurs, Foucault contends, because power relations are ubiquitous, in that they emanate from all points in a social 'field'; productive, or capable of being exercised by all social agents; and contingent, in that forces of domination tend to create the conditions for counter-flows of resistance to emerge (*ibid.*). Although Foucault's concept of plural and fluid 'power' potentially allows subordinated groups to regain agency, it remains a generalized proposition. Some political and feminist critics have notably argued that it does little to relate the constitution of normalizing and governing power to a discernible State apparatus (Poulantzas 1980; Fraser 1989) or the variation of social disciplines to which men and women are subjected (Sawicki 1991; Ramazanoglu 1993). This analysis, therefore, retains Foucault's concept of productive resistance, which supposedly reveals the provisional nature of prison power, but applies the feminist critique that the exercise of agency is bounded by institutionalized constraints, whilst acknowledging the tensions between these positions.

According to Foucault (1990: 95), resistance plays a key role as an 'adversary, target, support, or handle' in power relations. Foucault contends that acts of power and acts of resistance are symbiotic, in that the potential for resistance is always present at the frontiers of authority: 'where there is power, there is resistance, and … this resistance is never in a position of exteriority in relation to power' (*ibid.*). Here, 'power' is described in terms of a set of strategic possibilities that emanate from the social margins as well as from administrative centres, and is exercised by subordinated groups, rather than solely by those who occupy privileged positions (*ibid.*: 92–102). Not all groups are equally situated in a social field, but neither are they permanently fixed in dominant or subordinate positions (Foucault 1980: 142). The fact that power relationships are continuously under construction reveals the contingency of administrative or structural privilege (*ibid.*). Accordingly, domination, once achieved, must be continuously maintained and stabilized, and never attains complete closure.

Foucault (1979) rejected 'determinist' conceptions of governmental power by drawing a distinction between government as the apparatus of the State, and governance, which refers to the ways in which peripheral forces are drawn into power relationships and may act in conjunction with the State. 'Power', then, does not constitute 'a group of institutions and mechanisms that ensure the subservience of citizens of a given State [but] must be understood in the first instance as the multiplicity of force relations imminent in the sphere' of rule (Foucault 1990: 92). Accordingly, governance is exercised through the integration of 'small-scale, regional and dispersed' sites of social regulation into a centralized, bureaucratic system (Foucault 1979: 20). Far from being reducible to a State apparatus, governmentality, or the will to govern, is exponentially reproduced through 'an ensemble formed by the institutions, procedures, analyses and reflections, the calculations and tactics, that allow the exercise of this very specific albeit complex form of power' (*ibid.*). Viewed like this, the power of prisons is vested in the interventionist, bureaucratic and governing practices that they have accumulated, and which uphold the function of punishment. The State apparatus, however, acquires more a permanent organizational form through 'strategic codifications' of power that are clustered around identifiable social 'problems' – crime, sexual 'abnormality', mental illness – and 'deviant' social groups. Hence, his focus of analysis 'wasn't "institutions", "theories" or "ideology" but *practices* – with the aim of grasping the conditions which make these acceptable at a given moment' (Foucault 1980: 5, emphasis in original).

It follows that Foucault regards marginal and everyday social relations as key sites in which power is experienced. Furthermore, because 'power generates resistance', governing 'practices' are likely to be resisted at the junctures in which they are installed: 'but this does not mean that they are only a reaction or rebound, forming with respect to the basic domination an underside that is in the end always passive, doomed to perpetual defeat' (Foucault 1991: 96). Hypothetically at least, the revolt of the repressed and the many inventive practices that might be understood as 'resistance' become worthy of serious theoretical consideration. What is unclear, however, are the concrete transformations that might be achieved here, or how local resistance might deflect power back on to 'the entire network in which [it is] caught up' (*ibid.*: 27). If, for example, 'power creates other kinds of power', then the powerful are also capable of mobilizing superior strategies to counter opposition. Similarly, the transitory character of domination (and of resistance) ensures that the 'strategic field of power relations' is on a constantly shifting course (Foucault 1990: 102). Whilst this alludes to a dialectical relationship of power, the cycle of social struggle never comes to a finite conclusion; rather, 'resistance' amounts to pragmatic, incremental shifts or gradual adjustments that do not accomplish radical or long-lasting changes.

Bringing the State back in

Similarly, Foucault's view of social struggle has not been wholly endorsed by theorists who question the neat symmetry between domination and subversion, with little reference to the differential positions of the social actors involved. For political theorists, the emphasis on practices of power and resistance invokes the predicament of structure and agency that Foucault avoids. In shifting from 'massive binary divisions' to the 'multiplicity of force relations', Foucault (1991: 73–103) does not fully explain the ways in which State power is invested in these local sites of conflict. He may have envisaged that governance originated in social intercourse and accumulated into a grid of normalization, discipline and political order. But as Poulantzas (1980), Jessop (1990: 48–79, 338–69) and Garland (2001) have pointed out, this does not account for the privileged position which the State persistently tends to acquire in processes of normalization, nor with the ways in which State power gains cohesion and legitimacy from the social reproduction of discipline. This absence (or rejection on Foucault's part) of the State's primary role in normalizing itself is particularly glaring given the centralization of repressive powers and the deeply antagonistic character of penal relations during political conflicts or crises (O'Dowd *et al.* 1980, Darby 1983; McEvoy 2001).

One of the more perplexing (and contentious) of Foucault's observations is that whilst power inevitably creates the conditions in which 'it' is resisted, resistance can only mimic the dominant discourses of power that are already in place. These two characteristics of resistance – its open-ended character and its reactionary nature (because innovation is already determined by dominant interests) – are not reconciled. Whilst 'resistance' takes on the idioms of dominant discourses, there is no account here as to how subordinated groups (such as prisoners) might appropriate them for alternative purposes. Furthermore, these possibilities are abstracted from questions such as precisely what 'powers' and forces are drawn into conflicts relative to resisting women prisoners? What can we make of the normalization and coercion represented in procedures such as strip searching? When does normalization end and coercion begin in the control of resisting prisoners? These questions are explored in feminist explorations of the relationship between normalization, control of the body and women's resistance.

Retrieving the missing body of Foucauldian thought: feminist analyses of normalization

A key area of feminist engagement with Foucault has focused on his theory of the body as a primary object of power relations (Sawicki 1991; McNay 1992; Shilling 1993). Foucault (1991) held that with the emergence of social institutions such as schools, the prisons and asylums, the body was reconfigured as an object of empirical, disciplinary, punitive and other corrective interventions. The body thus became a defining matrix of modern governance because it unified the will to govern with the development of social and cultural techniques for disciplining its unruly drives and reordering its productivity. Whilst the body's status as an object of inquiry and verification has been central to criminology since the inception of the discipline, it was revived with renewed critical vigour in the 1990s as a field of explanation for political, social and cultural power. However, in spite of the promise that 'the body' held for this critical enterprise, feminist engagements with 'the Foucault effect' have been divided. Fraser (1989), Howe (1994) and Carlen (1994) regard his talk about 'practices' and 'relations' as a dangerous abandonment of a critical language for the material and institutionalized inequalities which persistently assault the poor, marginalized women, and minority ethnic groups. They point out that political, and especially penal, power is predominantly inscribed on the selves of the oppressed, and this empirical reality remains an essential core of their subjectivity. The importance of these criticisms is discussed later in this chapter. A second approach has established insightful and powerful links between the social control of women and institutional, judicial and sociocultural constructions of 'normative' womanhood. This tactic has entailed reading women's bodies back into normalizing and disciplinary structures by observing the multitude of sanctions that make women regulated and self-regulating subjects (Bordo 1993; Stanko 1996), and the sociocultural reinforcements of femininity that underpin judicial and penal practices. Bordo (1993: 181) has called this the 'political anatomy' of the female body in which the use value and ideological meaning of women's selves are developed within pervasive cultural conceptions of a 'domestic, sexualised ideal of femininity … The intelligible body and the useful body are two arenas of the same discourse; they often mirror and support each other'. Crucially, however, these ideological forms are penetrated by other structures of domination which entrap women in economic dependency, violent relationships, physical and emotional exploitation and abuse in the home and public spheres.

The political anatomy of the imprisoned woman

The bodies of prisoners retain their status as central sites of penal punishment. Foucault (1991: 131–3) identified three dominant 'techniques of penal power' which act on prisoners' bodies. These are 'sovereign' powers which target the body through the enactment of corporal punishment; 'disciplinary' powers, which regulate the body within legitimized spheres of conduct; and 'juridical' powers, which incorporate individuals into the representational or symbolic order of punishment. Their interrelationship has been the subject of contention. Bottoms (1983) contested Foucault's apparent claim that the imposition of pain became a marginal and secondary function of the penitentiary. Foucault did trace the shift in styles of punishment from marking the body to rehabituating the body, but did not claim that this shift necessarily implied that the pain of incarceration was insignificant. Rather, he stressed the interrelationship between corporal and regulatory technologies of punishment, pointing out that 'imprisonment has always involved a certain degree of physical pain' (Foucault 1991: 15–16). By extension, a second area of contention occurs where it is held that 'sovereign punishment' is cancelled out by disciplinary power in contemporary punitive systems (Bottoms 1983: 172–4). Bottoms' reading of Foucault, for example, argues that there is a suppositional distinction to be made between discipline as the 'voluntary' training of the body, and sovereign power as the coercive targeting of the body which separate these objectives into different punitive domains (*ibid.*: 177). Furthermore, this distinction occurs ontologically and spatially, because the 'inducement of proper behaviour and the subjectification of the body to disciplinary techniques' requires 'an administrative apparatus', and is 'weaker' in non-custodial settings (*ibid.*). Sovereign and disciplinary spheres are further separable, in Bottoms' view, from the 'juridical sphere' or the ideological conditions which mandate the 'representational technology to punish' (Foucault 1991: 131).

Feminists have contended that such analyses compartmentalize the effects of social sanctions that are generated outside legal institutions, such as racism, sexism or homophobia, but are reproduced within them. Furthermore, they overlook disciplinary precepts which are not necessarily embodied in laws or institutional codes, but are systemic and functioning as perceptible regulatory influences in the lives of women (Cain 1994; Smart 1995). Penologists have also applied a concept of the political anatomy of the imprisoned female to describe the mutually sustaining punitive fields that form the composite domain of women's prison punishment. As Stenson (1998) points out, disciplinary, juridical and sovereign powers coexist in contemporary governance, and from a feminist perspective, each modality reinforces the other (Hannah-Moffat 2000). With women political prisoners, these different grids overlapped and reinforced each other. Disciplining them involved the use of various methods for destroying their physical integrity before reconstituting them as 'docile bodies'. The violence that this frequently entailed supports the observation that 'sovereign', corporal force persistently reinforced the disciplinary economy of the prison. Finally, the use of these methods was inseparable from the ideological, patriarchal and sexual anxieties that supported the construction of female political prisoners as a conspicuously transgressive category.

The limits of bodily resistance

Whilst one feminist approach has explored the synthesis of powers that maintains women in a punitive grip, a second approach has turned to concepts of 'technologies of the self' to explore the status of women's bodies as instrumental and symbolic resources for resistance. Proceeding from the observation that bodies are vehicles for social agency, as well as sites for domination, Bordo (1993) has argued that individuals seek to recover elements of autonomy by exercising power over their own bodies. Drawing on the anthropology of the hunger strike as a weapon of the weak (O'Malley 1990), Bordo's (1993: 139–64) discussion of anorexia nervosa as resistance to ideologies of womanhood demonstrates the limits of self-deprivation as an act of freedom. Although fasting and self-denial enabled anorectic women to inscribe fantasies of self-control on their flesh, their actions ultimately 'functioned in collusion with the cultural conditions that produced their own oppression' (*ibid.*: 159), and were 'not merely undercut but utilized in the maintenance and reproduction of existing power relations' (*ibid.*: 168). Similarly, as discussed in Chapter 2, whilst the resistance of Republican women prisoners was intended to negate the prescriptions that laid claim to their bodies, their actions reinforced the 'pathologization' of female protest. Bodily practices of resistance, then, cannot aspire to a free field of autonomy. They are pragmatic expressions of refusal that are embedded in pervasive material and ideological constraints.

At this point it is useful to review the direction this analysis is taking. Its overall objective has been to respond to the unanswered question of the previous chapter regarding the conditions under which women act, have agency and attempt to alter their conditions in prison. My underlying premise is that women political prisoners did resist, they resisted the kinds of correctional forms that are also associated with controlling women more generally, but with the additional outcome that this overlapped with, and was reinforced by, conspicuous State interests in embedding order and conformity in prison. Nevertheless, it was observed that the punishment of women prisoners could not be fully encapsulated in conventional 'political' definitions as a struggle against the ideological and material power of the State. Rather, the gendered dimensions of resistance and punishment problematize the more general analysis of dialectical conflict in Northern Ireland's prisons. More accurately, then, this analysis is concerned with the overlapping grids of gendered and political controls that constituted the political imprisonment of women. For this reason, Foucault's notion of the generative effects of 'power' was utilized to trace the expanded penal powers that were unleashed by resistance to criminalization. At the same time, Foucault avoids crucial questions about routinized coercion and violence in the prison system, as well as the links between gender and normalization. These issues have been usefully explored in those feminist analyses which have focused on the social inscription of the regulated, punished, feminized body as the background to corporeal rebellion by women. However, this analysis has left us with additional problems. These are Foucault's insistence that some form of agency must be retained even in the context of overwhelming institutional power, and the weaknesses in some Foucauldian feminist analyses in accounting for the subsumption of resistance into dominant structures and discourses. These issues are taken up in the final section of the chapter.

Situating agency and resistance: revisiting the paradox of women's imprisonment

A key problem in considering agency and resistance in women's prisons involves the difficulties in trying to understand the conditions in which women are sustained in structures of penal punishment, whilst at the same time identifying how they might act against penal domination. Therefore, any account of power and agency confronts the paradoxical nature of women's imprisonment. Women's experiences of prison are paradoxical because they are understood to be a firmly enmeshed in penal vigilance against minor digressions from feminized norms as well as prison discipline. At the same time, and relative to the first observation, whilst discipline in women's prisons is largely exercised through informal and discretionary controls, it is frequently through these practices that women in prison create opportunities for exercising agency, and begin to construct counter-disciplinary positions (Bosworth 1999).

As the previous chapter showed, the analysis of women's imprisonment has largely focused on the coextensive relationship between these mundane controls and the development of 'suitable' regimes for women. More recently, Bosworth (1998: 10) has argued that women in prison deploy their standpoints or identities as cultural capital in resisting control. Hence, prisoners' separateness from penal ideals of womanhood is critical to the dynamics of resistance, as 'it was also through their (cultural, ethnic and sexual preference) variety that women managed to challenge some of the universalising restrictions of imprisonment' (*ibid.*). In this context, women in prison 'co-opt elements from the dominant notion of "femininity"' to 'reinforce their own sense of self and to challenge aspects of the penal regime' (Bosworth 1999: 156). Although administrative and criminological thinking is still underpinned by hegemonic notions of women's 'passivity', the possibilities for assigning alternative meanings to their identities and agency are not entirely closed off, she argues (*ibid.*). Rather, 'concepts of identity and resistance enable the criminologist to develop a feminist theoretical critique of imprisonment which can acknowledge the specificity of different experiences of punishment' (*ibid.* 151). This post-structuralist account of the significance of everyday acts of refusal is consistent, in one respect, with previous feminist approaches to penal power. That is, it suggests that far from being inconsequential, the hidden realm of social control forms the foundation of punishment (and therefore resistance) in women's prisons. As Worrall observed, women in prison:

> are effectively offered a contract which promises to minimise the consequences of their criminality by rehabilitating them within the dominant discourses of femininity (that is, domesticity, sexuality and pathology). Despite these programmes of feminization, such women, *it is argued*, attempt to resist such construction by exploiting the contradictions of official discourses (1995: 162–3, emphasis added).

Here, Worrall adopts a more sceptical approach to dramaturgical or performative theories of resistance. Similarly, Howe (1994: 166–77) rejects the exaggerated claim that they transform systematic, institutionalized relations of power, on the basis that their effectiveness is limited to disclosing the disjunctures, contradictions and normalizing drives of social 'discourses'. Brown (1995: 49) argues that they merely confirm the tendency of post-structuralism to suspend questions of 'larger power relationships … the contemporary vogue of resistance is more a symptom of postmodernity's crisis … than a coherent response to it. Resistance goes nowhere in particular, has no inherent attachments, and hails no particular vision; as Foucault makes clear, resistance is an effect of and reaction to power, not an arrogation of it'.

Similarly, in a series of influential articles, Pat Carlen has sought to rein back what she views as the premature theoretical optimism of Foucauldian and feminist theorists of prison resistance (Carlen 1994, 2002a, 2002b). Carlen argues against privileging small victories over the structural, punitive power of prisons, 'which exists and persists independently of the best attempts of (some) prisoners to defeat it via strategies of resistance' (1994: 137). Here, she directs a twofold criticism against 'claims to theoretical innovation' from 'adding in theories' that focus 'much more on racism, sexism and the social regulation of all women than on the specifics of State *punishment* for female offenders' (*ibid.*: 132, emphasis in original). 'Adding in' theories, she continues, lead to a 'specialising out' of 'the specifically penal powers, penal functions and penal dimensions of such relationships' (*ibid.*: 134). Carlen has been consistently sceptical about the 'nominalist essentialism' which emerges from making a distinct theoretical objective of standpoint theory, social 'difference' or identity politics as the basis for resistance. Rather, she argues:

[The] full recognition of the complex power relationships and penal practices within which *women's imprisonment* is constituted as such is no more to *deny* women prisoners the power to resist than it is to *endow* them with that same power. For the effects of theories do not occur *sui generis*. They depend rather on the political calculations and conditions in which they are realised (*ibid.*: 133, emphasis in original).

Carlen has reserved her most cogent critiques for those elements of the 'insistence on resistance brigade' (*ibid.*) who have sought to rescue female lawbreakers and prisoners from definitions of 'victimhood' by pointing to their 'survival', 'agency' and exercise of 'resistance' (2002b: 167). Hannah-Moffat (2001) has similarly shown that the contemporary reformative preoccupation with 'agency', 'empowerment' and working on the self allows women prisoners to be channelled back into a circuit of therapeutic and individualizing controls. Thus, in trying to move beyond victimism in criminological discourse, current resistance theory is being unwittingly revisionist in 'underplay[ing] those aspects of custodial power which are necessarily activated and enhanced by prisoner resistance' (Carlen 2002b: 167).

These are significant objections. First, by raising the predicament of structural determination over social agency, they invoke the tensions and difficulties between 'materialist' and post-structuralist positions with regard to the systematicity, or otherwise, of penal power, which is far from resolved in prison sociology (Howe 1994). Secondly, they point out that resistance theory frequently underestimates the extent to which internal challenges or alternative discourses are neutralized through productive, versatile forms of 'carceral clawback', and absorbed into the fundamentally punitive function of imprisonment (Carlen 2002a). The third problem concerns the fragility of 'resistant subjectivity' given the inevitable re-enclosure of prisoners' agency within hegemonic, repressive, 'therapeutic' or other forms of penal governance. However, these criticisms also open up additional questions. Whilst co-option and oppression are abiding features of imprisonment, 'prison punishment' cannot be defined outside its structural, historical and correctional functions, nor extracted from successive ideological and interventionist frameworks which are conceived of in relation to its fundamental 'problem' – the 'appropriate' confinement of prisoners. This suggests, as both Carlen and Hannah-Moffat themselves show, that punishment is not a stable or unitary force because prisons must necessarily engage in reauthorizing and relegitimizing their own punitive logics.

In one sense, these interventions echo the question raised by earlier generations of penologists, which is whether agency in prison is always and already foreclosed. But taken together, these arguments eventually point towards a dialectical framework which foregrounds, rather than invalidates, the role of resistance (real or perceived) as a key element in the causes of prison punishment, as well as the forms it takes. Prison power does not develop 'independently' of prisoner's strategies to defeat it (Carlen 1994: 137), nor are punitive practices or regimes fully developed and instrumentally coherent prior to being enforced. Carlen is talking about returning the terms of analysis back from concerns with 'difference', which endlessly defers the fundamental issue of 'punishment'. However, 'punishment' cannot be conceived as an undifferentiated force, but must be evaluated in terms of the historically situated causes and contexts in which particular groups of prisoners are punished. Consequently, far from obscuring the structural conditions of penal power, an emphasis on situated, local resistance is essential for evaluating the 'political conditions and calculations' (*ibid.*: 133) of punishment. Resistance may not be an intrinsic condition of imprisonment, but neither is acquiescence.

It is not my intention here to 'deconstruct' punishment to a point where it loses coherence as a sign of critical articulation. On the contrary, my point about the contingency and partiality of prison punishment is about trying to grasp the significance of punitive difference to political imprisonment. Punitive difference refers to the multifaceted political, gendered and penal controls that were aimed at women. I am arguing that it was these peculiar conditions that enabled punishment to regain its unifying rationale – its legitimacy. Prison punishment was dialectical *and* relational because State and prison power was continuously challenged on political and gendered fronts in Armagh prison and Mourne House. In this context, Foucault's idea about the contingency of authority supports the staying power of resistance in the face of the recuperative capacity of the prison system, the versatile strategies that were used on both sides, and the recourse to ever more repressive or desperate tactics, without implying an equivalence between the antagonists.

Nevertheless, these criticisms contain a warning about the promiscuity implied by 'resistance is everywhere', which far too frequently links different kinds of reactions together without sufficient regard to their complex, collusive relationships with the very conditions they act against. Bosworth's focus on 'the capacity for autonomy' in prisons attempts to bridge the relationship between personal and structural transformation that can be brought about by resistance. However, whilst she insists that the analysis of 'small scale attempts to disrupt penal power … is not an excuse to disregard the status quo' (1999: 130), what is absent from her analysis is a more detailed exploration of how they exert a reciprocal influence on structures of authority. Arguably, her focus on everyday practices already acknowledges the limited contexts and conditions of prison resistance, whilst also refusing the position that any emphasis on 'resistance' can be considered a denial or invalidation of penal pain. For Bosworth, there is a significant interplay between subjective awareness and practices of the self and the development of a collective consciousness amongst women prisoners. Similarly, the resistance of political prisoners involved the many mundane acts that signified their partisan or critical consciousness (McKeown 2001), their appropriation of subordinated knowledges in negotiating various punitive frameworks (Foucault 1980: 72–98) and their self-legitimation as politically conscious and gendered subjects. These practices point to a continuum of 'resistance' which connected everyday refusals with their premeditated and collective strategies, and which allowed individual resistance to be consolidated into a systematic campaign of opposition. These developments are explored in greater depth in the following chapters.

Note

1   Whilst Loyalists were also involved in protests for the restoration of political status after 1976, they were divided on the matter of potentially assisting the cause of Republicans (Crawford 1999: 55–6), and their protests generally lacked political and strategic coherence in comparison.

Chapter 5

'Nor meekly serve our time': a continuum of resistance[1]

Each of the following seven chapters examines a different aspect of the prisoners' culture of resistance. They are described as 'fields' of resistance, which implies that each one was a response to a different facet of prison power, and required different resources on the part of prisoners in confronting them. The first field, 'getting in', which is explored in this chapter, traces the pathways to political imprisonment for women. It is argued that the experiences of arrest, detention and trial were significant formative influences on women's awareness of the gendered and political dimensions of imprisonment.

However, the term 'fields of resistance' also refers to the interconnectedness of their oppositional practices. This idea of a continuum of social action is more usually associated with feminist analyses of domination which place the 'routine use of aggression against women' into a 'complex totality' of institutionalized power (Kelly, 1988: 29). Feminist penology also recognizes a continuum of punishment in the criminal justice system which brings together 'modes of controlling women within both social and criminal justice systems and society at large' and 'generic anti-social controls' through a 'variety of malign institutionalized practices' (Carlen 1998: 65). In this context, the controls that women are subjected to in prison establish a continuum which ranges from the 'penal hammer' of legally sanctioned coercion, such as handcuffing and strip searching, to the 'bureaucratic screw' of procedural subordination (*ibid.*: 110–45). Mandaraka-Sheppard (1986), similarly, tracked the 'career' of disciplinary procedures in women's prisons from the point at which the original breach of prison rules was detected, through the processes of adjudication and punishment. Her emphasis on the structural dimensions of punishment and resistance to discipline connects one set of social actions (rule-breaking) with their consequences (punishment), without reducing the relationship between them to simple cause and effect. Rather, she provides a compelling account as to why alternative methods for dealing with conflict did not, or could not, develop. The penology of women, therefore, assigns a central place to examining the institutional and localized regulatory structures that bind together the apparently contradictory goals of security, care and punishment in prison (Dobash *et al.* 1986: 146–58; Bosworth 1999: 37–52).

The continuum of *resistance* explored here proceeds from the general paradigm of continuity in the punishment of women, but applies the argument made in Chapter 4 that different domains of prison control are also intercepted and changed by prisoners. It reflects Foucault's theory of power as it extends beyond the usual meaning of negative enforcement to include the various social interactions that mediate (and renew) relations of power. Accordingly, because prisoners use as well as contest power, the tactics adopted by the women politicals can be argued to have formed a discernible sequence of strategic responses to different aspects of prison authority. Yet there are forceful reasons for criticizing the tendency in Foucauldian analysis to presuppose that the powers available to dominant and subordinate groups are reducible to one another. Equally, there are grounds for avoiding the temptation to impose a retrospective cohesion on the different tactics used by women political prisoners, whilst glossing over the more unpredictable or personalized conflicts that were no less a part of their experience than they were for others in prison. Not all their actions were examples of the kind of purposeful, ideologically informed responses that are normally associated with 'political' resistance.

Indeed, some of these more 'irrational' responses seem to go against the pervasive idea that (male) political prisoners are in possession of an impervious core of self-awareness which somehow endows them with an exceptional capacity to cope with imprisonment. One of the more problematic claims in the phenomenological literature on the 'conscionable' prisoner relates to the anticipation that there is a kind of seamless unity of purpose and action in their engagements with prison authority. Goffman's (1991: 166) description of the 'moralistic prisoner' illustrates the point: 'The issue of collaboration with the enemy is thus raised. Even a kind warden's polite request to show one's paintings to visitors may have to be rejected, lest this degree of cooperativeness seems to underwrite the legitimacy of the jailer's position, and, incidentally the legitimacy of his conception of oneself.' Whilst this is observably true, there is little room here for analysing the ambiguities or compromises that are brought about in the course of making endless decisions about whether to reciprocate or withdraw, or what meanings or consequences these decisions might generate. Furthermore, as neither political ideology nor paramilitary training can fully prepare prisoners for imprisonment, it is more appropriate to view the tactical or ideological development of women political prisoners as processes that were shaped by the experience of confinement and punishment. In a phenomenological sense, they became rather than began their sentences as political prisoners. It would be more accurate, then, to say that alongside their premeditated activities, each 'field' of resistance is made up of contradictions or inconsistencies which arose as prisoners crossed the lines between collaboration and subversion, or where conflicts originating in 'ordinary' differences of interest unexpectedly developed into 'political' issues. It can also be argued that their errors or the limitations of their tactics had a significant influence on the dynamics of prison conflict. These instances of apparent confusion or incoherence, then, do not contradict the generally dynamic drive of social action suggested by Foucault, but illustrate the sometimes inconclusive outcomes of encounters which did not arrive at a stage of closure or resolution, but created new conditions for further conflict.

These complex shifts between positions were also bound up with prisoners' reflections on their intricate situation as victims of penal repression, as well as survivors and resisters. The following chapters seek to reflect this complexity when describing their struggle for agency, but without abstracting it from their experiences of victimization, coercion or violence. Kelly (1988: 161–2) observed the transitions that are possible between 'victimhood', through 'survival', to 'resistance' by women who experienced sexual violence as a process in which 'coping may merge into political action where individuals or groups perceive that their distress has a social cause, the solution to which can only be social change'. Phoenix (1998) described the narratives of resistance, survival and the self-constitution of identity amongst women involved in prostitution in terms of their 'making sense' of the paradoxes inherent in their situation, arguing that the meanings of 'survival', 'risk' and 'escape' emanate from their concrete material and gendered conditions. These kinds of subjective shifts between the roles of 'victim', 'survivor' and 'combatant', as well as those of 'mother', 'friend', 'supportive comrade' also occur in the stories of Republican and

Loyalist former prisoners. Their accounts, as well as those of prison staff and administrators, prison welfare personnel and the representatives of political prisoners, form the basis of the following chapters (see Appendix I). As the narratives relate to events that occurred between 1972 and 1998, it is acknowledged that neither penal policy and governance, nor the composition of the prisoner body, remained the same over those 26 years. In order to accommodate any discontinuity, the fields of resistance are organized to correspond generally to the different phases of penal administration – internment, criminalization and 'normalization' – which were discussed in Chapter 2. However, it is also understood that many conditions remained substantively consistent between 1972 and 1998, and were thus sufficiently durable to support an analysis of a continuum of prison conflict.

Getting in: resisting internment, interrogation and detention

As discussed in Chapter 1, the 'reactive detention' of the early 1970s had specifically gendered effects in terms of extending the reach of criminalization to the margins of paramilitary activity, and sweeping up women under wide-ranging laws. 'Getting in' commences with Nora's account of being interned for 10 months in 1974. Her story reflects those of other working-class, Catholic women who made the transition from civil disobedience to active participation in paramilitarism. Nora's family were known to the authorities as active Republicans. They were one of a number of Catholic families that had been burned out of the Divis housing estate in West Belfast by Loyalists in 1969. Before being interned, she had been 'arrested a few times in town' for selling Republican newspapers and collecting donations. Nora's experiences also reveal the wider social implications of interning women with children, and the strategies that they, their families and communities devised to sustain their family structures. The predicament of being 'lifted' out of her social networks, then, connected Nora's subjective strategies for coping with the pains of imprisonment with a broader context of familial, political and communal struggle.

Nora's story

They just came one night. They raided the house that often that you just got on with it and started again. This night they come and took curtains and cupboards and all down [to search for concealed weapons]. I knew it was serious … Then they took me to Townhall Street (police station) for three days, and then to Armagh. It was during the Loyalist strike in May 1974.[2] There wasn't a sign of life about, only me in this cop car with two women cops. I wasn't beaten or anything, but talked at … talked at for hours and hours and hours. They were trying to get information on men that you knew, and they just kept on and on at you. I couldn't honestly say I got beaten up or anything, I didn't. But the very fact that you were there was bad enough.

My husband was already interned, and I had children of my own and foster children.[3] So that was seven kids left. My sister was already in jail at this point. There was nowhere for them. Nowadays children have rights so that can't really happen to them … My brother-in-law took some of them, and the rest went to my mother. But the strange thing about it all was that anytime I put in for parole to see the kids, they never used to give it to me, but they gave it to my husband. They gave him access, maybe every other weekend, to come out and check on things. If I had had no parents, or my husband didn't have brothers, these children would have been left with nobody. It didn't cost the authorities a thought. When it [detention] happens to one person it affects everybody.

There is a direct relationship between judicial assumptions about women who have elected to commit acts of extreme transgression, for that is how they are represented, and notions that they have relinquished their claim to the roles of womanhood and motherhood. Denying Nora access to her children was an additional dimension of punishing women who, to paraphrase Carlen (1998: 67–8), are deemed to be both out of place in the masculine realm of political action, and out of the bounds of normative ideologies of womanhood. These women are subjected to 'the different dimensions of the "anti-social control of women" [which] emanate from one fundamental mechanism for keeping women "in their place"'. Nora's case was taken up by human rights advocates in Belfast, but she turned down an offer for immediate release on licence, on the basis that she was required to sign an agreement to keep the peace, which implicitly required her to accept a criminalized status:

With my case, and all of the children, it was an embarrassment … They sent lawyers to say that the British government was trying to work on my case, and that if I could get people to say that I'd agreed to their terms, they could see a way of releasing me.

Basically they proposed that the [Detention Review] Commission would let you out if you guaranteed you wouldn't commit any crimes.

I said I was an internee, and why should I apply for bail to get out? I told them that I didn't do anything to get in here, so I don't need anybody to vouch for me to get out. If their evidence was so strong, why didn't they take it to court and do it? No, I wouldn't say it, it would have been my principles down the chute to do it. You're not going to let anybody criminalize you by saying that [they] can get a bailsman to let you out if you agree to their terms.

Getting to Armagh was traumatic, but once you got in you could settle. My sister was already in. My friend had also been lifted the day after me, but I didn't even know she was arrested until she arrived the next day. She was held in Townhall Street too. There was a good few younger women from Divis there, so you weren't going into a jail full of strangers. That probably cushioned it that wee bit, that you knew all these people that you had been about with, in the jail. Then I just fell into the prison life, organizing your cell and so forth. You could go to classes. Most of the night-time was taken up with welfare visits and arrangements for what was happening to the kids. It was a bad time family-wise, but it wasn't such a bad time that I couldn't cope ... it didn't make me depressed. You could cope with what they threw at you if you hadn't had the added pressure of neglected kids. Then you could say, 'well, to hell with it, I'm here now'.

The women in our time, it was different certainly. If I had been in prison during the strip searches, maybe because I'm a wee bit older, but I don't know how I would have handled that ... But in some ways the pattern was set then, and they were able to work upon it later, and then pass it on down. That makes sense to me, that we laid the bricks and it was followed on. And yet, you don't have any experience at the time of what to do. It's just your instinct, that when you get there you realise, 'well, I can't go any further than here'. You have to put up with that. You can't lie at night wishing you were out of there. Not that you didn't wish to be out of there, but [you kept it] always to yourself, in case somebody else wasn't feeling good, and you made them feel down. Always, if you felt that way, you kept it to yourself, not to lumber it onto anybody else (Nora, internee, Armagh).

Interrogation

According to Robin Evelegh (1978: 138), who was commanding officer of the Royal Green Jackets (Third Battalion) between 1972 and 1975, and an influence on counter-insurgent thinking in Northern Ireland, the prevailing view of senior military intelligence staff was that using torture or ill-treatment against suspects was counterproductive as it rarely produced valuable information, and was, rather, a crude and 'regrettable' expression of brutality. Nevertheless, he conceded that it 'would be ingenuous to suggest that torture, or the threat or mild practice of "beating up" do not produce information' (*ibid*.: 137). He continued, 'in a sense, "beating up" and "time to question" are in counter balance. The greater the time for questioning the less the need or temptation to resort to brutality' (*ibid*.: 138). Whereas his original point upholds the polarity between coercion and the rational objectives of intelligence-gathering, he goes on to show that in practice the distinction between them is removed. In this sense, the practices of interrogation integrate the body of the detainee into the State's sovereign *and* rational functions. As Foucault (1991) argued, torture presents the sovereign powers of the State a direct route through the body, whilst the reordering of the body within rational-disciplinary mechanisms enables it to become an object of bureaucratic processing, intelligence-gathering and the combat of 'terrorism'. For Feldman (1991: 115) coercion 'render[s] State power tangible, immediate and circumscribed' because the 'performance of torture does not apply power; rather it manufactures it from the "raw" ingredient of the captive's body. The surface of the body is the stage where the State is made to appear as an effective material force'.

Brown (2002: 404) has similarly argued that the 'pre- and anti-modern' forms of brutality and harshness which continue to perforate the 'punitive restraint and rationality' of modern government are signs of the 'sovereign mode of State action [which is] characteristic of late-modernity'. The fact that contemporary liberal democracies 'periodically make recourse' to the tools of repression, containment and exclusion (*ibid*.: 405) is less of a historical anomaly than it initially appears. But 'what distinguishes modern forms of penal excess from monarchical violence … is not the fact or absence of its brutality, but the strategies adopted for its justification, regulation and distribution' (*ibid*.: 416). The 'recursive' characteristic of repression was reflected in the use of internment and suspension of *habeas corpus* four times in Northern Ireland's history in 1921–2, 1938–9, 1956–62 and 1971–6 (Boyle *et al*. 1980; O'Dowd *et al*. 1980; Farrell 1980, 1986). Furthermore, the awareness that agents of the State had been historically allowed to act outside the law prompted civil liberties groups to document infringements of the civil rights and bodily integrity of detainees (Amnesty International 1973, 1978). Denis Faul and Raymond Murray, then the Roman Catholic chaplains to Armagh prison, collected and published their 'Black and Blue' dossiers on the incidences of custodial mistreatment of men and women at various police stations and interrogation centres in the 1970s and 1980s (Faul *et al.* 1975; Faul and Murray 1975, 1978a, 1978b; Faul 1978, 1983). A recurring theme in the testimonies of female detainees was the ways in which the pervasive threat of violence intersected with expressions of sexual dominance during their interrogations. Faul and Murray, for example, recorded cases of intimidation and verbal abuse, the use of sexual innuendoes, psychological disorientation, assault and sleep deprivation.

Whilst none of these experiences are gender specific, some additional details emerged in the women's testimonies, including the fact that women were shown photographs of the fatally wounded and injured, and berated by their interrogators for their 'failure' to show compassion or remorse for their alleged culpability (Faul and Murray 1975: 56). Other stories circulated that pregnant women had been threatened or assaulted whilst in custody (Faul and Murray 1978b: 133–4). Although my respondents did not report this kind of mistreatment, their accounts of being interviewed by male officers are suggestive of the larger backdrop of the sexualization of interrogation which is organized around the social construction of feminine passivity and masculine power. Theweleit (1996) has drawn parallels between the cult of sexual sadism amongst the German *Freikorps* and the humiliation and rape of women in their custody in the 1930s, whilst Franco (1992: 109) has examined how torturers in the Latin American dictatotorships of the 1970s forced male prisoners to act 'as if they were women … to be constantly aware of their bodies, to be ridiculed and battered'. Women detainees also described the inscription of sexual power into the interrogation process:

> Different tactics were used against women. I remember when I was in Castlereagh [an army and police interrogation centre]. Getting hit didn't annoy me but it was the sexual innuendoes that did. The Special Branch men, they were saying that this is what they were going to do to you. And you knew. What was to stop them? I mean they could beat you and they could verbally abuse you. But they could have, they could have …! And that was an extra thing they used when they were interrogating you. Even if they didn't, they made the threat of it all the time I was there (Áine, sentenced prisoner, Armagh).

Here's how they did things. One sat really close beside me, literally touching me bodily, and the other came from behind, put his hand on my shoulder, and I swear to God he had his face up against the back of my neck, and he said, 'do you not remember me?', and he mentioned my old school. I couldn't think. It was someone that I knew years ago when I was going to school. He was Catholic, obviously. But the ones who interrogated me were all Northern Irish. They sometimes had the British army. That was always the threat in the entire set up, that there was always the sexual threats they made (Meg, internee, Armagh).

The PIRA Training Manual, or the 'Green Book', warns members in Active Service Units that if they are captured 'the enemy forces will not hesitate to use extreme methods of both physical and psychological torture to extract information on yourself and/or your organization. The Army expects that Volunteers won't disclose information on themselves and others' (O'Brien 1995: 351–2). Accordingly, a member was obliged under PIRA General Army Orders to 'refuse to give any account of his [sic] movements, activities or associates, when any of these have any relation to the organization or personnel of Óglaigh na hÉireann', and 'refuse to make or sign any statements' (ibid.: 355). The minimum penalty for a breach of these orders was 'dismissal with ignominy', unless the disclosure was so serious as to amount to a charge of treachery, which carried the penalty of execution.

Female detainees appear to have been regarded as the weakest point of entry to the primary source of (male) power in the PIRA on the grounds that they were subjected to both stringent paramilitary discipline and patriarchal authority in their organization. As Seifert (1994: 59) has argued the position of women as 'an element of male communication' and exchange is magnified during times of war and conflict, 'where many men regard their masculinity as compromised by the abuse of "their" women'. The women's accounts of their interrogation are consistent with Evelegh's (1978: 133) thesis that the 'art of interrogation' had the symbolic as well as practical function of disrupting the operational effectiveness of paramilitary organizations by exploiting any signs of disarray or lack of morale within them. This entailed recruiting minor figures as informants, matching interviewees with an interrogator of a similar 'rank', and exploiting the familiarity that officers might have of suspects' localities and backgrounds: 'The mistake is often made of ignoring the contact intelligence that can be gained from quite junior defectors … What is in fact required for successful interrogation, ending in useful information and possibly a defection, is an intimate knowledge of the milieu in which a suspect moves' (*ibid.*).

> There was also an element in Castlereagh that thought, say, if a girl was lifted with a couple of men, the mentality was that she was the weak one. Their thinking was, 'move on her first'. But nine times out of ten it was the women were the strongest. And you got to know what way they were thinking and what they were doing. Even in Castlereagh, when they were coming around to us, I knew that they were thinking, 'she is the weak link here'. But I wasn't the weak link (Anna, sentenced prisoner, Armagh).

> They were always picking on the women thinking 'she's going to break'. This is what they actually do now when they're raiding a house or arresting a man: they're lifting the wife too. They still have the mentality that the women are the weak link, or can be used as one (Meg, internee, Armagh).

> What they said to me in Castlereagh was, 'if you don't sign or if you don't confess you're going to go away for a long time. You're going to take the rap for this. You're going to be looked on as the ring-leader'. It was laughable. But it was that type of psychological thing they were waving about you (Áine, sentenced prisoner, Armagh).

The trial process

The political trial is one of the central stages where the contest for legitimacy between the State and political prisoners is played out. In an important sense, it retains those elements of the spectacle of State power that, according to Foucault (1991), had otherwise disappeared with the abolition of public execution and the concealment of punishment in correctional institutions. However, the public arena of the trial places defendants in a position to speak, but only if they submit to judicial investigation and implicitly acknowledge the legitimacy of the proceedings. In addition, a woman's demeanour in court may contribute to assumptions about her guilt if she does not demonstrate sufficient remorse, compliance or willingness to reform herself. Studies of the trial proceedings of women by Worrall (1995), Allen (1998) and Ballinger (2000) support the argument that a woman's failure to submit to male or family authority or demonstrate acceptable sexuality and 'respectability' has a prejudicial effect on the interpretation and summary of the evidence. Thus, the dilemma of being tried as a woman is that any defence or case for clemency can only be rendered intelligible within a narrow, reductive set of judicial discourses:

> The female lawbreaker is routinely offered the opportunity to neutralize the effects of her lawbreaking activity by implicitly entering into a contract whereby she permits her life to be represented primarily in terms of its domestic, sexual and pathological dimensions ... The effect of this 'gender contract' is to strip her lawbreaking of its social, economic and ideological dimensions in order to minimize its punitive consequences. Many female lawbreakers accept this deal; some reject it outright (Worrall 1995: 31).

The rituals of resistance which are common to political trials, such as refusing to recognize the court or testify in self-defence, interrupting proceedings or making statements from the dock, placed women defendants in a contradictory position. They had to choose between relinquishing their political identity by engaging with the court, even if only to refute its legitimacy, or take the risk that their cases would be mediated through judicial 'discourses of femininity (that is domesticity, sexuality and pathology)' (*ibid*.: 163). Republican women defendants thus entered into a double quandary in refusing to recognize the court, as their lack of co-operation tended to support the prosecution's case that their silence was conclusive evidence of extensive paramilitary involvement. Consequently, the rates for conviction were high (Boyle *et al*. 1980: 61). The practice amongst Republicans of refusing to recognize the court declined sharply after 1976 in line with a more pragmatic shift towards engaging in a legal defence strategy, and to avoid the potentially detrimental effects of losing experienced operatives (McEvoy 2001: 145–7). Nevertheless, the refusal to engage with the trial proceedings fostered in defendants 'a sense that their prison resistance had begun', that they 'had a responsibility to continue the struggle' and to minimize the risks of 'significant military or internal security information coming out during the trial' (*ibid*.: 143). Furthermore, the defiance of women internees who were brought before the Detention Review Commission contravened the values of judicial paternalism as much as the authority and legitimacy of the tribunal:

> When you were in for so long, they asked you to go to the Commission. These were held in Long Kesh. You needed a barrister. I had appeared in a documentary and I had said some

things like 'the answer to British occupation is if they don't get out, blow them out'. So, on the day my barrister said, 'they've got TV screens in here'. You know, you just don't think that they're going to go back into these things. And lo and behold, all this stuff that I had said, they showed it on the television. So I was re-detained as a danger to the public. There was nothing you could do about it – there was no right of appeal. I was brought back twice, and it was renewed both times. The last time it had just been renewed coming up to Christmas time, and I got out on the Christmas Eve, quite unexpectedly (internee (name withheld), Armagh).

When they brought me in front of them, for the first time, they brought us there by helicopter, into the 'Kesh. There was a big ring of British soldiers, with their weapons poised, and I got out of the helicopter … and they took one look at me and I think they were disgusted. But the Commissions themselves were a farce, an absolute farce. I refused constantly to recognise the Commission, but I had a bit of pressure put on by certain solicitors there: 'you should recognise it, just to get out' (Eilís, internee, Armagh).

At her hearing, Meg (internee, Armagh) broke away from the witness box and managed to tear down a screen which concealed a military intelligence officer who was giving evidence against her: 'The whole thing was a joke! You just sat there, and there was this Commissioner who sat up there. There was somebody who would sit behind this screen giving evidence against you. It was ridiculous.'

Resistance at the gateway

The functions of reception to prison are directed towards stripping away the unique histories of incoming prisoners, and reassembling them into a compliant unit within the general mass of other prisoners. Moreover, an incomer's records or previous reputation will also determine the degree of 'thoroughness' and vigilance with which these mortifying and alienating practices are conducted. Even during the period in which special category status was in operation (1972–6), incoming political prisoners claimed that they encountered various levels of official denial that their political structures existed, or were even recognized by administrators. Prisoners cited disputes with reception officers who insisted upon allocating them to a 'reception cell' overnight until they agreed to be interviewed by the governor, which was the standard procedure, rather than allowing them to see their commanding officers immediately, as they usually demanded. For Meg, an internee, the humiliations of reception were intended to get individuals to waver in their demand to be treated as political prisoners. Accordingly, she played for time and the opportunity to recover her resolve by refusing to strip off for her medical inspection: 'I would only tell them if I had distinguishing marks.' The women then had chlorine baths, in tepid or cold water, 'but I was in such a state after three days in Castlereagh, I didn't mind' (*ibid.*). Prisoners intermittently attempted, unsuccessfully, to refuse to remove their clothes. Hanna (sentenced prisoner, Maghaberry) described the compulsory undressing and washing at reception in terms of her initiation into a new moral order: 'When I walked into reception, they told me to strip naked, to get a shower – "wash the dirt off you" – and everything else like that.' For Anna and Winnie, reception confirmed the all-encompassing dominance of institutional life:

> When you go into reception, it's very strange. There were usually about four screws there waiting on you, all women. The men do the circle. You went in, were told to strip and get washed. You were thrown into a bath with a globby lice soap. Then I was taken in and a sheet put 'round me, and checked for scars and marks. There was no doctor there. The sheet was taken off. That was another intimidation tactic, because nobody likes to stand there naked in front of a complete stranger, and they check you for scars or moles, and this is all written down. The morning after you see the governor, you were taken and photographed. They checked the colour of your hair, eyes, if there was [*sic*] any facial scars, and that was all written down on your record (Anna, sentenced prisoner, Armagh).

> You do feel quite small. Armagh is one of the old Victorian jails, massive high walls and ceilings. When you walked through that door, you felt about two inches high. You were surrounded by total strangers who literally despised you for what you are, and you could feel that. You were against everything that they stand for. You know as soon as you walk through the gate that that whole system [was] there to break you down as soon as humanly possible. It is frightening. Anybody that says they walked into Armagh feeling cocky are liars, because it is an intimidating experience … It would be like me walking up the Shankill Road

with a sign around my neck saying I was a Catholic (Winnie, sentenced prisoner, Armagh).

Winnie was committed to Armagh after political status had been revoked and the Republican sentenced prisoners had already spent a year on their non-cooperation strike. Her insistence on her political affiliation and her request to be taken to the Republican wing indicated her intention to join the protest:

> The tactics they would try to use when you first went in to Armagh, they knew from being at the courts what way the land lay as far as you were concerned, if you were going to work and conform, or if you were going to go on protest [*sic*]. Rather than let you associate with protesting prisoners on reception, they would put you in a cell on your own the first night. It was an intimidation tactic, because you hadn't the back-up of the rest of the women. It was to see whether or not you would conform, because the next morning you were sent for to see the governor. He would [outline the rules]: 'you have to work from such-and-such a time', and 'you are allocated privileges ... and what are you going to do?' It was your choice to tell him politely where to shove it, or conform (*ibid.*).

The question of self-nomination to a political structure was still subject to some ambiguity after women prisoners were transferred to HMP Maghaberry in 1986. As discussed in Chapter 1, the regime at Mourne House was designed to curb the influence of the political factions. In reality, tensions arose as a consequence of the imprecise and discretionary arrangements under the general objectives of the 'normalization' policy, which allowed senior prison staff to engage with paramilitary prisoners, whilst stopping short of formally acknowledging their status in political or legal terms. Hanna described how she negotiated the ambiguities between formal policy and discretionary authority on the matter of recognition during her reception in the early 1990s:

> You have to go through a strip search. They try to undermine you, and try to get you on to the non-political wings, where the criminals ... frauds and stuff like that are [*sic*]. So I had to turn around to them and say, 'I'm a political prisoner and I want to go on the political wing'. 'We have no political wings here', was their first reply. So I said, 'I want to see my OC'. That's a no-go area. So they asked me did I know anybody in the prison.

Obviously I knew every prisoner that was in the jail. So I named them all off. After about half an hour I was straight on to the wings. Walking on to that wing, it's just a great feeling, because you always heard so much about these women. And about prison – you always tried to imagine what prison's like. But from day one, once the others start calling out 'Tiocfaidh Ár Lá' ['Our day will come'],[4] and 'go on, girl', you just know you're a political prisoner (Hanna, sentenced prisoner, Maghaberry).

Although her claim to political status was negotiable within a framework of informal official obstructions, the political prisoner's subsequent concerns lay with her application to join her own factional structure. Political prisoners underwent a double initiation into prison, because, after being processed through the official channels, they had to be debriefed by their own political officers. Debriefing involved a secondary cross-examination by the prisoner's commanding officer to acquire details about interrogation techniques, ascertain the thinking of military intelligence, and to establish whether any information about operations, the identity of others or organizational structures had been revealed under interrogation. Whereas debriefing might have been regarded as a necessary precaution by the PIRA, there were inevitable, disturbing similarities between the procedure and the hostile questioning which incomers had previously undergone. For Hanna, this was a greater existential test of her soundness than her original interrogation:

It was the longest hour and a half of my life – [I was] shaking. Because when you go into prison someone comes and gives you a breakdown. Somebody comes in and speaks to you – goes through the whole thing, day by day, or what they [interrogators] asked you, what you said. They need to know the information about what they're thinking in Castlereagh. And you're trying to convince them, 'I didn't say anything, I didn't say anything'. And that's the most I was frightened of, that our own people wouldn't believe me. (*ibid.*)

The procedures of 'getting in' have been extensively noted by penologists in terms of their depersonalizing effects (Goffman 1991), or as preliminary, instructive rites of delivery into prisonhood (Heffernan 1972). Whilst these are relevant to the experiences of women detained for political offences in Northern Ireland, functionalist or phenomenological analyses largely assume an uncontested passage into institutional alienation. This chapter has explored how Republican women prisoners negotiated, and at times subverted, elements of prison discipline in their initial encounters with it. It connects their responses to their previous resistance during their arrest, trial and interrogation, which had instilled in them a sense of opposition to the conditions of their sentencing and confinement. This is not to suggest that every woman entered the prison with a fully developed consciousness or foreknowledge about penal power, or that possible strategies for resistance were readily available to her. Rather, it points to the potential junctures between gender and political consciousness which were sharpened by their experiences of the criminal justice system, and informed the techniques of opposition they subsequently refined in prison.

Notes

1 The chapter title is from the Republican prison anthem 'Nor meekly serve my time'.
2 The general strike organized by the Ulster Workers Council which led to the collapse of the power-sharing Executive in Northern Ireland after six months.
3 Some details removed at interviewee's request.
4 Slogan of the Republican movement.

Chapter 6

'Making space for ourselves': reconstructing a prison community

Prisons are well defined disciplinary spaces that are meant to be impervious to appropriation by their inmates. However, this chapter examines the development the territorial strategy adopted by Republican women prisoners for marking out a separate space. It explores the tactics of demarcation and exclusion that allowed them to establish their internal disciplinary and social systems, manage relations with other prisoners, and exclude staff and Loyalist prisoners.

Since its inception as a social experiment, the penitentiary has materialized the ideals of an orderly and 'rational' environment for inculcating moral reform and accomplishing the complete regulation of its inmates. Although, in practice, the operation of elaborate and expensive 'separate systems' such as those at Millbank and Pentonville was shortlived (Hirst 1995: 245–6), the concept of prisons as all-encompassing monoliths has tended to prevail in the seminal theories of confinement. Thus Goffman (1991: 17) describes the asylum as a 'total' institution, where 'various enforced activities are brought together under a single rational plan purportedly designed to fulfil the official aims of the institution'. Foucault's (1991) 'total and austere regime' summons up Jeremy Bentham's Panopticon with its combination of a formal architecture of control and the meticulous organization of prisoners along the lines of 'scientific' uniformity, total silence and absolute segregation.

However, if the early correctional utopians thought that the problems of disorderliness and nonconformity could be controlled by reorganizing social space, they were also inspired by changing ideas about humane intervention and reform. These developments were reflected in new prison designs that were influenced by contemporary theories about the appropriate environment in which different groups of prisoners could be restored to their proper social function. The shared history of 'benign' social control and architectural innovation underpinned later developments in prison design. For example, the 'new' human-scale women's prisons that were constructed in the 1970s reflected the resurgence of paternalistic and domesticated ideologies in the post-war period. The proposed construction of New Holloway, London, as a therapeutic prison reflected decades of penal ideology which positioned women prisoners primarily as psychiatric or medical cases (Rock 1996). Similarly, the planning of Mourne House demonstrated the repressive results of merging a 'community house' unit into the structure of the maximum-security prison complex.

The reconstruction of prison space is also profoundly relevant to prisoners because it provides them with reference points for explaining their captivity. For example, the surreality and infantilism of psychiatric units in women's prisons are summed up in the prison argot, 'The Muppet wing' or 'Fraggle Rock', so-called after the children's TV programmes. Dobash et al. (1986: 196–204) noted the metaphors of mental and bodily invasion that are part of the language of women prisoners, whilst Sim (1990: 169) cites correspondence with a woman prisoner in HMP Durham who referred to 'H' wing as a 'submarine'. Carlen's respondents (1998: 105–6), as well as the women interviewed here, referred to the 'strip cells' as a zone of sexual humiliation, and as a physical and psychological barrier through which prisoners had to pass when travelling on and off their wings.

This awareness of the repressive topography of institutional life allows prisoners to create an alternative imaginative, communal and intellectual viewpoint which they accommodate alongside the realities of their confinement. There is a long-standing history of prisoners collectively reshaping their environment through the violent seizure of space in riots and disturbances (Scraton et al. 1991; Adams 1992), the adaptation of communal areas into zones which support illicit economic activities and 'fraternizations' (Giallambardo 1966; Heffernan 1972), and the use by prisoners of prison yards and wings for political organisation (Jackson 1970: 48–52, 212–21, Davis 1971: 36, 1988: 61–2; Seale 1991: 296–322), 'teach-ins' and assemblies. The spatial politics in Northern Ireland's prison system conspicuously revolved around sectarian divisions and exclusion. This involved different forms of occupation as the prisoners extended physical control over their own blocks or wings, and created an alternative political meaning and practical functioning for the prison environment. McEvoy (2001: 108–36) and Feldman (1991: 265–9) have examined the significance of intimidation and violent exclusion to the occupational strategies of Loyalists and Republicans in the Maze. Whilst the use of violence was an element of the women's experience, their strategies for accomplishing territorial autonomy were more fluid, and involved various levels of cultural and ideological expression as well as mutual opportunism and conflict between staff and prisoners (Corcoran 1999).

Constructing a political community

In the early 1970s, the practical determination of establishing clear control over political prisoners in Armagh prison was obstructed by two combined factors. First, the complete segregation of prisoners was difficult to sustain because of overcrowding, which caused governors to apply remedies such as subdividing the wings with wooden barriers and restricting access to work, exercise and visits to prevent interned, sentenced and remand prisoners from associating. The second factor was the commitment of incoming prisoners to generate constant reminders to the authorities of the political character of their charges. Eilís, a former internee, noted that the initial drive to organize collectively followed the military discipline and factional segregation that were in practice at the compounds at Long Kesh. However, the practical and symbolic elements of the 'traditional' Republican prisoner structures had to be adapted to the specific contexts of Armagh:

> Before we gained political status, you had that attempt to maintain control over us. But with more and more women coming in, plus the fact that on 'A1', there was no more room, they had to open up and give us political status anyway, so it was only a matter of time. So they didn't really oppose it too much, because if you counted us up, there was nothing they could do about it. We had our own system in place. [Name withheld] was in charge, and there was our officer system, and she would have been naming who mediated with the governor on anything. My brother was inside and they had refused to wear the uniform, so that was a natural decision that you weren't going to wear any uniforms, that you weren't a criminal, as they called us (Eilís, internee, Armagh).

As discussed in Chapter 2, the prisoners' organization originally took the form of a self-disciplining structure which was grafted on to the normal prison routine and mirrored its rituals and disciplines. Yet, there is a striking paradox in this alterity between the early Republican social structures, with their hierarchical lines of command, rigid routines and internal discipline, and those of the official prison regime. Eilís argued that the routine was necessary for uniting a disparate and inexperienced group of prisoners, whilst Winnie noted its function in embedding paramilitary discipline and authority:

> As an internee, you didn't know how long you were going to be there, so what you needed was a routine, and you needed your plans and you needed to carry them out. You weren't going to adhere to the prison system's routine, so you formed an alternative regime, which they ended up having to come to terms with. What that involved was a prison structure. We had our OC, a public relations officer and somebody in charge of people coming in. There was a good system going. And to this day I still admire it, because at one stage there was 230-odd women, and still our own system worked (Eilís, internee, Armagh).

> It became very militaristic after a while. For instance, we would have fallen-in every morning, and the OC and the Adjutant went around and checked your cells and made sure it was spotless. The screws could never walk in and say things like, 'that one over there has not done their duties'. We had floors that were like skating rinks, they were so highly polished. And they went in and they checked one of the cells, down behind the furniture. It was like being in the army or the navy, with the OC checking that everything was just so. We did that every single day. Every day we fell-in when you got out for lunch at 12.30, and then you were dismissed, and the food trays would come up. And just before lock-up, all the women would stand outside their cells. The OC ... would have brought everybody to attention, and you were dismissed, and went into your cell for lock-up for the rest of the night (Winnie, sentenced prisoner, Armagh).

The time and space continuum that exists in correctional institutions works as a key technology of control. For Foucault (1991), the radical atomization of the prisoner is ensured by the spatial distribution of inmates, their fear of constant visibility and the division of time into ordered activities. These techniques inspire alienation, submission to routines, and orderly and submissive behaviour in prisoners. Thompson (1991) observed that the 'time and work discipline' of modernity established a similar hold over the collective consciousness, destroyed concepts of seasonal or 'natural' time, colonized human creativity and subordinated individuals to 'useful' and 'reforming', compulsory occupation. Faced with months or years of routinization, the 'ownership' and management of time was a vital defence against the disintegration of community. Republicans, in particular, placed a great emphasis on using the prison education facilities to develop skills and acquire qualifications which would be of use to them and to the movement after release. If this appeared to conform to dominant penal values of the productive expenditure of time, prisoners used the idea of 'doing time' to facilitate a longer-term political trajectory:

> I used the prison system, my time, to my advantage. I did my exams out of it. I was at school when I was arrested. I finished off my 'A' levels in jail, did a couple of other courses, and planned what I was going to do on getting out. So, I think I was quite focused in that way. I set up our own library. We used to read anything from Mills and Boons to Angela Davis and Jackson, Che Guevara. We used to think we were really revolutionary! But, at the same instance, most of the women were very, very focused with what they wanted to do. The whole political awareness – it was amazing to see it develop (Eilís, internee, Armagh).

> In jail what can be used against you is your ignorance. Republican prisoners realised that very early on, and decided to use the education not as a support thing, but to widen our horizons and to broaden ourselves. By broadening themselves politically and everything else they were actually strengthening what they believed in. For a lot of them before, it was an idea, but they never actually looked at where the idea came from, or how it was formed, or even why they were doing what they were doing. When we went into jail and started to become educated and started to understand what was happening, and looking at the parallels and so on, it actually strengthened our beliefs … Prisoners who had gone on to university would have given lectures in different things. Somebody else would have studied something else, and given lectures on that. It was educational and it broke the monotony, literally. Later on it progressed, but at that time it was making the ones that weren't so aware of why they were involved in the first place, more aware (Winnie, sentenced prisoner, Armagh).

125

But the prisoners' enthusiasm for turning their cells into classrooms did not always allay official anxieties. A 1977 television programme that showed UDA prisoners in the Maze drilling, receiving political instruction and weapons training led to an outcry about 'universities of terror' (*Sunday Independent* 21 September 1977). The education of women, in the meantime, continued to experience more familiar obstacles well into the 1980s, as Kathleen (sentenced prisoner, Maghaberry) explains: 'they didn't want us to have education, and they certainly didn't want the remands to have it. They wanted to have us all contained. Any education they gave it was like "let's do cookery class, let's do the needlework class" – the wee, safe sort of subjects. We wanted law and politics.'

In his book, *Invented Communities* (1991), Benedict Anderson explores nationalist myths of origin, arguing that the idea of a 'national community' is essentially mediated through the invention of 'tradition', which is in turn made plausible and intelligible through formalized cultural rituals. The construction of 'imagined' communities cements the fiction of collective unity, and supports the claim to exclusive occupation of a territory or 'homeland'. Anderson's point about the constructed nature of cultural memory and identity does not only explain the emergence of a Gaoltacht as a space of political or cultural revival, but also its role as an expression of separatist power. The 'Gaoltacht' took its name from combining the arcane English word for prison, 'gaol', with the Gaelic suffix '-tacht' (place) to signify a unique Irish cultural colony within occupied territory. Within this 'zone', Republican prisoners organized self-instruction in the Irish Gaelic language, Irish history, political theory and operational training. Although communicating through the Irish language was a useful tool for allowing intelligence to be transmitted without being intercepted by staff, its usage also connoted resistance (McKeown 1996: 46). This system of self-education continued even during the no-wash protest or times of lockdown, when prisoners shouted the vocabulary and grammar through the vents on their cell doors, with the words and phrases being repeated by occupants of the other cells. Winnie explained the symbolic importance of Republican prison culture:

> We had parades in the yard, because before we went on the 'no-wash', we were allowed out for a couple of hours of association. That was keeping your Republican identity. We had our Easter parades and other commemorations on the Republican calendar. We used to practise marching and drills for weeks and weeks. And the ones that were actually doing the parade, because we

were marching in the yards, which was in breach of the rules, were put on 'hard time' because of it. It was like a display for the rest of the prisoners. On the day we did it, we were in uniform, and had the colour party, and we went out and did it. We all lost a month's association and a month's remission, but that didn't make any difference because we knew we weren't getting any remission anyway. So it really didn't make that much of a difference. For a conforming prisoner, losing a month's remission would have meant you were in jail longer. Because we knew from the outset that we were going to end up doing all our time, it didn't worry us (Winnie, sentenced prisoner, Armagh).

Excluding the punitive other: the limits of organized group violence

The history of prison conflict in the course of the 'Troubles' demonstrates the extent to which organized, pre-emptive violence and disturbances were strategically integrated into the prison campaign (O'Malley 1990; Feldman 1991; Campbell *et al.* 1994; McEvoy 2001; McKeown 2001). However, the body of work on organized physical resistance or group violence in women's prisons is relatively underdeveloped. Newton (1994) relates this to the highly masculinist tradition of prison analysis, whilst Shaw (1995) argues that the problem is rooted in definitional and theoretical shortcomings when talking about the differences, contexts and meanings of women's use of violence. This is compounded by official silences and the tendency for authorized versions of events to segue easily into systematic assumptions about women's violence and disorderliness. Thus, women's aggression or anger can be explained away in 'individualised and pathologised' terms rather than the complex 'social and situational events' that contextualize them (Shaw 2000: 63). Shaw continues: 'for women in prison, there are *additional* problems because of the greater willingness to see aggressive or violent behaviour by women as "unfeminine" and (almost) by definition pathological' (*ibid.*: 64, emphasis in original).

The few, existing accounts of collective violence in women's prisons show that it is generally a spontaneous, but short-lived, response to group punishments and perceived injustices, provocation, constant security checks and the arbitrary implementation of the prison discipline system against trivial infractions (Mandaraka-Sheppard 1986: 135–6). The level of violence also escalates when prisoners defend themselves during cell and body searches and as a consequence of the deployment of male riot-control officers to enforce orders which prisoners have

127

refused (Arbour 1996). As discussed in Chapter 2, there were violent disturbances in Armagh prison throughout the operation of special category status and during the non-cooperation and no-wash strikes, as well as in Maghaberry prison in 1992. The record of institutional repression against violent disorder showed that the consequences of using confrontational tactics were overwhelmingly negative, and led to collective punishment, injuries to prisoners, the introduction of more stringent security procedures and the lack of adequate inquiries into these events. Three of the women involved in the failed escape (1973), and the hostage-taking incident at Armagh prison (1974), described the nature of the problem of engaging the administration with a collective show of force:

> They [male police officers and army personnel] just stuck the hose through the cell door and the force of the water, it just went all over. At that stage you were able to get your fingers around the spyholes and we were just about able to hang on to the door. They batoned us; my fingers were up with swellings from my knuckles the whole way along. I was black and blue (Meg, escapee, Armagh).

> A couple of girls got out and they went up the stairs, but they couldn't go anywhere because it had all been blocked off with wood. So they actually had their protest, and they all got hosed. They did this to the whole wing. They [uniformed staff and special support unit] were just going mad all over the place (Anna, involved in the hostage-taking incident, Armagh).

> You always knew it [official violence] was a possibility, but it wasn't always foremost in your mind. You didn't think about it, because if you had then you couldn't have persisted, if you thought every waking minute, 'I can't bear this, and I can't get out' (Meg, escapee, Armagh).

The expulsion of the political other: strategies of mutual exclusion by Loyalists and Republicans

Group cohesion in prisons is also motivated by perceived or actual violence from other prisoners and staff. In women's prisons, as in men's, collective unity is enforced through the exclusion of individuals who do not adhere to group values, the expulsion of informers and the use of other methods for removing 'layers of pollution and stigmatisation' from the prisoner body (Feldman 1991: 268). The social hygiene of the community is imposed through various forms of group justice, including boycotts, intimidation and using violence against those who have been sentenced for 'unacceptable' crimes, such as crimes against children (Carlen *et al.* 1985: 157–8; Bosworth 1999: 111). Republican prisoners in Armagh prison endorsed the use of 'preventive' violence as a 'necessary' means of self-defence, and as a signal deterrence to staff. For example, they organized protective alliances by partnering more experienced prisoners with those who were viewed to be more vulnerable, as a safeguard against intimidation:

> There were two [prisoners that] got picked on all the time, so we split them up ourselves. I moved in with [name withheld], and [name withheld] went in with [name withheld], so the bigger ones went in with the smaller ones. [Staff] thought twice about kicking the cell doors in and dragging them out 'cos they knew there was somebody there that would take them on. It was trying to work out things like that. But again, we changed it around, putting the less confident ones in with the ones who'd be a bit more confident with themselves, and back them up. It made them a bit more, not ferocious, but determined that nobody was going to get the better of them, whereas, if there was two of them that was constantly getting beat, they'd wear each other down (Winnie, sentenced prisoner, Armagh).

The rationale of self-defence established a dual logic of external protection from physical assaults, and for ensuring moral differentiation from, and political antagonism towards, Loyalist prisoners:

> We were on the wing with the Ogilby murderers.[1] Coming up to the Twelfth[2] and about then we used to get a bit of hassle from them … but it was a case of proving your point from the beginning, that nobody was going to push you around, and that included them. They were at the bottom end of 'A1' wing, we were at the top end. We chose to keep separate from them. Another [non-political] prisoner was there at the time, who got the Queen's pardon for killing her father. The day she was pardoned, I was in the toilet, and I came out and was standing washing my hands, and [a Loyalist prisoner] says to me 'what do you think of [the other woman] getting the pardon?' I says, 'fair play to her'. She said to me, 'Oh you watch out for her,

129

she's evil.' I says to her, 'she killed her father who was abusing her. You battered a woman to death with a breeze block. Piss off out of my face or I'll put yours in the toilet'. That was the mentality, so we kept our distance from them completely … To me, it was my own principles and standing up for survival and for what's right. And when you got on to the wing and into the unit as Republican prisoners, it was that comradeship, because you always watched someone's back in every circumstance. There were a few incidents, Loyalist prisoners chancing their arm and pushing it. They sort of inadvertently fell into baths and things. But it was a case of, 'don't chance your luck, because if you hit one, you hit them all'. Because you could have the whole lot of them hitting on you. It was always that show of us against them. You attack one; you attack them all. That was everybody, right across the board (sentenced prisoner, Armagh).

The construction of Loyalist prisoners as the penal and political 'other' was a reflection of the psychological effects of the Loyalist campaign of random terror in targeting Catholic 'civilians' and 'combatants', as well as the iconography of defilement and the mutilation of their victims associated with the Shankill Butchers and the Ogilby defendants (above) (Taylor 1997: 187).[3] Such distinctions between 'combatants' and 'non-combatants', or between the 'sectarian' basis of Loyalist strategies and motives and the 'politicality' of Republican ones, are problematic and perhaps semantic, but were nevertheless significant reinforcements of difference to Republican respondents. The objectification of Loyalist prisoners included observations about their physical appearance (some Loyalist women were prominently tattooed), their 'intimidating' demeanour, 'aloofness' and 'sectarian' exclusionism, and references to the offences for which they were committed. Rather than being straightforwardly sectarian reactions, however, these observations derive from the larger political mythology and relational practices of violent conflict, amplified by the threats and dangers presented by proximity to the political 'other'. Nevertheless, as Feldman (1991: 4) suggests, this kind of antagonism does not sustain 'relations of uninterrupted linearity', as some elements of mutual familiarity arose between Loyalists and Republicans in the context of the encompassing experiences and the patterns of socialization (enforced or voluntary) arising from confinement:

Then the UDA women came in. They were in for the Ogilby murder. There was about eight of them, and then you had the

UVF crowd, that was it. And you could see a total difference. The UDA ones tried to communicate that bit more, but the UVF were staunch Loyalists (Anna, sentenced prisoner, Armagh).

UDA prisoners came up for Irish classes. One wanted to learn Irish, so she came up to one of our officers to learn Irish from us. She also wanted to learn Irish history because she said that [in] the history she had been taught, there was big gaps. So she came up to our education officer, and she taught her Irish history and Irish language (Áine, sentenced prisoner, Armagh).

Although there were occasions when Loyalists and Republicans in the men's prisons agreed on combined strategies, there is little evidence of any corollary working relationship between women prisoners, except where they were commonly victimized by administrative actions.[4] The Loyalist women's tactic of disengagement and self-segregation was related to the fact that their numbers at any stage were very low. There was, for example, no formal UDA or UVF structure in Mourne House after the early 1990s, although Loyalist women were imprisoned for various 'criminal' offences. Loyalist prisoners were also 'impeded by the political difficulties of aligning themselves with Republicans to achieve progress on the same issue[s]', and consequently 'focused almost exclusively on segregation, separation from the enemy' (McEvoy 2001: 104). Furthermore, the rare presence of women in Loyalist active service units and prison structures, their minority status as a prisoner group vis-à-vis both 'ordinary' and Republican prisoners, and the lack of acknowledgement they received from their community provided clear reasons for their insularity. Louie explained:

Once you're in prison, a lot of the prisoners know exactly what you're there for. There's two ways they'll treat you; they'll either treat you with contempt and completely ignore you, or they will basically acknowledge you're there and just get on with it. At the end of the day with the female side, the attitude was, 'you're there for a reason, and just get on and do it'. There's a lot of things first in your mind, and that type of thing was secondary … I wouldn't say they [other prisoners] were awe-struck at all. I think shock would be the word. Curiosity. Sometimes you'd get into conversations or a few debates about some issues and if you could hold your own, then OK. God help you if you made a mistake (Louie, sentenced prisoner, Loyalist).[5]

Interviewer: Did you ask to have facilities separately from the Republican prisoners?

Yes. They declared war on me. This is an enemy. I was not prepared to sit down and speak to people who were butchering my people on the streets. There wouldn't have been any engagement, no. As for association with the non-political prisoners, that did not arise. Although, sometimes when you would ask for segregation and it wasn't issued, there was a form of self-segregation where you could keep yourself to yourself and say, 'no, this is the direction I'm taking', and if anybody else is there you just don't recognise them at all. They don't exist (Louie, sentenced prisoner, Loyalist).

Stresses within the Republican community

Margaretta D'arcy's *Tell Them Everything* (1981) is, to date, the most comprehensive 'insider' account of the Republican no-wash protest. D'arcy, who is a feminist activist and writer, refused to pay the fine that was imposed on her for public order offences committed during a women's vigil outside Armagh prison in 1979. She was imprisoned for three months in Armagh in 1980, where she elected to 'join' the Republican strike. She observed that the IRA prisoner structures in Armagh operated according to exemplary democratic principles of open discussion and collective decision-making: 'I was very impressed by the way these meetings were conducted. There was time and confidence for everyone to put their viewpoints before the vote was taken' (*ibid.*: 101). D'arcy's account needs to be read with some caution, as it compares PIRA structures to the self-consciously 'organic', 'egalitarian' and 'empowering' political associations that sprang from feminist, environmental and new social protest movements (Enloe 1983; Liddington 1989; Roseneil 1995). The characteristics of the latter include an emphasis on group democracy, the willingness to challenge asymmetries of power within the group, leaderlessness, skill-sharing and collective responsibility. These principles are intended to form the 'centreless' base for radical political development, and more effective methods for challenging the hierarchical lines of power in bureaucracies, the military and corporations. Arguments such as D'arcy's have, in turn, been subjected to criticism of their idealistic precepts about power and their presumptions about the 'natural' lack of support amongst women for authoritarian or militaristic organizations (Carroll and Welling-Hall 1993; Howes and Stevenson 1993).

It would be difficult to argue conclusively that the women's prison structures were not constrained within the vertical command structure and ethos of the Republican movement. However, its military discipline and hierarchy had been increasingly called into question by prisoners themselves as the prolonged protests between 1976 and 1981 revealed its weaknesses. It gave way in the late 1980s to 'supportive', 'co-operative' and 'proactive' modes of collective decision-making (McKeown 2001: 136–7). It would be more accurate to say that the transition from rigidly demarcated roles to the collective ethic had been motivated by the inadequacy of the older style of command for responding to the individualized kinds of punishment to which the small group of women had been exposed. Furthermore, the counsel of restraint that the outside leadership had adopted during the protests against criminalization had prompted Republican women to use their resources and structures more effectively, as well as broaden the sources of political support that they could count on.

Similarly, whilst McKeown (*ibid*.: 160–70) has accounted for incidents of expulsion or resignation within the IRA structures at the Maze, I came across no evidence of internal punishments imposed upon women prisoners by their peers.[6] However, their demanding, insular and exclusive group meant that individuals were exposed to informal pressures to relinquish aspects of their personal autonomy and social difference to the collective consensus. There were internal conflicts within the Republican grouping in Armagh during the mid-1970s over the stringent internal discipline and the leadership's style, and what was perceived by some prisoners to be the political and social dominance of Provisional IRA members over other affiliates. Apart from the problems of factionalism and resistance to dominance within the Republican group, there was conflict because of interpersonal rivalries or the difficulties that arise generally from prison life:

> I was approached by two women who said, 'we would like you to be with us'. Some of those were people that I had worked with outside, but when they went inside, decided that they weren't going to fall in with the Republican group, and were going to have their own group. They stayed away from the main group. But that wasn't for me, that sort of dissension. It didn't do anybody any good or make their sentence end any quicker. It's what you believed in. You were staying with your doctrine, and weren't going to be side-tracked with what somebody else thought you should. My beliefs were Republican straight down the line. And what was happening with these women had nothing to do with

the wider picture. Whatever happened these women, whether they didn't like the OC or what, I didn't want to be part of that. My Republicanism didn't embrace that sort of splinter attitude … because if you don't try and keep together, you've had it. If you start letting the stresses fragment it, forget it, there's no point in doing anything. If you didn't stick together, they might have won. It just sort of worked out, and nobody bothered with the three or four others (Nora, internee, 1970s).[7]

These claims of unbroken solidarity raise the problematic figure of an idealized, 'highly conscientized', and 'moralistic prisoner' who maintains an irreproachable political distance from the divisive influences of strangers outside the group (Goffman 1991: 165–6). They also obscure the individualistic, unorthodox or resistant behaviours that may be perceived to contravene the broader group ethos, as well as exclude diverse or alternative forms of self-validation that are not available within the structure. Some individuals did avoid other prisoners, withdrew wholly or in part from the group as a coping strategy, or decided to serve their term without being involved in the more 'political' activities. One sentenced prisoner reflected on the isolation and the loss of support which she risked by situating herself on the margins of the PIRA structure:

> I suppose you had to conform in a sense, as well … I'm trying to be objective about this because I personally had some bad experiences in prison. I would have done my own thing and that's not accepted, you know. I purposely, unlike most of the prisoners, stayed on my own. I didn't double up. I had the choice. I read an awful lot. I went to classes … so that kind of thing was a focus. [But] I wasted my fuckin' time in jail, the four years I was in, in a sense. Well, not wasted, that's wrong, I was probably a bit more introspective or whatever, and kind of reflected more on stuff. I mean if you talk to women who probably done time from the late 70s, early 80s, they'd be more politicised or more focused, and knew what they wanted. But … and it's my opinion, most of us, all of us, internees and all … fuck, it was murder-pitch at times (sentenced prisoner, Armagh).

In detracting from the orthodox account of Republican solidarity, this respondent pointed to the dangers of fragmentation in Armagh in the early 1970s. She attributed the isolation and marginality of the women's structure to the social conservatism of Republican thinking and the lack of a coherent strategy for supporting younger prisoners and women in prison, as well as the political inexperience and absence of women in leadership positions at the time:

> I think women had a harder time in jail. The very fact [was] that we weren't politicised, we weren't politically aware. Again, I'm generalising. We hadn't got the cop-on and the maturity. There was a lot of infighting and backbiting. There wasn't the kind of strong united front that there would appear to be in all the accounts you'd be given. It wasn't that bad either, but underneath it, we could have used our time more productively, if we had more experience, and we could have been more focused. It doesn't matter what your physical surroundings are, you're still doing time. You're still locked up with people, you still have all those problems. The fact [is] that we were not politicised, and because we had all this time on our hands … When you have time on your hands, and you don't know what direction you're going in, and you're not really focused, that can create some problems. You are doing your time hard that way … We were just the products of conservative backgrounds, this Catholic, Republican, very conservative, right wing ethos about women's role and that. We were bringing that inside. And you had all these issues coming up there. And because we couldn't really articulate what was going on, I think there were major problems (sentenced prisoner, Armagh).

This chapter described the remaking of political communities in prison. However, the comments from the 'sentenced prisoner' above also capture the ambiguity of this struggle for women who were suspended between the inherited traditions of prison resistance and the practical opportunities that were available to them. The prison structures of both Loyalists and Republicans were based on familiar forms of boundary-setting in prison, such as group violence, self-defence, exclusion and moral validation, which did little to radically alter the larger regulatory framework of the prison. Additionally, the legitimacy of their communities was continuously renewed by the observance of political orthodoxies and individual self-discipline. This was related to the levels of silence or circumvention that individuals maintained about instances of 'collaboration' with staff or political 'others', or when internal divisions threatened to undermine their narrative of collective unity. However, these early structures were not simply reactionary microcosms of the prison. As discussed in Chapter

10, they led, especially for Republicans, to the future development of more sophisticated levels of self-organization in the subtler governing environment of the 1990s. Furthermore, the levels of segregation that prisoners practically achieved was an important element in fostering their ideological opposition to the stigma of 'criminality'. The following chapter discusses the relationship between the emergence of a 'political identity' and resistance in prison.

Notes

1 Ann Ogilby was killed whilst being interrogated in a UDA club in July 1974. The case gained notoriety when one of the defendants referred to the incident as a 'romper', taken from a children's TV programme, *The Romper Room*. One man and 11 women were jailed for the killing, including the UDA's female commander. This case accounted for the largest single admittance of Loyalist women into the prison system.
2 The annual commemoration of the victory of William of Orange at the Battle of the Boyne 1690, which takes place on 12 July, and is celebrated by Protestants and Unionists.
3 The 'Shankill Butchers' was a group of UVF members who were involved in the abduction, torture, mutilation and murder of 19 Catholics between 1972 and 1979.
4 Chapter 2 described two such incidences: the hostage-taking in Armagh in 1974, and the disturbance in 1980 leading to the no-wash strike, when three Loyalists were also injured by staff.
5 Certain identifying details, including the prison in which Louie was incarcerated, are omitted.
6 There is no indication that the 'resignees' from the strikes in Armagh between 1976 and 1980 were disciplined by the Republican movement. They tended to refer to 'forced withdrawals' on health grounds and under pressure from the prison authorities (*Belfast Telegraph* 1 September 1978; *Irish News* 9 April 1980; *Irish News* 7 October 1980). However, the comments of others who stayed on the protest did involve some implicit criticism in the observation that by withdrawing, those individuals had made their own position worse.
7 The women concerned later became members of Republican Sinn Féin, which broke away from Provisional Sinn Féin in 1986 over the latter's decision to end the historic Republican policy of boycotting electoral politics.

Chapter 7

'We are not criminals': political identity as resistance

Categories of identity … become both potential sites of resistance to the universalism of penal control, and sites of possible conflict within the prison population (Bosworth 1999: 111).

Political identification, it's also justification for what they did. They know that the world sees them as murderers or bombers or what have you, which are very negative things, and a bit of that has been conveyed to them in various ways. I think that while they can reinforce the political motivation to themselves, they almost, in a way, can excuse themselves, sort of validate what they did, and sanitise it to themselves (official visitor, Maghaberry).

Penologists have long recognized that a core site of contention in prisons converges on whose definition of identity prevails. However, the sociological analysis of identity in prisons, whilst correctly pointing to the dangers of psychological deterioration for long-term prisoners (Cohen and Taylor 1981), the erosion of personal autonomy and intensive stigmatization (Sykes 1958; Goffman 1991), or the distortion of parental, familial and social identities amongst the damaging effects of imprisonment (Coulter 1991; Clarke 1995; Jamieson and Grounds 2002), tend to emphasize the negative institutional determination of the self. There are, indeed, compelling reasons for qualifying any claims to the radicalizing or resistant effects which imprisonment may have on prisoners. As previously discussed, such critical restraint is evident in the work of the 'adaptive' and 'subcultural' theorists who emphasize the circumscribed boundaries within which prisoners express solidarity or commonality, and in the later feminist analyses of the deep structuring of gendered and punitive subjectivity. Furthermore, the violent repression of prison protests in Britain, France and North America in the late 1960s and early 1970s revealed that radical or collective prison movements were as frequently deterred from becoming sustainable oppositional forces as they succeeded in providing a basis for resistance (Jackson 1970; PROP 1976; Scraton *et al.* 1991; Seale 1991; Adams 1992: 88–90; Churchill and Vander Wall 1992).

In *Engendering Resistance* (1999), Bosworth re-engaged with the long-standing debate about agency in prison by arguing that identity provides an important explanation for the ways in which prisoners reshape power relations in confinement. Thus, 'within ... inmates' limited ability to control the ordering of relationships in prison, ethnicity, age, religion, sexual orientation and offence become categories through which women define a prison identity' (*ibid.*: 110). Two positions arise from this analysis. First, as imprisonment freqently reinforces various forms of discrimination (on the basis of 'race', class, sexuality, gender or nationality), prisoners develop a consciousness about, and come to use their subject positions, or 'identities', to construct alternative forms of agency in prisons. Secondly, it follows that identity and agency in women's prisons are intertwined and mutually constitutive, denoting 'both their specific subject positions or agency, and their ability to act. To have agency is to preserve the ability to negotiate power and to resist' (*ibid.*: 130). As these relations are woven into the regulatory and punitive demands that are placed on prisoners, 'identity' does not resemble an essentialist position from which prisoners resist control (*ibid.*: 98). Rather, identities are formed and re-formed in a continuous interplay between 'socio-structural locations ... and the manner in which individuals perceive themselves'.

However, as discussed in Chapter 4, the idea that 'identity', as a loose alignment of oppositional reflexes, resistant consciousness and identity politics, can constitute a valid basis for radically altering the material basis of penal power, has been contested. Rather, Bosworth's detractors noted the powerful discursive role which criminal justice institutions play in (re)defining the terms within which prisoners' agency is understood – as 'needy' or 'dangerous', as 'clients' or therapeutic candidates – which legitimize 'new' and versatile forms of penal governance and, ultimately, the institutional viability of prisons themselves (Hannah-Moffat 2001; Carlen 1994; 2002a). These ideological and structural forces are crucial for understanding the contested dynamics of identity and resistance in Northern Ireland's prisons. They are reminders of the different interests that were invested in retaining the legitimacy of stigmatization and punishment. Furthermore, they underline the difficulties of defining 'prison identity' as a categorical entity which is separable from the other aspects of identification, such as a sense of community or nationalist ideology, which were formed before imprisonment and with which political prisoners sought to reconnect.

The irony of subjective resistance or identity politics in prison, moreover, is that they cannot fully escape the parameters of criminalization or other forms of personal deconstruction that are central functions of confinement. Resistance to 'prison identity' in Northern Ireland, in so far as the term can be grasped, developed some identifiable characteristics under these conditions. First, political prisoners drew on a variety of ideological and sociocultural resources for rendering their imprisonment intelligible as part of a legitimate political struggle. Therefore, the idea of the 'prison struggle' established a sense of purpose and meaning which translated the deprivations of confinement into a wider historical and collective event.

Secondly, the meaning of being a political prisoner became evident in the ways in which women prisoners came to understand and resist prison subordination in terms of a national and gendered struggle. In this sense, political identification gave them access to an alternative set of explanations for the reasons they were imprisoned, the forms their punishment took and their reactions to actual or perceived challenges to that identity.

Thirdly, the development of resistant agency was contingent and progressive. The prisoners themselves acknowledged that their political identity was not a given entity, but was claimed and fought for. As seen earlier, one woman spoke of the problems of 'becoming' a political prisoner by referring to their 'ignorance' and confusion in the early days of forming a political structure. Another prisoner, Anna, related the processes of developing a political consciousness with the politicization of everyday acts of resistance: 'we didn't know about how to work things like that until we were there. It was gradually by trial and error. I think that it was really strict routine with us.'

Finally, the ambiguities of being 'political' and 'women' prisoners forced them to confront the boundaries between those positions. A defining characteristic of the women's prison campaign was its role in mobilizing new constituencies of support amongst feminists, anti-imperialists and the political Left by redrawing some of the terms of debates about gender oppression, State violence and paramilitarism. At the same time, these debates had inevitable consequences for prisoners themselves in their gradual acknowledgement of the subjectivity they shared with non-political women prisoners, as well as with men in their political organizations.

Criminalization: personal and political implications

One of the unforeseen dangers of issuing criminal or other unwelcome labels is that they cannot be relied on to maintain their original meaning. The introduction of the criminalization policy in 1976 is a case in point because it redirected prison conflict in Northern Ireland on to more conspicuously ideological grounds, and further clarified to the prisoners the necessity of resisting 'criminal' subjectivity. For Winnie, the refusal to take on a 'criminal' identity extended from the historical and ideological basis of Republicanism, but she also describes how this consciousness was deepened ('politicized') by the experience of imprisonment:

> With what I was charged with and because of my views which were Republican, I seen myself as a political prisoner, and there was no way I was going to conform to the British government's idea that because of my beliefs I was a criminal. So, it was just a case of following through from that. Certainly, I had thought about what was happening in the jails because the prisoners play a very big part in our society. It's like most things; if you haven't been in jail yourself, there's a relative or somebody belonging to you [who has], so there's always been a very close association with the prisoners. And because of my views, I didn't see any of the prisoners as being criminals. I didn't like the badge being put on them, and certainly nobody was going to put the badge on me. And it wasn't through any sense of being very politically aware, because I would be lying if I said I was. But I had very strong Republican views, which do not necessarily go hand in hand with being political, if you know what I mean. But it offended me; it offended my sense of pride and dignity as a person, and if I had conformed, I would never have been able to look at myself in the mirror in the mornings. Conformity starts with accepting the label. Like a lot of other people, I had a lot of friends and family who were killed over the years because of the Troubles. And it was a case of, if I had conformed, not only would I be belittling

my own integrity, as far as I was concerned I would be belittling their memory as well (Winnie, sentenced prisoner, Armagh).

Although both Loyalists and Republicans objected to criminalization, their perspectives on the policy reflected fundamental differences in their understanding of State legitimacy and justice. For Meg and Anna, both Republicans, the policy was consistent with a broader authoritarian sweep against nationalists, and this element of mass discipline on the part of the State was directly connected to the processes of disciplining in prison:

> It was a political decision with the government … because Thatcher was giving concessions like jobs and all that, to try to make things normal on the outside, and on the inside to criminalize anybody that disagreed with it. It was all part of the struggle. The whole system was part of the struggle (Meg, internee, Armagh).

> Part of the idea to take away the status was to make it a more or less strict regime to deter these people, because imprisonment wasn't a deterrent. There were a lot of women back in for a second time, so they seen it wasn't acting as a deterrent to these people. So they made the rules even harsher as a deterrent, really (Anna, sentenced prisoner, Armagh).

For Loyalists, the alienating effect of criminalization took a different trajectory. Whereas for Republicans it represented a deliberate act of official exclusion, Loyalists were alienated by their perceptions of the *failures* of the State in its inability or unwillingness to protect her community. Louie, who uses the third person (and male) voice here, argued:

> You must remember that political prisoners don't see [that] any of our fellows committed a crime. What they did was an act of self-preservation and survival to a situation they were put into, and was put upon them. This was not addressed by a government that was supposed to be protecting us … I would say they [Loyalist prisoners] weren't guilty of a crime, they were found guilty of self-preservation and survival (Louie, Loyalist).

Political imprisonment has undoubtedly had a significant effect on the experiences of working-class Republican and Loyalist communities in Northern Ireland, and this informed a wider consciousness about criminalization as a form of collective stigmatization and punishment.

The idea of prison struggle as part of a historically embedded and collectively shared experience was a significant factor in sustaining their campaign. Respondents frequently described their motivations in terms of a communal imperative – which paralleled the experiences of violent conflict by their communities outside – and as a historical imperative – by which their prison struggle affirmed the continuity of national resistance. For Winnie, conformity would have denoted both a personal failure and a betrayal of these obligations. In the context of these potent social and historical motives, imprisonment was a rational outcome of political involvement:

> You knew what the story was if you were going to end up in jail. It just wasn't on the periphery of your consciousness. You were doing what you were doing and you never thought about the actual details, until you actually went into the jail and the door shut on you. Then you thought, 'I'm in jail' (Nora, internee, Armagh).

> I don't really understand their thinking. They [the authorities] don't realise that when Volunteers first join the struggle they know that they're either going to go to prison or they're going to die. Why did they think that any sort of measures that they bring in are going to stop people? (Meg, internee, Armagh).

Republicanizing feminism and feminizing Republicanism: the contradictions of political and gender solidarity

> I've never been penalized or stopped from doing something because I was a woman. In fact I was encouraged to, and I was afforded every opportunity. I know myself, on a personal level, there was an awful lot of respect there. But the contradictions were huge, I mean, they were huge (Kathleen, sentenced prisoner, Maghaberry).

Despite the stated assurance of women former prisoners as to the equality of their role in the prison struggle, they were continuously obliged to confront their contradictory positions as women in the prison system, and as women who were Volunteers in their own organizations. The active participation of women as combatants and supporters of violence has been one of the more contentious areas of feminist engagement with paramilitarism. Whilst the feminist movement in

Northern Ireland, as with feminism generally, cannot be understood as a homogeneous entity, the problematic question of women's allegiances to nationalist, patriarchal and violent organizations created significant divisions within it. The women's movement took organizational shape with the founding of the Northern Ireland Women's Rights Movement (NIWRM) in 1975, which tended to condemn what they perceived to be the dual oppression of women through 'State patriarchy' *and* paramilitary violence. More damningly, women paramilitaries were accused of having aligned themselves with violent organizations that were complicit in the subordination of women within the 'armed patriarchy' of Northern Ireland (Edgerton 1986: 74). Indeed, the issues of the 'armed struggle' and class were at the root of a series of splits in the NIWRM and the emergence of new groups such as the Socialist Women's Group and the Belfast Women's Collective. These latter groups also agonized over whether campaigning for social and economic equality, reproductive rights and legal reforms could be relevant to ghettoized nationalist women if feminists continued to sideline the struggle against 'British imperialism'.

Whilst the debates within and between feminism and Republicanism over the issues of political violence, the Armagh prison protests and strip searching have been explored in detail elsewhere (see McCafferty 1981; Loughran 1983; Buckley and Lonergan 1984; Fairweather *et al.* 1984; Ward 1986; de Brun 1988; Shannon 1989; Connolly 1994; Aretxaga 1997), the issue of women's position within Republican ideology and strategy developed in relation to a number of influences. First, the intersecting questions of gender and the 'national struggle' were broadly framed by the historical phases of political and ideological development within both movements generally. In the first instance, feminist ideas and politics were being transformed by internal challenges to the domination of white, Westernized and middle-class assumptions about 'women's oppression' in early second-wave feminism. In practical terms, the dangers of talking about 'women' as a single group gave way to an analysis of the intersecting gender, class, sectarian, ethno-national and other forms of subjugation that different groups of women experienced in Northern Ireland. Equally, whilst the dilemma of 'Republicanizing feminism' and 'feminizing Republicanism' remained a problematic and contested area of political debate, the Armagh prisoners' protests had demonstrated very publicly the consequences of the Republican leadership's failure to address or support these questions in the 1970s and early 1980s.

A gradual engagement between feminist and Republican thinking commenced with the founding of Women Against Imperialism (WAI) in 1978, which was concerned with 'safeguarding the advances made by women in the struggle for total liberation', whilst being 'opposed to the British presence in Ireland and supporting the liberation struggle' (*APRN* 8 July 1978). In 1980, Sinn Féin opened a Department of Women's Affairs (later Sinn Féin Women's Department), and published a policy document, *Women in the New Ireland* (1981), which sought to forge alliances between Republicans and feminists on the grounds that 'women's liberation is an integral part of national liberation' (*Iris* November 1981: 57–9). However, at the launch of the policy at Sinn Féin's annual conference in 1981, its first co-ordinator and former political prisoner, Rita O'Hare, argued that 'the struggle against the oppression of women has yet to be understood and then incorporated into overall Republican policy' (*ibid.*: 60). Even with the development of these hybrid feminist and Republican strands, permanent tensions persisted between them on the issue of the use of violence for social transformation, as distinct from violence as a tool of patriarchal oppression.

Yet in an important sense, the disputes and uncertainties about violence also led to some points of uneasy co-existence between feminists and Republicans when the meaning of 'violence' tilted towards the victimization of women by State forces. This tenuous alliance was crucially reflected in a succession of campaigns in which feminists in Sinn Féin and WAI aligned with other women's organizations over security force intimidation, the fatalities and injuries that resulted from the army's use of plastic bullets against civilians, and the strip searching of prisoners. Such events were regarded as evidence of armed aggression against nationalist women by an 'army of occupation' (de Brun 1988: 323). Kathleen, who was in prison in Maghaberry in the 1990s, described her route to reconciling these perspectives:

> It all depends on what adjective you use that gives you your perspective, feminist-Republican or Republican-feminist. But I had massive problems with the themes of feminism, because I saw it as more post-feminism. It was as if something happened to a load of middle-class women in the late '60s, early '70s that I just couldn't relate to at all. Being a feminist for me was resisting, like what we were doing in the jail. And my decision to become a Volunteer was actually to do with my *feminist* background, rather than the other way about. The thing that actually influenced my decision to become a member was the women on the ground, the women who were running their homes single-handedly, running their kids, going to the jails, and were very instrumental

in the political campaigns on the streets. And to me they were the resistance of the Republican movement (Kathleen, sentenced prisoner, Maghaberry, emphasis in original).

Although the prisoners directly challenged the disabling paternalism within Republicanism, their contradictory positions as women and combatants were not so easily reconciled. According to Eilís, their struggle for legitimacy and equality began when they challenged the implicit preconceptions that they would have a peripheral status within a centralized command structure directed from the Maze prison:

You had a growing realisation, 'we are here because we made our own decision to be part of the whole struggle'. But we have a single movement. What you had at the time was 'comms' coming from the 'Kesh, giving directions. At one stage we called a big meeting in Armagh saying, 'hold on, that's all right, a number of directions being given, but we also have a voice here, and we also have decisions to make as well' … So we got a very slow but sure realisation that women are an integral part of the struggle, and it was like a strength. There's also the contradictions, but comradeship too between ourselves and the men. We always had, not tensions, but we were extremely aware of asserting our rights, our autonomy, not just falling into their command structure as well. We might have been all IRA Volunteers, but, and the 'but' was significant, we deliberately had our own publications, our own writings. We had our OC as contact, our OCs rather than their OCs being spokespeople for us all. We always made sure that we were represented. Even though they've never done anything to misrepresent us, we felt it was extremely important for us (Eilís, internee, Armagh).

But according to another Republican prisoner, 'the blunt truth of the matter was that we were all there, young kids who were reacting to the political situation outside, being caught up in if for whatever reason, but hadn't thought it through. My politics didn't emerge until I was out of jail'. The differences between this respondent and Kathleen do not just reflect 'generational' developments in Republican thinking between the 1970s and the 1990s, but also points to the variety of individual responses to the predicaments of their dual marginality. For the 'Republican prisoner' above, gender consciousness was suppressed by Republicanism, for Kathleen and Eilís, it was a means of inscribing themselves into a renewed idea of Republican struggle. A third or intermediary position also emerged amongst other prisoners that womanhood (as it was targeted by the prison regime) was a weakness because it exposed prisoners to a punitive onslaught. As a consequence, surviving and resisting prison was best achieved by making their gender subsidiary to political identity.

The escalation by the Armagh women of their protests to the no-wash strike and the first hunger strike in 1980 was the crucial turning point, as it confronted the broader Republican movement with the legitimacy of their group, as well as establishing the political visibility and meaning of their prison protests in the public domain. However, this was frequently resisted by the Republican leadership:

> It was a pushing and shoving sort of thing. We decided through discussion and everything else to try to escalate it [the protest campaign]. The Army Council outside wouldn't allow us. But we wanted to escalate it, because we thought we weren't doing enough to help the men up on the 'Blocks. We thought if we escalated it because we were women, we could be used as propaganda for the better. Like most things, you can say it's sexist or not, men are seen to be able to take it, the women aren't. This was the way we were thinking. We fought very hard to get [clearance from the Army Council], and they wouldn't allow us to do anything. So we were very frustrated because we weren't allowed to escalate anything. At that time the men in the Crumlin remand were getting hammered. So it was a case for us of, 'we're sitting here with no visits, no parcels or anything like that. We're losing our remission, but we're not doing anything else'. It was as if they were out there fighting for us and we weren't doing very much for ourselves (Winnie, sentenced prisoner, Armagh).

> But then the word came that when Bobby [Sands] went on hunger strike, the no-wash would end in all the jails. So when I went over, we were on a no work protest. The women had been on hunger strike the previous December, while they were still on the no-wash, but during this hunger strike it was decided that it would be better if the women did not participate on it. I think probably at that stage, they knew they were really going to be up against a very tough type of regime, and while I don't think there was any kind of belief that women would not go through it or anything, maybe it was felt that the administration would manipulate it. The women reluctantly agreed not to participate then (Elizabeth, remand prisoner, Armagh/commanding officer, Maghaberry).

Loyalist women prisoners were positioned within even finer grids of difference, both within an experience of penality that was primarily articulated by Republican women, and within overwhelmingly masculinist Loyalist structures. Opposed to criminalization and claiming political status on the same ideological grounds as her male peers, Louie none the less consciously rejected the relevance of gender difference to Loyalist political goals:

> The difference between Loyalist prisoners and Republican prisoners is that war was declared on us, we did not declare war on anybody. War was declared on us. We have been victims of created suffering. It is a case that we were politically motivated to stand our ground and say, 'we've got to protect ourselves and our areas'. We are not terrorists. That's the way it would be seen. We are political prisoners, and should be treated as such. There's a reason behind it and the reason was basically the protection of our heritage, culture, and identity ... I would actually say that we have the greatest respect and high regard for our political prisoners, and they make the decisions. The decisions that are made by Loyalist factors [*sic*] come from the prisoners. Because the prisoners are the ones who have suffered, who have given their life and they will have a very strong say in the way forward. What I am saying is that, in one respect, there is a place for women, but they [the Loyalist leadership] will not exploit them to the tune of sticking them out front waving flags and rattling a bin lid. There will be a certain amount of respect (Louie, sentenced prisoner, Loyalist).

In her explanation of women's role as Loyalist Volunteers and political prisoners, Louie emphasized that women's engagement in 'frontline' or combat roles disrupted the intersecting constructions of nationhood, kinship and tradition that Loyalism sought to defend. The connections she makes between masculine authority, military hierarchy and territorial defence are consistent with the objectives and ethos of 'conservative', counter-revolutionary and 'defensive' paramilitary organizations (Drake 1996), and which constitute the classical apparatus of male dominance. Furthermore, whilst the broader mobilization of nationalist women enabled their role to be represented as a legitimate contribution to the 'war effort', Loyalist organizations had arguably not placed comparable emphasis on widespread community mobilization until the 1990s (Ward 2002), nor had Loyalist prisoners engaged in the 'radicalizing' debates equivalent to those which had impinged on

Republican ideological development in the prisons (Stevenson 1996). Whilst the Republican respondents at least consciously addressed the dilemmas and ultimately challenged them within their organizations, Louie argued that the Loyalist women's non-confrontational approach was consistent with the broader political ethos of Loyalism. None the less, her critique also pointed to the obstructions which Loyalist and Republican women faced in their struggle for gender equality, political visibility and organizational legitimacy.

Relations with non-politically affiliated women prisoners

It was not only towards male peers that political women prisoners felt themselves to be constructed as the 'other'; they also compared their positions with those of 'ordinary' women prisoners. As previously discussed, women are considered to be out of place in organized prison resistance because of the taken-for-granted androgyny of the category of political prisoner. Equally, they are implicitly conceived of as exceptional to the general paradigm of subjectification (victimization) that is applied to women in prison. These ontological tensions continuously shaped the ways in which women political prisoners negotiated the sometimes conflicting obligations which arose from sustaining allegiances both with their external organizations and with 'non-political' or 'ordinary' women inside. When discussing their exposure to security practices such as strip searching, for example, the politicals voiced their shared susceptibility with other women prisoners to gendered forms of surveillance, discipline and to the sexual meanings of invasive security procedures. Others noted that, whilst all women in prison were subject to categorization as aberrant and socially inadequate, they were different from other prisoners in that they were treated as uniquely manipulative, and more likely to undermine or compromise prison order. Similarly, whilst the paradigm of prison discipline reacts to women in prison as emotionally dependent, capricious and non-compliant, the politicals 'were different' in that their 'manipulativeness' was viewed by staff as capitalizing on their political status and identity:

> They would have said [that we were] intimidating other prisoners on the wing or disobeying an order, that was the classic, 'disobeying an order'. If we'd have stopped and said, 'hello' to somebody you were told to go back up to your cell. If we ignored them you were disobeying an order. It was totally petty. It actually frightened some of the prisoners who were just in for ordinary

things. We used to stop to try to talk to them. They were scurrying away. I could understand that because they just didn't want to be locked up or brought up in front of the governor and all that. To us it was nothing, well it wasn't nothing, it was difficult enough being locked in all day. But we could apply ourselves to different things in the cell – we were used to lock-ups. That's basically what it was. And we were used to jail struggle (Winnie, sentenced prisoner, Armagh).

In applying the language of victimization to 'ordinary', 'criminal' or 'non-political' women prisoners, Republican women simultaneously invoked the subordinated figure of the women prisoner, and expressed their rejection of the subjectivity it implied. Jennie described the 'ordinaries' as the 'real' victims of penal subordination, arguing that political prisoners occupied a relatively 'privileged' position within the prison regime:

We had this attitude that there's no way we should be in here, so who the hell were they to take it away from us? It would have been different if you had been in there as an ordinary prisoner, and had to obey the rules, and had to know what the regime was about. But we were going straight in there after fighting and reacting to the situation outside. So we just thought this automatically, we didn't give it a second thought in some senses, until we actually saw the ordinary prisoners, what they had to go through, and how privileged we were in some senses. That would be a personal thing. I had total sympathy with them. I don't think I even thought about it politically. I just thought that it was wrong that those people, through circumstances beyond their control, were in there (Jennie, sentenced prisoner, Armagh).

At the same time, political difference was not incompatible with conceiving of themselves as being subject to some elements of shared subordination with other women prisoners, nor did it foreclose the potential for mutual recognition between them. Nora, for example, pointed out that Republican prisoners extended their influence to protect 'non-political' prisoners from the more casual forms of disciplinary intervention: 'If anything, we were very protective, for example, [with] screws trying to make it difficult. They came in under our wing, sort of a protective wing, so the screws couldn't order them around, or order them to do something that they didn't want to do' (Nora, internee, Armagh).

The serial character of political and gender resistance

These acts of Republican solidarity with women outside their group bring to mind postmodern and feminist political theories which conceive of political struggle in terms of contingent and strategic alliances that emerge in relation to specific issues, or as a response to common contexts of subordination (Carroll 1992). To the former school of thought, postmodern politics is characterized by the clustering of fluid and temporary groupings around 'non-traditional' political causes related to race, gender, the environment and neoliberal globalization. This kind of political action has the advantages, as far as its proponents are concerned, of ideological 'pragmatism' that avoids the divisive identity politics or factionalism to which conventional movements fall prey. At the same time, it is at least questionable whether the subjective or expressive freedoms envisaged in postmodernism are available to those in the repressive correctional settings of prison. Similarly, as Cooper (1995: 147–8) observes, equality between groups in any struggle 'becomes difficult to measure … either because a grouping is disadvantaged through its location within several organising frameworks, or else because there is a strong correlation between a particular organising framework and the structuring of a specific terrain, race and the economy, for instance', or in this case, gender and punishment.

In an effort to think beyond either the 'false unity' of essentialism or the fragmentation of politics into single-issue pragmatics, Iris Young has sought to explain how women who are divided by class, race or other lines of difference can still be viewed as collective actors. Young (1997: 31) proposes that women constitute a social collective because of their common positioning in systems of representation, reproduction and the sexual division of labour (*ibid*.: 28–9). Those who are positioned within the category 'women' do not have to affirm that they are engaged in a shared enterprise with other women, nor seek to establish common histories, experiences or identities with others. 'Being positioned by these structures as "women" does not itself designate attributes that attach to the person in the series, nor does it define her identity' (*ibid*.: 29). Rather, 'individuals move and act in relation to the practico-inert objects [i.e. material resources and social relationships] that position them as women'.

Here, Young develops Sartre's notion of 'serial collectivity' to describe the way in which women are unified passively as a group 'in series with others in that class [and] in relation to work, exchange and consumption' (*ibid*.: 26). The idea of women as a 'serial collective' captures the conditions that define them in relation to the other social groupings to which they belong so that 'the concept … provides a useful way of thinking about the relationships of race, class, gender and other collective structures to the individual person' (*ibid*.: 31). However, Young is also concerned with the circumstances in which women 'form themselves as a group of mutually identifying agents' under specific conditions (*ibid*.: 21). These are, first, that the category 'woman' is a load-bearing one that can accommodate multiple differences, yet at the same time signify common contexts of subordination. Secondly, she draws attention to the 'objective' material and social forces that establish the actuality ('facticity') of gender as a shared reality in women's lives. In this sense, women might be defined as collective actors even when they do not conspicuously subscribe to feminist or other consciously political agendas. Thirdly, even though the category of 'woman' has rightly been challenged to admit differences, a notional collective category must be retained because 'without conceptualising women as a group in some sense, it is not possible to conceptualise oppression as a systematic, structured, institutional process' (*ibid*.: 17).

Applied to Northern Ireland, the series 'women in prison' describes the range of positions and situations which 'ordinary' and 'political' women occupied as prisoners, and which were manifested in the material and ideological organization of women's punishment. For example, the serial character of prison punishment applies to the collective control of women as a group as well the reinforcement of differences amongst them in categorization systems, the development of regimes and the justifications for applying disciplinary techniques. In this sense, 'seriality' also brings together the political and gendered axes of women's punishment that have previously been kept apart and creates a context for analysing these intersecting experiences. Young's concept of seriality as a political strategy usefully addresses the practical, if limited, examples of solidarity across the lines of politics and gender in prison. It explains the penal structuring of differences between the Loyalist, Republican and 'non-aligned' women, whilst also retaining a sense of their common positioning and mutual recognition within gendered penal frameworks. The overlapping dimensions of punishment, and common interests in resisting it, also led to occasional alliances between them without obliging them to relinquish their differences or enter into more permanent, and problematic, relationships. Although this book has not embarked on a comparative analysis of the experiences of the different groups of women prisoners, neither has it been assumed that the experiences of political women prisoners can be detached from the gendered formation of prison punishment. Equally, seriality confronts the disqualification of women prisoners as political actors within their paramilitary structures. As identities derive from social engagement and action rather than intrinsic categories such as 'political prisoner' and 'women in prison', their struggle referenced the multiple meanings of resistance within these two domains. Rather than choosing between political and gendered identities, women political prisoners reshaped them into plural, mutually transformative positions.

Chapter 8

The turning of the screw: active disengagement, intimidation and the conditioning of staff

This chapter returns to the paradox of women's agency in prison discussed in Chapter 3, namely, how politically affiliated women in prison developed sustained, collective agency in a system which customarily relies on individual discipline. The question invokes the predicament of gendered penal subjectivity whereby women in prison are not understood to exercise effective, long-term collaborative agency, or where women's resistance is viewed to be most successful at the level of personal subversion (Bosworth 1999: 130–1), but rarely impedes the larger punitive functioning of prison establishments. Equally, the collective agency of female political prisoners defies the androcentric precepts of 'inmate subcultural' theories. These have either failed to register the peculiar constraints which shape relations in women's prisons, and thus conclude that resistance is either absent from their social arrangements, or advance essentialist explanations for the apparent fragility of female communities in prison. Similarly, the scholarship on political imprisonment in Northern Ireland, whilst acknowledging the Republican structures in Armagh and Maghaberry prisons, represents the question of gender (as well as applying 'gender' to women's penality only) as an unresolved problem in the study of political imprisonment (McEvoy 2001: 8; McKeown 2001: 236–7).

Whereas the previous chapters examined different facets of internal consolidation and self-affirmation on the part of Republican prisoners, this chapter examines the role of their structure in organizing 'external' relations with the prison administration and discipline staff. In particular, it examines the complex functions and meanings of boundary-setting and exclusion as strategies for limiting the kinds of disciplinary interventions that have customarily eroded solidaristic structures in women's prisons. The term 'active disengagement', which prisoners applied to their strategy, sums up its sophistication as both a defensive and an offensive tactic. In the first instance, it amounted to a boycott, or collective withdrawal from direct contact with prison officers, as a means of minimizing the kinds of interpersonal controls that are mediated through socialization and mentoring relationships with staff. In addition, 'active disengagement' was meant to diminish the collective influence of staff as a bureaucratic-regulatory layer between Republican prisoners and senior administrators. This supported the prisoners' objective of asserting their political status by extracting from prison governors a direct acknowledgement of their structure as the sole entity through which they, as well as welfare and discipline staff, had to engage with inmates. However, staff–prisoner relations are themselves sources of insecurity because everyday interaction creates opportunities for prisoners to exert both direct and clandestine influences over officers. In this sense, the 'human dimension of security' becomes a field of intensified regulation which ties together the policing of prisoners' interactions with staff with vigilance against 'inappropriate', mutually exploitative or collusive relationships between them. The second part of this chapter explores the more conspicuous methods for conditioning individual personnel through collective censure, intimidation and violence. The discussion concludes with an analysis of the gendered dimensions of conditioning for both staff and prisoners.

Active disengagement

The dynamics of conflict in women's prisons, as Mandaraka-Sheppard (1986), Dobash et al. (1986), Carlen (1998) and Bosworth (1999) remind us, are often purposefully locked into local or interpersonal disputes between members of staff and individual prisoners. Their arguments arise from the observation that the disciplinary paradigm in women's prisons resembles a circuit of normative gendered expectations and institutional practices which reinforce the infantilization of prisoners, and which endorse highly personalized forms of correction, scrutiny and regulation. Moreover, the primacy of loosely defined 'security practices' creates resentment on the part of prisoners at 'petty' and 'aggravating' aspects of the regime, as well as contributing to stress, anger and disempowerment at their inability to exercise basic personal decisions. The possibility that 'A' Company in Armagh prison could unravel because of peripheral conflicts arising out of personal contact with discipline staff was validated by the initial experiences of the regime in Armagh prison:

> We were not allowed a radio at first, and then a radio was allowed, but not a tape recorder. The radios were checked, and after three days they were handed over...The screws used to mess with the parcels. They used to mess with your letters. Sometimes you'd be waiting on your letters, and you wouldn't get the letter for three weeks. And then they'd be censored with the big black lines through them. Some of them would be vindictive about that. If something happened, they wouldn't let you know. But it would be the wee things, say when you'd be waiting for a visit. And if they interfered with the parcels, you'd know that that screw had done it. If you had a letter missing, you knew that it was taken on you [sic] (Anna, sentenced prisoner, Armagh).

As Dobash *et al.* (1986) and Hannah-Moffat (2001) note, 'good order' in prison is bound up with the assumption that women prisoners are susceptible to the 'beneficial' influence of personalized concern about their welfare. Female officers are encouraged to implement systems of formal and informal rewards and to foster compliance through 'mothering' and related strategies for legitimizing their position of control. Women in prison are generally not allowed to disengage from interacting with staff, nor erode the vertical lines of emotional and social dependency that are constructed in the course of contact with staff. Carlen (1983: 102) critically observed the injunctions on individual women to become entrepreneurs of their own rehabilitation by establishing confidential relations with members of staff in which 'the good prisoner opens up to the officer and doesn't think she is any better than the other women'. Walker and Worrall (2000: 33) noted that the obligation to 'be yourself' or to 'express yourself' is self-incriminatory because prisoners know that 'their actions [a]re monitored and that whatever they did would be written about in reports'. Self-disclosure, as Carlen (1983: 102) puts it, entails a double bind because 'there is resentment and suspicion of the women developing a private realm of consciousness, yet at the same time there are bars to sociability which prevent them developing a public realm of consciousness'.

Furthermore, as political imprisonment implies intersecting subjective and collective domains of consciousness, the prisoners argued that social intercourse with staff was not only concerned with returning them to docile femininity, but was also with breaking down the political character of their alliances. Active disengagement, therefore, involved a range of practical methods for circumventing staff power, refusing to obey orders that were not transmitted through their elected leaders and questioning officers' instructions. In other instances, individual prisoners were assigned to make contact with certain members of staff 'in a psychological kind of way', by alternately establishing friendly relations and then unexpectedly withdrawing or changing their attitudes towards them (Elizabeth, commanding officer, Maghaberry).

Whilst disengagement or distancing are more frequently connected with passive forms of resistance, active disengagement can be viewed as a form of constructive disobedience which involved extensive, calculated methods for refusing the obligations that are placed on prisoners to know their place and recognize authorized structures. Áine noted that their refusal to validate the most minor, symbolic forms of interaction, such as refusing to reply to officers when their numbers were called out until they were addressed by name, inverted the norms of disciplinary inculcation and 'broke down' the embedded institutional practices and deferential mores that sustained staff morale and authority:

> What they tried to do was enforce their rules on us. Like the screws making us call them 'Miss', and making themselves one step higher than you. We'd respond by calling them by their second [family] name. It was a constant battle to see who was going to get the upper hand all the time. We did quite a few times. They did quite a lot of the times. But it was a constant battle (Áine, sentenced prisoner, Armagh).

Anna argued that Republicans regulated staff behaviour by taking grievances directly to the governor. She further noted that the strategy compelled officers to revise their normative expectations about relating to prisoners and to check their own conduct, and in addition, accomplished the objective of making staff show some 'respect' for prisoners' space and property:

> It depended a lot on who was doing the cell searching what aggravation was caused. You maybe had a screw coming in who was pretty decent. They'd have been nearly afraid, taking the

stuff from your locker and going through it. Other ones would just come in and turn the place over and put everything on the floor. Then we won a concession there too, insisting that they had to put everything back. We decided we weren't going to let this happen any more. If some of the screws can come in and conduct themselves right searching the stuff and putting it back, then why is there a need for these other screws to go in and just wreck your cell? That's where it came from. Then they had to adhere to the code (Anna, sentenced prisoner, Armagh).

Exclusion was also connected with pragmatic concerns about curtailing the observational and advisory roles of welfare staff and discipline officers, who might otherwise acquire information about the prisoners' political activities, or gauge their morale. Stringent adherence to their structure also preserved individuals from the problem of potential collaboration, which can occur through what Goffman (1991: 165–66) calls the 'self-defining implications of even the minor give-and-take in organisations', which grants the 'legitimacy of the other's line of action'. As Anna explained, 'you never approached a screw for anything; you always went through your [political] officers'. Winnie added:

It was all a power struggle, even with the welfare coming up, you always went through your OC. She contacted the welfare. You didn't go to the screws to get them. You went to her. She got the screws to get them up. If the governor sent for you, she went in your place to find out what the craic [situation] was. It was to keep that distance from them (Winnie, sentenced prisoner, Armagh).

As discussed in Chapter 2, although the political structures were nominally recognized after the introduction of special category status, the practical implementation of the policy provoked a deep reluctance from senior and uniform staff to confer legitimacy on an alternative authority and rival power structure in prison. Furthermore, staff found it difficult to distinguish between 'regular' and politically motivated insubordination, which reinforced their hostility and suspicion. Respondents who were involved in the initial phase of political organization during the 1970s also argued that their strategies were directed at altering the entrenched, paternalistic ethos of the regime, in the context of extensive administrative problems and the inexperience of staff in dealing with a 'new kind of prisoner' (Meg, internee, Armagh prison):

The screws hadn't a clue, nor indeed did the governor, of how to go about treating us, because we would have never been in except for the political struggle. They were caught unawares, totally unawares. They did not know what to do. So, although there was a conflict because they were trying to maintain a regime that they were used to for years, we were saying, 'no, that won't do, that doesn't suit'. And we were putting continual demand on the regime, which were demands they had to meet, because they didn't know any different [sic] (Eilís, internee, Armagh).

It would have been a real antithesis for most of the governors. They resented having this group of prisoners telling them what to do, how to run a prison. So they were having to get used to the idea as well, having to come to terms with it. Well, they were trying to cope with the situation as well. They had prisoners who were totally new, and they had nobody to look to, either. It was a very testing period when you think about it, and it probably would have been really dead on if political status had been there after '76. They were getting their act together when, next thing, the criminalisation policy came in, and threw everything up in the air (Jennie, sentenced prisoner, Armagh).

According to some respondents, staff acknowledgement for their group was grounded in pragmatism and expedience. Jennie (sentenced prisoner, Armagh) commented that 'it was easier to manage, like what's happening now.[1] It's easier for them to let the prisoners control the situation. It makes the screws' time easier, and easier all round for everybody'.

You had their regime and our regime. But again their external one could only come in where they could keep that in place, you know? You did have situations where there were controls. You had no control over your mail coming in, you had no control over your visitors, because that's a situation that was out of our power. The likes of visits to your relatives [in other prisons] was within their remit. But for the most part, if anything was dramatically wrong, you negotiated the position within the jail. Very often they succumbed a lot [sic]. Even the warders, they would have known who to approach on our own staff, if something happened, whether there was a row between prisoners and a screw. They would have approached our staff and said, 'sort it out'. But they always approached our staff. Officers couldn't override that because it was black and white. This is the way you worked. I mean it was fairly straightforward (Eilís, internee, Armagh).

For some reason the administration … if they saw that working too well they had to come 'round and do something just to stop it. All through the whole struggle and all the protests there were certain ones that we had a working relationship with. They knew the reality of it, because we were going to say to them, 'go and see our OC'. They knew there was no point in coming to see us individually (Winnie, sentenced prisoner, Armagh).

Violence, intimidation and the 'socialization' of staff

Unlike most prisoner populations, political prisoners have substantial external capacity to exert direct and indirect forms of intimidation and violence against staff both within and outside the prison. Since the publication of the Mountbatten Report (1966), a succession of inquiries identified the 'suborning' or 'conditioning' of staff as a significant factor in major escapes or breaches of security (Woodcock 1994; Learmont 1995). In Northern Ireland, the question of safeguarding 'the human dimensions of security' on a day-to-day basis was reinforced by the realities of intimidation and violence by paramilitary organizations against prison officers outside prison establishments. The lethal effect of intimidation by Loyalist and Republican paramilitary organizations was manifested in the assassination of 29 prison officers, including two women, between 1976 and 1993. All except one were killed whilst off-duty, at home, travelling to or from work, or in the vicinity of Belfast and Armagh prisons, whose perimeters were relatively more difficult to secure because they were situated in urban locations. Twenty-seven officers were killed by Republican organizations and two by Loyalists.

The first murder of a prison officer during the 'Troubles' occurred on 8 April 1976, six weeks after special category status was revoked (*Irish News* 9 April 1976). Prior to this, the Provisional IRA had issued warnings to staff recruited from the prison services in Scotland and England and Wales that 'they were setting themselves up as a prize target', stating that, 'until now there has been no hostility by political prisoners or internees towards the men whose job it was to guard them, apart from a few isolated cases' (*Belfast Telegraph* 9 January 1972). PIRA also issued warnings in response to allegations of the mistreatment of prisoners by officers. In 1971 they had threatened to 'shoot a prison wardress [*sic*] who was allegedly ill-treating women political prisoners

159

in Armagh Jail' (*ibid.*). From the early 1970s, Republican and Loyalist prisoners used the sanction of 'naming', or disclosing the names and movements of individual officers to their organizations, or issuing statements alleging mistreatment by specific administrators, as an indirect and extended form of intimidation. In 1973, Republican women prisoners had released the name of a male officer at Armagh prison, a 'Mr Quigley', whom they alleged had been involved in the assault of women prisoners in the aftermath of their attempted escape. This prompted members of the Board of Visitors to condemn 'the mental anguish' caused to the officer and his family, 'especially as he has received threatening letters' (*Irish News* 20 March 1973). Republican women in Armagh prison repeatedly issued public criticisms of one Dr Cole, the medical doctor in attendance at the prison during the no-wash and hunger strikes, in statements smuggled out to supporters and the press. Whilst the 'naming' of individual members of staff did not always result in their being killed, the strategy opened up another set of possibilities for conditioning prison personnel. Eilís argued that use of naming and intimidation was connected with their attempts to resolve specific and intractable contentions about conditions or treatment. Nevertheless, her account also indicates that their appeals to the leverage of external violence, whether intentional or not, were intended to have a deterrent effect on staff aggression:

> There was always the threat of male screws. We didn't want them in but they brought them in after the escape. We may have got hurt, but so did they. And we had to have that underlying threat all the time. If they did anything on us, if they tried to overstep their mark with us, it mightn't be this week, it mightn't be next week, or it mightn't be the month after, but sometime when they weren't expecting it, we moved. The time we captured the governor proved the way that we could move as one, which we did … After criminalisation the prisoners got a much harder time. They also still didn't break their own regime, though. A lot of it was sheer control, random, then you got the conflict, the real power, intense conflict … But that happened in key stages (Eilís, internee, Armagh).

McEvoy (2001: 112) and McKeown (1998: 286) argue that there is no direct or reductive correlation between the levels of staff fatalities and specific incidents of violence between prisoners and staff. According to McEvoy (2001: 112–13), whilst some violence was 'clearly strategic' and directly related to 'the broader conflict between paramilitaries and the

British State', other incidents were inspired by 'the range of institutional, personality, and other variables which could be found in any prison setting.' Nevertheless, the timing of assassinations was clearly a factor in the complex causes of conflict and violence in the prisons. From 1976, the assassination strategy shifted from individual reprisals to pressurizing the authorities to revoke the policy of criminalization. Eight prison officers were killed in the first two years of the criminalization policy, between 1976 and 1978 (NIPS 1978: 9). The highest level of staff fatalities in a single year was in 1979, when nine officers were killed by Republican organizations, during the height of the Blanket protest in the Maze, and the non-cooperation strike at Armagh prison, and the year before the first hunger strike (NIPS 1980: 7). These included the first fatality of a prison officer, Agnes Wallace, who was struck along with three other women officers in a drive-by shooting and grenade attack. The only prison officer to be killed in 1982 was a woman, Elizabeth Chambers, who died on October 7 in an ambush by the Republican splinter group, the Irish National Liberation Army (INLA)[2]. Threats had previously been issued by the Provisionals against Thomas Murtagh, the governor who had been appointed to Armagh prison in 1981, and had been at the forefront of implementing the segregation policy there. Although it is difficult to establish a precise relationship between specific events and the targeting of staff working at Armagh prison, it is clear that the cycle of violence and conflict during the women's prison protests in previous years had created the desire for reprisal on the part of staff and prisoners:

> The only time the staff felt vulnerable was when they put the bomb outside Armagh jail. We heard the bomb go off, and then it came on in the news. Our immediate reaction was, 'Yes!' And everybody said the same thing. And they were raging. Christ they were raging. We used to say, 'it doesn't matter where you are, if we want to get you, we'll get you'. We would use tactics like that. And we always had this conviction that we would win. And we would say that to individuals, 'when we win, you're snookered, 'cos I will hunt you and personally lock you up'. It wasn't a case of it's going to take us years, it was going to be tomorrow (prisoner on protest, Armagh).

> Naturally when things were at a flashpoint outside, when there were shootings and bombings and so on, there was a great upsurge of annoyance and in some instances, animosity. It undoubtedly had an effect, because members of staff also had

family members in the 'Specials' [*sic*] [part-time RUC] and the Royal Irish Regiment. There were individual threats made against warders in the prison. There were allegations from a number of warders. Then again, don't forget that there was one of them shot, and there were attempts made on a couple of them. I was there one day and they were shooting outside and the big deal was to get them home safely, as quickly as possible (official visitor, Armagh).

The killing of prison staff was politically counterproductive. Hillyard (1978: 137) noted that violence against prison officers produced 'far greater unity' amongst staff and afforded greater legitimacy to the Prison Officers' Association (POA) as 'a powerful and influential organisation' which was prepared to challenge the authorities, 'not only in relation to working conditions, but also in relation to the development of policy'. During the 1970s, the POA responded to the murders of colleagues by initiating work-to-rules and applying blanket temporary stoppages on supervising visits, exercise and education, or clearing mail. Although the prison inspectorate described the 'customary practice' of temporary bans 'as a mark of respect ... and not as a protest action' (Home Office 1979: 114), they were also purposeful reminders to the government of the dire consequences if the POA withdrew its co-operation, or if it contemplated a retreat on the criminalization policy.

In the aftermath of the 1981 hunger strike, Republican prisoners embarked on an apparent shift of tactics from random violence against staff to 'breaking down the human contribution to security', by suborning individual officers as preparation for the eventual escape of 38 prisoners from the Maze in 1983. The Hennessey Report (1984: 14) into the incident subsequently noted that 'in this they [Republicans] were largely successful. It seems they began a policy of conditioning staff in order to reduce their alertness. This they did by lowering the tensions ... and avoiding, where possible, confrontations with staff'. In what amounted to a swingeing critique of the poor management of security in the Maze, Hennessey pointed to the inadequate levels of training and supervision that had contributed to lower standards of vigilance, lax habits and poor attitudes amongst ordinary-grade staff prior to the escape. Hennessey was equally categorical in his criticisms of failures in the management of security at the most senior levels which 'fell markedly below an acceptable standard ... at all levels, the quality of managerial control, direction and leadership proved inadequate' (*ibid.*: 47–8). The Colville Report (1992: 7) on Belfast prison identified the continued influence which paramilitary prisoners exercised collectively on staff throughout the 1980s as a major threat to security, concluding that, after eight years of conflict over the integration policy, the 'suborning of staff' remained 'a horrible reality'.

Moen (1999) has argued that the preferred term for staff conditioning amongst Republicans, 'socialization', introduced a broader meaning than the usual, instrumental one, as it reflected their conscious effort to shift the ideological basis of power relations between them and officers. Socialization, he contends, involved the longer-term objective of inculcating officers and administrators into the normality of the prisoners' worldview, attitudes and expectations, by utilizing 'mentoring' or 'advisory' tactics that are normally the province of staff. This included, for example, encouraging individual officers to talk about their morale, working conditions or troubles with management, with the view to gathering valuable information and drawing officers and their confidantes into a shared empathic range. McKeown (2001: 118) described the socialization offensive in terms of alternating tactics of appeasement and orchestrated confrontation towards ordinary and senior staff. Crucially, however, confrontational or physical strategies were not as readily available to women in prison, for whom such 'aggression' and 'subversion' would have led to reprisals. Furthermore, relationships in Armagh prison had seriously deteriorated as the disputes against enforced integration had become interwoven with conflicts over the introduction of random strip searching. As a consequence, the dynamics of socialization in Armagh prison acquired specific, interpersonal dimensions that were shaped by overt conflict.

Socialization as a gendered strategy

The prospect that the personal authority of female prison staff might be subverted because individuals may adopt illegitimate forms of contact with prisoners or relax, at their discretion, elements of security and discipline, has exercised senior administrators since the early penitentiary system. As a consequence, the demeanour and behaviour of discipline officers and staff towards prisoners have been rigorously scrutinized in order to prevent undue familiarity with inmates. However, an internal contradiction in the management and definition of 'appropriate' engagement arises in prison regimes for women because 'familiarity' and 'empathy' between individual prisoners and members of staff are sanctioned and encouraged. Thus, the mechanisms of familiarity are integrated into maintaining order through their 'setting personal example, gaining prisoner's trust and instilling personal loyalty ... in theory, at least, every effort [is] to be made to encourage moral reform by a process that combine[s] an uneasy mix of coercion, encouragement and manipulation' (Zedner 1998: 309). Nevertheless, 'the common assumption that women [are] more susceptible to personal influence' has emerged as a concern which implicates female staff as well as prisoners (*ibid*.). Hence, the meticulous supervision of relations between them has arisen out of a perceived need to renew continuously the lines of demarcation between legitimate intervention and improper or unsafe contact.

For Newton (1994), Lord (1995) and Zimmer (1997), these predicaments are apparent in the different strategies adopted by women officers as they negotiate the gendered occupational structures of the 'guard role'. Excluded from immediate access to the 'traditional' ethos of rule enforcement, and deprived of the legitimacy to present themselves through a grid of masculinist 'authority', 'physical competence' and 'personal dominance', female officers integrate more acceptable 'feminine' roles into their occupational performance. In doing so, they become 'more likely to have a social worker's orientation towards the job', and reinforce personal authority through 'the development of friendly, pleasant relationships with prisoners as a way of generating voluntary compliance' (Zimmer 1997: 291). However, although Zimmer suggests that female custodians might curb their professional power on the basis of mutual recognition as women within structures of institutional authority, prisoners may seek to pursue other alternatives out of this possibility. Republican prisoners adopted strategies for confronting female officers with the extent of gender subordination connected with doing their jobs. May, Winnie and Kathleen explained their tactic of pre-emptively challenging the personal motives of staff conducting strip searches:

> At that stage we had tried to turn it 'round on the screws, because they were using it to get on top of us. We were trying to turn it 'round, and use it by saying, 'you're a woman and you're doing this – you're starting this on another woman?' – portraying it more that way at that time. Because no matter what else had been done in the past, it was suiting them too much, so we were trying to take another line at it. We were told to do it this way, just to try that and see what it would make them feel, as a woman to woman thing. But they didn't. I suppose the ones that were chosen for that job just ... I don't know what type of people they were ... but it didn't change. No matter what line you went with them, they didn't respond (May, sentenced prisoner, Armagh).

Literally, that day of the month when you know your visit's up, you're automatically preparing yourself psychologically that you're going in there for a digging match. You know it's not going to be an easy transition; you're going in there to defend yourself. At one time I stood like that with my hand on my hips and sort of smiled at them and said, 'are ye enjoying yourselves now? I always knew ye were a lot of dykes anyway', and I just put my clothes on and went out on my visit. That was just bravado. Again, a lot of women came back from stripsearching, and it took them a while to psychologically get themselves into gear again (Winnie, sentenced prisoner, Armagh).

I would try to embarrass them with my nakedness. And they hated it. They hated it because we made them feel more uncomfortable with what they did (Kathleen, sentenced prisoner, Maghaberry).

The failure to persuade officers to relinquish authority on the basis of their womanhood attests to the ways in which 'doing gender' and gender solidarity is shaped by, and constrained within, the hierarchical structuring of institutional power (Zimmer 1997: 290–1). In this context, most of the respondents accused female officers of being unlike 'women' because they deviated from conventional constructions of 'feminine' empathy, restraint and 'justice' towards other women. Historically, random strip searching was implemented at a point when routine antagonism had become embedded in the preceding five years of resistance to the criminalization policy. Moreover, in a prison setting, sexual censure and homophobic discourses are complex expressions of actual and potential violation. They produce levels of differentiation by identifying other prisoners or staff who transgress the highly normative sexual and gendered values that are reproduced in prisons. Conversely, accusations of sexual abuse have been conventionally viewed by the authorities as tactics which prisoners use to obstruct staff from inspecting prisoners or from 'patting them down' during routine searches. Censure also assists in reordering a shared moral and ethical value of physical and psychological integrity. In the prisoners' accounts above, the visual objectification of their bodies by other women amounted to an illegitimate transference to female scrutineers of the powers usually naturalized through the hegemonic 'male' gaze. The allegations of collusion by female officers with the dominant gendered, surveillant order assisted in inscribing the otherness of prison officers.

The prisoners' censure also cemented other forms of political and emotional antagonism towards staff, which involved various condemnatory manoeuvres for supporting the transference of moral integrity and political authority from the staff to themselves. Some forms of personal differentiation hinged on routinized forms of bigotry, for example, in the reductive explanation offered by some respondents of the 'mercenary' and 'sectarian' motives of staff:

> Again it all goes down to your self-worth. You knew what you were there for. We weren't there for money, for glory, you're not there for anything else bar your principles, and believing in fighting for your country, which makes a big difference. In retrospect, the screws were there for the money, solely for the money. They were like Judas, they could be bought for money. You couldn't buy us. It was a great time of pride because of that. It was a case of, 'your establishment can throw whatever the hell you want at us, but we're going to take it' (Winnie, sentenced prisoner, Armagh).

Even some external scrutineers tended to endorse elements of this argument. In the words of one member of the Board of Visitors:

> I think that a vast number of the staff went in to gain money. I don't think they really see it ... in fact, I'm quite sure that very few of them get job satisfaction. Because there's nothing, there's no aim for them beyond containment. The political prisoners, because they organise their own day and their own lives, are not institutionalised, and therefore don't rely on the officers for anything ... I would say, some of the officers would certainly hold their own very sectarian attitudes, just formed the same way as the prisoners have, because they're coming from the same background, and the influences that led to the prisoners joining the paramilitaries are still influences in the lives of the officers. There is, dare I say, limited intelligence, but that's a dreadful thing to say (official visitor, Maghaberry).

The provocative nature of these remarks obscures the more substantive structuring of power relations between staff and prisoners. The recruitment of prison staff during and after internment from the armed forces and working-class Protestants had reinstalled the historical, classed and sectarian precedents of drawing communities with Loyalist or Unionist affiliations to the security structures (Farrell 1983). Furthermore, there was a widespread perception amongst ordinary-grade staff that they ultimately had to cope with inconsistencies in the approaches of senior management, as they appeared to alternate between confronting and conciliating paramilitary prisoners. Although an analysis of staff adjustments, their conceptions of their relationships with prisoners, and the sectional and political influence of the POA requires a separate study, some brief observations can be made concerning the structural positioning of lower-ranking officers. The succession of official reports which had pointed to the dangers of conditioning or illegitimate contact with prisoners as a primary contributor to disorder and breaches of security had led to demoralization and resentment amongst staff. Furthermore, the precautions taken by senior management to reduce conditioning by turning the behaviour of officers into objects of security and surveillance contributed to their loss of a sense of professional status. Moreover, the complex lines of exclusion from access to the political groups, and the subsequent loss of personal authority over prisoners were exacerbated by the fact that senior administrators and governors were negotiating directly – 'over our heads' – with the paramilitary factions:

> The reality is that you wouldn't get interaction with paramilitary prisoners because they've their own command structure and they won't recognise you as a prison officer … But it's a known fact that these paramilitary organisations do co-operate very closely in prisons. They work hand in hand. They also co-operate with the officers in their own way. But actually, it's got worse. In the old days, in the compound days, there was a very good relationship. There is no relationship now. The only relationship now is that paramilitary prisoners use officers to condition them for information. And that's another point. If the officer's not there, they can't be conditioned, can they? (male prison officer, Maghaberry)

The claim that prisoners might have voluntarily engaged with staff during the operation of special category status is spurious and contrary to historical fact. However, the reference to the 'old days' before criminalization denotes a kind of nostalgic resistance to the increasingly technocratic demands of doing prison work, as well as the subtler shifts in bargaining power that were taking place as a consequence of the 'normalization' policy. It must be noted, too, that many of the claims and counterclaims of staff and management were connected with the waning influence of the POA over managerial decisions from the late 1980s, and the increasing tendency of senior management to equate staff alienation with their failure to embrace the new managerial climate.

The negative portrayal of most prison officers as a reactionary and obstructionist core, inimical to progress and motivated by sectional interest, had gained currency in surprising quarters by the late 1990s. Moreover, the observations of senior managers, governors and official visitors (members of the Boards of Visitors) sometimes took on an extraordinarily personal character. Senior administrators claimed that the low entry qualifications to basic officer grades were factors in their 'reactionary' attitudes and inability to cope with radical change. For some official visitors, the restriction of their role to mere 'turnkeys' confirmed the belief that ordinary officers were little more than functionaries. Ironically, these views chimed with those of political prisoners, who talked about the 'incompetence' and 'inadequacy' of staff in similar terms. However, their respective interpretations of these same 'facts' also revealed important class and ideological differences. For example, whereas the official visitor patronizingly observed that staff–prisoner conflict was related to their mutual recognition within the same class and social background, prisoners argued that officers had sought to escape these conditions by seeking a privileged position within structures that sustained sectarian inequality and injustices.

In this broader, antagonistic context, Republican prisoners inverted the standard assumptions about the social aptitude, intellectual attainment and organizational competence that usually legitimize the authority of staff:

> They had low levels of education: good with their fists but couldn't string a sentence together. And when they came in to us, we used to cut them to ribbons. And you'd have had an eighteen year old talking to a forty year old as if she was a child, and the forty year old would have taken it because she didn't have the education or the vocabulary to argue back with her! They did feel inferior to us and that's probably why they kicked the crap out of us and enjoyed it so much. It was their way of getting back. We did feel superior to them. No matter what they did, such as bullying or playground tactics, it was like most bullies, they're more to be pitied than laughed at. I think that was my attitude. Some of the other ones would have cut their throats (sentenced prisoner, Armagh).

These critical and personalized comments also constituted a perceptible series of strategies for repositioning themselves as politically aware and conscious subjects of prison order. Eilís argued that the political prisoners were more successful and powerful agents within the custodial environment in so far as their resistance to institutionalization prevented their being conscripted into the various constraints and personal compromises that underlined the 'false consciousness' of staff:

> Their regime could not have coped. Our regime coped because there were a number of things we wanted out of it, and number one was that whole learning process. We wanted to politicise ourselves. At the same time too, it was very personal, we wanted to produce arts and crafts, get exams, whatever. So that's what we put in place (Eilís, internee, Armagh).

> Because at the end of it, they were as much in prison as we were. Where they went was curtailed because the IRA was starting to stiff screws. So there were only certain places they could go, and they knew that those certain places could be attacked, because the IRA knew where they were. It was a case of they could have got them anytime they wanted. In that respect the high rates of pay and all the rest of it, it was as if they were compensating themselves because they couldn't get out of it. It's not like a nine-to-five job. Even within their own communities, being a prison officer is frowned upon. It's not only here [West Belfast], if you're a prison officer you'd be shunned there [East Belfast]. So I think all the trimmings was to try and build themselves up and to build their self-esteem up (sentenced prisoner, Armagh).

Although couched in reductive, demeaning, victimizing and violent terms, the censoriousness levelled by prisoners against staff powerfully conveys the structural dimensions of sectarian and political differences as they intersected with penal and gendered relations. Simultaneously, the concluding and anonymous comments cast some insights into the disturbing realities of anger, fear and conflict that emerge from the intensely personalized domains of penal governance. If, as Pickering (2001) has argued, 'emotionality' is an important way of knowing and understanding the social world, then the prisoners' reactions are valid expressions of subjectivity and resistance. The penal colonization of the emotional domain has predominantly been understood as having invasive and victimizing effects on prisoners. Feminists and Foucauldians, moreover, have pointed out that this is a perverse achievement of the intimate regulation which is endorsed and sustained in the confinement of women. The penal organization of the emotional realm also implicated the well-being, personal integrity and morale of staff. The construction of their emotional fallibility, susceptibility and corruptibility, which had to be guarded against, also implicated them as a primary problem in maintaining 'good order' and security. The long-standing administrative preoccupation with 'conditioning' in the Northern Ireland prison system, then, was primarily informed by a narrow vigilance against possible breaches in security either through the 'failures' and 'weaknesses' of staff, or the intentionally subversive motives of prisoners. Feminist explanations, by contrast, apply a broader concept of 'disobedience' to codify the range of anxieties, transgressions and displacements of normative and clearly defined roles that arise from resistance to voluntary association with prison staff or other 'beneficial' and authorized influences. In this context, the subversion of staff–prisoner relationships was not reducible to a functional or instrumental understanding of 'conditioning'. Rather the transgression of these relationships emerged from the very conditions of controlling and punishing prisoners.

This chapter has explored the social construction and meanings of solidaristic techniques for reversing some elements of the economy of personalized correction that characterizes women's imprisonment. However, in doing so, it has raised some further questions about the limits of such tactics, especially in the light of the capacity for prison punishment to reinstate good order by shifting from disciplinary to coercive strategies. The following chapter examines how this transition was mediated through the bodies of prisoners.

Notes

1 This interview was conducted in 1997.
2 Names taken from the Commemorative Roll of Honour, POA Headquarters and McKittrick *et al.* 1999: 782, 916.

Chapter 9

'Our bodies are weapons of war': a penal dialectic of the body

They used our bodies against us. That's the only thing they had against us was our bodies. I suppose that was a threat too. Not only did they take your freedom away, they actually took the right of your body away. They have a say about that, when you can change, when you can have your clothes on. So you didn't even feel your body was yours (Hanna, sentenced prisoner, Maghaberry).

Throughout the prison campaign women prisoners sought to retain control over their own bodies in the face of discipline, punishment and routinization. As the disputes over criminalization hardened into overt conflict in the prisons, their bodies assumed a central place in the prison struggle. This chapter examines the relationship between the more extreme expressions of corporal resistance, such as the no-wash and hunger strikes, and the direct, physical repression of women prisoners. As Foucault (1980: 56) reminds us, the body is a two-way conduit for forces of domination in that 'after investing itself on the body, [power] finds itself exposed to a counter attack in that same body'. This dual meaning of the self as a 'weapon of war' emerged where women described their bodies as both objects of retribution and as instruments of resistance. The first part of this chapter examines the contradictory and risky implications of women using transgressive strategies in the 'dirty', or no-wash, strike. It then analyses the implementation of 'random' strip searching in the women's prison as a reassertion by the prison administration of its privileged jurisdiction over the bodies of the confined. The final discussion considers the wider meanings of institutionalized sexual violence in pursuit of a conclusion to the insurrection of women prisoners.

The gendered body of prison resistance in Northern Ireland

The idea that prisoners used their bodies symbolically, instrumentally and strategically at different points in their struggle is probably the most extensively discussed aspect of the Northern Ireland prison protests (Coogan 1980; D'arcy 1981; Beresford 1987; O'Malley 1990; Feldman 1991; Campbell *et al.* 1994; Aretxaga 1995). The no-wash and hunger strikes, in particular, dramatized the status of the prisoners' bodies as representative of a historical contest between State oppression and the resilience of the suppressed. According to Feldman (1991: 204) 'each stage of politicisation and ideological attainment [of the prison campaign] corresponded to a radical deconstruction and reassemblage of the body ... new political representations and insights emerged that could be traced directly to the technical ... reorganization of the prisoner's body'. However, the conditions under which women protesters were able to establish a corresponding, radical praxis of the body were more ambiguous. Aretxaga (1995: 125) criticized Feldman's account for belying those 'questions of subjectivity' which are 'not only a product of the disciplines of the body used in prison' but play 'an important part in the excess of violence characterising those disciplines'.

This question of subjectivity as it is analysed in this chapter, then, relates to the particular definitions of disorder that were attached to the women protesters, and were manifested in the methods of corporal punishment that were used against them. It is argued that distinctive forms of punitive closure emerged which reflected the gendered and political anxieties that were provoked by the entry of women on to the stage of prison resistance. Therefore, whilst Feldman connected radical practices of resistance with progressive phases of ideological development amongst men prisoners, questions of punitive and sexual difference have to be brought into consideration to explain how the bodies of resisting women prisoners became signs and instruments of the penal crisis during this period. Furthermore, each point of transition in the women's prison campaign – between reactive containment and criminalization, and later during the period of 'normalization'

– opened up new opportunities for the administration to apply novel and intensified forms of intervention. These included the attempts to erode their political structures through the extended use of individual adjudication and regulation after 1976, the physical and disciplinary containment of prisoners on the no-wash and hunger strikes of 1980, and the enforced submission of remand and sentenced prisoners to compulsory visibility following the introduction of random body-searching in 1982.

The second consideration entails breaking with conceptions of the passive, 'feminized' body in prison, by interpreting the practices of the self deployed by women as examples of their transition from abjection to resistance. However, it is not my intention to make the claim that the bodies of political prisoners were 'authentic' sources of resistance, or representative of the innate defiance of the confined. Instead, the analysis examines the interplay of suppression and resistance that privileged the body as a site of power and conflict.

The origins of the no-wash strike

The incident that triggered the no-wash protest in Armagh prison in 1980 was the sentenced prisoners' refusal to attend disciplinary hearings to find what punishments they had incurred in the course of refusing to conform to the 'convict' regime. This had previously led to a series of confrontations between the (male) governor and the prisoners, and eventually broke out into open conflict when members of staff were ordered to bring prisoners by force to their hearings. However, Winnie and Áine also argued that the underlying cause was their refusal to conform to the codes of personal deference and compliance that normally uphold the prison hierarchy:

> So there was a bit of aggro. We decided that the ones that were put on report would refuse to see the governor. You had to go to the governor; the governor wouldn't go to you. They refused to go to the governor so he had to come up to them … It really went against his grain having to come up, because he had to do the report at the cell door, while you were lying on the bed totally ignoring him. It was a victory for us, because he came up to us, we didn't go down to him. It was this type of 'on-off' all the time, with us trying to get one over on them, and them trying to get one over on us. That was constant (Winnie, sentenced prisoner, Armagh).

173

It was because [the governor] couldn't give way, and we wouldn't go up to see him. That's what I took out of it, because as far as he was concerned we were belittling him by making him come and see us, and he was going to prove differently, so he was! The main thing was his authority was confounded, and his idea of himself was offended, and he was determined to make an example of us, and that was that (Áine, sentenced prisoner, Armagh).

Winnie, who subsequently spent nine months on the no-wash strike before being released from prison, continues:

[A prisoner] took a dose of diarrhoea and had asked the screw to let her out of her cell to empty her chamber pot ... They opened [her] cell door and one of the screws made some crack about she could shit anywhere. So she threw [the contents of the pot] over her. She was immediately put on report. Again, we refused point blank to go and see the governor. If he wanted to adjudicate us, he could come up and do it. So that day we were all standing in 'B1' at the hotplate because the meal was coming up ... We heard the gate opening and thought it was the special category prisoners coming back. But it wasn't, it was the riot squad coming through. We were completely surrounded. They were heaped.[1] We were quite calm, we looked around and thought, 'shit, what's happening here?' One of them grabbed a prisoner, and the place just went berserk (Winnie, sentenced prisoner, Armagh).

We were all locked in the Association Room, and they took out the ones that had to be adjudicated. They trailed each one of us into the governor, and held her steady in front of the governor while he read out what he had awarded her – a month's lost remission and all this crap, and then took them out and threw them in the ante-cells in 'B1'. So, there was absolute murder. Everybody that was taken out was filed into a room and searched with a male screw standing at the door. They said they were looking for uniforms [of the PIRA]. The whole point of them coming in was to bring the five or six prisoners that had to be adjudicated in front of the governor. That's what instigated it (*ibid.*).

When we got out for exercise, four of us at a time, we found the bathrooms locked. You had full chamber pots, nowhere to wash yourself. So one of us went down to Mairéad [Farrell] and she said to us, 'chuck it down the wing'. And that's how the no-wash protest started in Armagh (*ibid.*).

Excremental resistance: the gendered politics of dirt and protest

A central aspect of rehabilitating women involves cultivating normative aspects of femininity in prisoners who are deemed to have lapsed from that category. In this sense, prison discipline still plays a residual moral function in inculcating cleanliness, discipline and self-improvement in its inmates. At the same time, the practical struggle to maintain personal hygiene and self-care is denied because of the multifaceted invasions of privacy in a prison setting. Even before the protest, these problems had been compounded in Armagh prison by overcrowding, the deteriorated and insanitary conditions of the institution, the degrading daily process of slopping out and the inadequate washing and laundry facilities. Additionally, the government argued that the no-wash protest warranted the special measures of monitoring the prison on public health grounds, disinfecting and steam cleaning the soiled cells, and isolating the protesters because they constituted an 'unacceptable health hazard to other inmates, staff [and] the community' (*Commons Written Answers* 19 December 1980: 341–2). For the women on the no-wash protest, the loss of access to sanitation and opportunities to maintain basic bodily care created significant personal stresses. As Winnie explains, this did not just involve risking physical and psychological disintegration, but also profound alienation from their bodies and the forfeiture of standards of self-care which they connected with their identity as women:

> The first time I actually had to spread my own excreta on the wall, I cried, because it was debasing. I was thinking, 'Mother of God, what the hell am I doing?' It was like most things, you sort of pull yourself out … you're doing it because you've been put into it. You didn't ask to be put into that situation, you've been put into this situation, make the best of it. But like most things, the human spirit is phenomenal at blocking things out, and accepting things as normal … it's not that you accepted it as normal, you just accepted it. It had to be done, and that was your choice. If you didn't accept it, you went. You came off protest [*sic*]. It wasn't even the consequences. The way I looked at it, I had gone through two and a half years or so of a system trying to knock the crap out of me. And because this had escalated, if I had given in the system would have won. To me that's what it came down to. Call it sheer stubbornness or whatever, but there was no way the system was going to beat me (Winnie, sentenced prisoner, Armagh).

We used to write stories and read them out. They would have been passed around the wing. Literally anything to keep you sane, because if you're sitting in a cell that's twelve by six, with another human being, and that space is crawling from floor to ceiling in excreta, and it's dark brown, it's like being in a coffin. There's no light getting in because the windows are boarded up, and it's just like being buried alive. So you have to do something to keep yourself sane (*ibid.*).

Practices of deliberate self-neglect are part of the repertoire of prison protests generally, alongside strip strikes and hunger strikes, violence and environmental destruction, although these more extreme forms of protest are uncommon amongst women. Prisoners also use less visible methods for obstructing the jurisdiction of prison regimes over their bodies, such as self-mutilation and suicide, drug abuse and non-cooperation with welfare or clinical staff. These are generally related to prison-induced stress, and they may not necessarily be directly motivated by protest. However, whilst they invoke different levels of compassion and institutional support, responses to them tend to alternate between punishment for 'anti-social' behaviour or pathologization and psychiatric labelling, and sometimes involve both (Sim 1990; Leibling 1992). As seen in Chapter 2, the women's protests were defined by a nexus of disciplinary and medical discourses which distinguished between the 'genuinely unfit' prisoners who merited official clemency and the recalcitrants who presented their 'self-inflicted' conditions. By 1980, Republican prisoners on the no-wash strike were alleging that they were being routinely denied access to medical facilities on the grounds that they had rescinded their normal entitlements as long as they remained on their protest:

When we were on the no-wash we were all checked. Well, not checked; the doctor looked into the cell and went out again. We were all designated as being fit during the protest. Before no-wash, you were called once a month to be weighed. There was no blood pressure taken or anything like that. But when we went on the no-wash there was nothing. Say for instance your menstrual cycle. They took the towels and things out of the boxes and just lobbed them into the cell. This meant, because they weren't in the boxes, if there was urine or anything on the floor, it was defunct, you couldn't use it a lot of the time. There was no medical care at all. It was to see if they could break us (Winnie, sentenced prisoner, Armagh).

As Sim (1990: 164) has indicated, the apparently incompatible relationship between neglecting the clinical needs of women prisoners, and the hyper-pathologization of the troublesome few, emerges from the interlocked parameters of 'security and control on the one hand and the psychiatrization of women's behaviour on the other, [which are] dominant pivots in the regimes designed for women prisoners'. Two prisoners left the no-wash strike on health grounds and transferred to the 'non-political' wings. Úna Nelis later alleged that she was harassed and intimidated by prison officers (*Irish News*, 9 April 1980). Pauline McLaughlin, who had been on protest since her imprisonment in 1976, left the strike in the summer of 1980. McLaughlin, who was 23 years old, and had anorexia and claustrophobia, subsequently suffered a heart attack in Armagh prison on 27 October 1980. She was returned to the jail from Musgrave Park Military Hospital to resume her sentence as an 'ordinary' prisoner. According to her supporters:

despite her poor health, she [had] continued her no-wash protest and as a result, doctors and medical staff at Armagh refused to give her any medical aid. When it became clear to the doctor at the prison that Pauline, who was unable to keep any food in her stomach, was gravely ill, or unfit for work or punishment … she automatically regained her right to medical treatment, a weekly visit and a food parcel *without giving up her protest* (*Irish Press* 1 November 1980, emphasis added).

The apparently ambiguous detail that McLaughlin recommenced a sole protest whilst separated from the strike proper is consistent with Republican claims that those prisoners who left the strike were still part of the prison campaign and that they continued to offer moral support to their peers. However, it also points to the localized official accommodations that were being made to ensure that any sign of desistance could be claimed as evidence that the majority of prisoners were conforming. For example, the fact that prisoners on the 'ordinary' wings were not fouling their cells was frequently cited as evidence that they were conforming, despite the fact that many Republican remand prisoners there actively supported the strikers:

No disrespect to the women who had come off protest, but the administration seemed to look on them as if they had broken them. They hadn't really, it was just through family things and health reasons, different reasons, the women had to come off. But there was a sense that [the administration] were trying to hold these people up to you as a role model. Like, 'if you're good, this is what you can get', trying to discourage you at all from having any participation in the prison struggle. That was what they were trying to do, to criminalize you (Elizabeth, remand prisoner, Armagh/commanding officer, Maghaberry).

Furthermore, those who continued with the protest were motivated by immediate and pragmatic considerations:

Even had it crossed my mind to come off protest, the smug look on the screws' faces would have stopped me right away. Because there was a couple of girls came off the protest, and the verbal abuse they got from the screws, 'you're only ordinary criminals now', that sort of thing. I think with a lot of the women there, the harder you hit them, the more they came back. It was a case of showing them that they hadn't got one up on you. Fair enough, they'd give you a beating and all that, but you'd recover from it and still be where you were, because they weren't going to get you off that protest (Winnie, sentenced prisoner, Armagh).

Amongst the compelling images of daily life on the no-wash protest is a smuggled photograph of Mairéad Farrell, who led the strike as PIRA commanding officer in Armagh prison. Farrell is depicted standing in her cell beside an iron bed. The walls behind her are streaked with arcs of dried excrement, which form a backdrop to her blurred figure and indistinct facial features. This image is a composite representation of the symbolic and material presence of dirty and polluting substances that summon up a variety of social fears. As anthropologists and historians have pointed out, discourses of social hygiene have had long-standing connections with cleaning up, or eradicating 'contaminating' forms of contact with racial, classed and gendered 'others' (Douglas 1984). Similarly, notions of 'purity' have historically supported the idealization of women in the bourgeois domestic sphere as the crucible of moral and environmental order against a rising tide of social decay (Hoy 1996). The revival of 'polluting' discourses in various commentaries on the strike reinvigorated historical anxieties over the 'dirty Irish' and reinforced them with a horror of women's secreting bodies. Such analogies were seized upon by the right-wing London press in their descriptions of the Armagh women as 'the effluent brigade which has tried to prove something or other for Mother Ireland … by sitting in its own excrement' (*Daily Telegraph* 27 August 1980).

In one sense, the strike succeeded in drawing the other occupants of the prison into the prisoners' world of degradation. However, it failed to bring the prison to an operational standstill. Specialist teams of male prison officers equipped with protective 'space suits' and using steam-cleaning equipment were drafted in from the Maze to clean the dirty cells. The NIO also issued denials that male 'Loyalist orderlies' had been given extra remission to clean and maintain the Republican wings in Armagh, stating that they were selected because they 'were willing to do the work, are considered suitable for it, and for no other reason' (*Irish News* 9 September 1980). A former official visitor who mediated between the prisoners and authorities observed the incomprehension and revulsion which the women's strike provoked:

> The staff just couldn't understand how women messed up themselves like that. To the female staff it was just beyond understanding. The men certainly didn't want to clean up the mess. The women, as women, couldn't understand it. The men had to clean it up, because they had to scrape and paint the walls [and] had a rota to do so many cells at a time (official visitor, Armagh prison).

Whereas the 'Blanket men' and the male hunger strikers converted the stigma of defilement into a narrative of endurance (O'Malley 1990; Feldman 1991), the women's no-wash protest was discredited because it transgressed codes of feminine propriety. As the anthropologist, Mary Douglas (1984), has pointed out, the cultural values assigned to 'clean' and 'unclean' objects, and the ordering of pure and tabooed spheres, are designated in specifically gendered terms. Even in the political and humanitarian interventions on the prisoners' behalf, the legitimacy of their protest was subjected to different interpretations about the character and meaning of the *women's* strategy of degradation. From the prisoners' perspective, their extreme form of protest connected the denial of their political rights with the sexual and physical humiliation produced by the conditions of criminalization. On the other hand, their involvement in degrading practices also played out the ambiguity noted by feminist analysts of political conflict (Stiglmayer 1994; Jamieson 1998) that the idealization of the 'nation' in patriarchal political culture is invested in the bodily and sexual sanctity of women. Furthermore, as Meg points out, the women prisoners were conscious of these possibilities for redefining the paradigms of 'clemency' and humanitarian intervention, mobilizing public outrage and drawing politicians and the prison administration into negotiations:

Men are expected to go to jail, men are expected to fight, men are expected to die, men are expected to get battered. But when a woman does this, it's something different. *So everybody uses that.* I always think that people in the struggle use that also, I mean, 'our women are being treated like this'. On the other hand, the oppressors could say they'll take it easier on the women as a concession (Meg, internee, Armagh, emphasis in original).

Aretxaga (1995: 144–5) asserts that the women's no-wash and hunger strikes failed to achieve commensurate status with the protests in the Maze because they placed demands on their supporters to reconcile these cultural and political contradictions. She adds, 'despite the shared political consciousness and goals of men and women prisoners, their protests had [a] different significance. While the men's protest was articulated through an intense dynamic of violence, the women's protest was crystallized around the meaning of sexual difference'. Although my analysis departs from the suggestion that the women's protests did not entail a significant dynamic of violence, the distinction that she draws between 'sexual difference' and 'intense ... violence' reveals the wider disengagement of sexual humiliation from definitions of institutional violence. There are no equivalent accounts from Armagh of the experiences of male prisoners 'on the Blanket' who were subjected to enforced antiseptic baths, or the use of the 'mirror-squat', where they were forced to squat over mirrors so their rectal cavities could be examined, nor of the (illegal) use of body-cavity searches with fingers or implements and the beating of their genitalia during these procedures (Campbell *et al.* 1994: 53–91, 215). Nevertheless, the persistent implication in academic and 'popular' accounts that women prisoners did not undergo comparable levels of mistreatment with men played a part in converting their experiences from being regarded as an issue of institutional violence into a question of sexual, and gender-specific, violation. Even sympathetic commentators such as Tim Pat Coogan, then editor of the *Irish Press*, the Republican-leaning Dublin newspaper, identified the outrage that was being visited on Irish womanhood as the most manifest element of the women's protest:

The 'dirty protest' is bad enough to contemplate when men are on it, but it becomes even worse when it is embarked on by women, who, apart from the psychological and hygienic pressures which this type of protest generates, also have the effects of the menstrual cycle to contend with (Coogan 1980: 114).

The women's no-wash protest was constantly beset with the problem of being overshadowed by the Blanket protest at the Maze. In part, this was because the symbolic and instrumental effects of the Blanket protest were not immediately transferable to the no-wash protest, and in part because of gender-specific and culturally embedded prohibitions that surrounded the acceptable use by women of their bodies and sexualities both publicly and politically. Yet, these social prohibitions were also catalysts for articulating underlying doubts about the *political* legitimacy of the women's protest. The no-wash strike ceased to be explicable only in terms of straightforward State repression once the women's fight for representation revealed more ambiguous layers of marginality and exclusion which implicated their own movement and supporters. This introduced opportunities for the authorities to play on the illegitimacy of the Republican campaign by representing the Armagh protest as hysterical, attention-seeking, trivial, and an unnecessary distraction from the principal drama being played out in the Maze. The generalized inadmissibility of the women's protest, of which public bafflement and Republican discomfiture were symptoms, was encapsulated in the contention of one observer that all they had achieved was a dubious equality in degradation:

> There was a lot of one-upmanship in it. It was a matter of, 'anything you can do we can do better'. It didn't amount to very much. It didn't have much effect, it didn't last very long, and it didn't have any real objective or purpose, in a sense. I thought at the time that it was just a gesture … the main gesture was *to* the Republican movement.

> I appreciate what the women were endeavouring to do, to get the rights to wear their own clothes and other things. When I met Humphrey Atkins I made sure that he was clear that the women were looking for equality of treatment with men. But some were more equal than others.

> I don't think the Republican movement considered the women at all. Their [the women's] decision was inverted snobbery. The women went on and tried to do more than the men, when they already had the conditions to a large extent. But it was complicated by the fact that they wanted recognition for all the political prisoners. It was a mixture of the misunderstanding by the authorities that they let the thing develop, because they gave

political status and then they withdrew it (official visitor, Armagh, emphasis in original).

Strip searching: remoralizing the unruly body

The rest of this chapter discusses the continued centrality of controlling the bodies of women to the project of reconstructing prison order after the no-wash and hunger strikes. It argues that the transition from conflict to 'normalization' from the early 1980s and into the 1990s coincided with the introduction of penal techniques for re-establishing surveillant and disciplinary access to women prisoners. As discussed in Chapter 2, conflict resumed in the Maze in 1982 over accusations that the gains of the 1981 hunger strike were being reneged on and the phasing in of the 'integration' policy. The transition from overt conflict to the period of bureaucratic-administrative normalization created a distinctive shift in governance in the prisons. As Gormally and McEvoy (1995) and McEvoy (2001) argue, 'normalization' entailed an ambiguous and administratively defined redirection of penal policy towards managerialism and conflict reduction. Rather than neutralizing the organizational capacity of political prisoners, however, 'normalization' at best shifted the basis of contention on to legalistic and bureaucratic grounds (Rolston and Tomlinson 1988), and at worst advanced an equally antagonistic climate of disruption and organized violence over the issues of segregation and enhanced security into the 1990s (McKeown 2001).

Nevertheless, if the period of stark physical resistance and coercion appeared to have reached a critical turning point with the conclusion of the hunger strike in the Maze, the introduction of random strip searching in Armagh prison 13 months later led to a resumption of intensified conflict there. Prison governance developed in a different direction in Armagh prison because the use of strip searching between 1982 and 1986 brought to the fore a renewed focus on controlling the unruly bodies of women prisoners. Elizabeth, who was a remand prisoner at Armagh before becoming PIRA commanding officer at Maghaberry, analysed the use of strip searching in terms of a remoralizing and redisciplining turn in penal governance, and as a surrogate method of containment. She argued that the initial introduction of random strip searching for remands in Armagh, and at the male prisons of Magilligan and Belfast, was an attempt to divert attention from the Maze to the more vulnerable 'margins' of the political prisoner population. These observations are consistent with the official determination at the time to prevent the renewed influence of the political structures in the prisons.

The female prisoner population had begun to rise as a consequence of the widespread civil disorder and increased recruitment to the PIRA during the 1981 hunger strike, and with the increased numbers of defendants remanded on the evidence of 'supergrass' witnesses:

After the hunger strikes ended, there was a conscious decision taken by the prisoners to go into the system, for to try and break the system down. That was where you seen, I think, almost the parting of the ways between the way they treated the men and the way they treated the women. A major factor was the governor. He introduced strip searching and forced integration. I think that at that stage, there were only 24 of us, and they felt that they couldn't do it with the men because they were too many. And you see, they had this thing too – because they brutalized those men so much and they let ten of them die – those prisoners were now going to get out on to the wings. And they knew that those prisoners weren't going to forget that. Therefore, I think they started panicking a wee bit in the 'Kesh, that they had to give some concessions to keep the men quiet, or whatever. Whereas, they did the opposite in Armagh – a stark contrast, you know. They started being actually more brutal, with the strip searching, and the fact that they started the strip searching on the remand prisoners. Because at that stage you had a lot of remand prisoners in on supergrass evidence, you had a bigger number of prisoners on remand than there had been in a long time. Also, it was like the pound of flesh, 'we have yet to change things in the 'Blocks, but we can still get in here and come down hard on them'.[2] I think it was just part of their policy, coming down hard on the remands at that stage. They had done it with the sentenced prisoners for years, now they were starting on the remands. They appear to have taken the decision at that stage [that], 'we're not going to break these people. These ones that have already been here have been through this hunger strike, maybe we should start on the new ones' (Elizabeth, commanding officer, Maghaberry).

They came down hard on the ones they thought were vulnerable. Their idea was that from now on these were going to be the showcase regimes. They had this plan later on with Maghaberry. They'd lost the 'Kesh, and they thought if they worked a bit at us, they could still break the women. Then they could show people, 'look how these prisoners can all mix together, integrated'. They seen normalization as a twofold thing, as a punitive thing for the outside: 'if you're going to come into jail, don't think you're going to get it easy', and also in the sense of trying to reform you, trying to integrate you back into society again. Not that they ever did anything to try and do that – anything positive – it was all the negative side of it. I think by this stage the whole administration was of the view that they didn't know what to do. They didn't know how to cope with prisoners coming off this no-wash (*ibid.*).

Strip searching: engendering State violence

All the prisoners who spoke about the experience of being strip searched considered the practice to be a defining example of State violence against women in prison. Whilst the compulsory exposure of their bodies was unambiguously connected to sexual domination, its timing, conflictual context and the zeal for implementing it led prisoners to place strip searching firmly in the sphere of political retribution and deterrence. The irony of the claim that the practice enhanced safety and reduced violence in the prisons did not elude the prisoners. Rather, many considered that their resistance to strip searching to be the critical moment in which the women's bodies were placed on the frontline in the wider struggle against coercion across the prisons. Moreover, in describing the mass strip search of women prisoners at Maghaberry in 1992 as 'rape', Kathleen also pointed to the multiple dimensions of bodily invasion as a 'symptom' and 'consequence' of institutional repression and gender subordination:

I connect strip searching to the struggle in the prisons which in essence was won by ourselves through the hunger strike. Because for the first time the whole world knew what was happening in the North of Ireland, and they knew what was going on in the jails, and the hunger strike was the culmination of all that. It was an unfortunate process where people had no other choice, and you could rationalize that and put it into a clear context, and with strip searching, I can also do the same. Because our struggle was also a part of the prisoners' demands, and they knew they were going to be met, and they [the prison administration] knew that they were losing that power as such. In that context they then introduced strip searching and that had the same effect. They were hoping that it would be done in such a subtle fashion, in the backdrop of all the other stuff that seemed to have a priority. Strip searching was kind of slipped in there, out of the blue ... I would say strip searching is a symptom or a consequence of their overall policy, but it doesn't make it any easier for me as a person to accept strip searching as such. You know having all the rationalizations doesn't ease the pain of being abused and humiliated in that context (Kathleen, sentenced prisoner, Maghaberry).

I've always viewed rape as a violent act rather than a sexual one. It's the ultimate act of violence, 'cos it's all about power and control. You know, it's not about fucking ejaculation, it's all about power, and control and containment. And revenge. We were getting penalized for being political women, first and foremost. That's what that was about. And the aftermath was all about being penalized, and that mostly because we had the audacity to resist … It's the ultimate weapon they have against us. You see a group of women who are extremely strong, highly politically motivated, highly personally motivated, and it's a way of containment, just a way to remind us that they have the power and control. It's got fuck all to do with security (*ibid.*).

Kathleen's comments powerfully convey the collision of the State, sexual violence, penal power and the bodies of confined women. This relationship exemplifies the long-standing feminist critique of the institutionalization of violence against women. Feminist theories of the State have sought to dismantle its idealization as an autonomous, abstracted and rational entity by moving towards an analysis of it as a strategic actor in mediating power relations, including gender relations (MacKinnon 1989; Pateman 1989). Although 'the State' and 'gender' are systematic, although not corresponding, structures, feminist theory has revealed how gendered relations are partly constituted in the realms of the law and the criminal justice system, and welfare, economic and social structures. An alternative approach has centred on the dual role of the State as a strategic actor in perpetuating violence against women, both by failing to intervene in crimes of violence against women as well as through the direct involvement of its agents in inflicting violence. Crawley (2000: 92) summarizes the argument: 'The State … plays a critical role in instigating and perpetuating violence against women through both its own acts of political repression and through condoning and/or failing to prevent the patriarchal oppression of women.'

Crawley further argues that the failure or refusal by the State to act in preventing violence 'is equivalent to' the commission of an act of violence 'because, in its failure to respond, the State gives the abuser freedom to act with impunity' (*ibid.*: 99). This draws together those direct and indirect roles which define the culpability of the State in terms of authorizing or licensing frameworks which may develop, tacitly or otherwise, alongside more active forms of official violence. The analysis, then, becomes concerned with revealing the distancing processes and justificatory positions which hold that abuse or violence arises from localized and unauthorized malpractice on the part of elements within police, security or penal services, and cannot be equated with the actions of the State. Furthermore, these arguments are concerned with establishing a language of accountability in the context of systematic institutional secrecy and the protection of public servants. A central objective of the feminist criminological project entails dispelling the climate of disbelief which surrounds violence against women across both 'public' and 'private' institutional domains. As Arbour (1996) and Shaw (2000) have also shown, the official silences that surround incidents of violence against women in prisons are facilitated by the construction of institutional 'privacy' in terms of 'internal' matters that are deemed to be beyond admissible public concern, and which in turn reinforce low levels of accountability.

Feminist theory has been concerned with the institutionalization of gendered power and sexual violence since radical feminists proposed that they are central organizing instruments of male domination, supported by the State's policies and practices (MacKinnon 1989). Brownmiller's (1974) argument that sexual violence is a structured dimension of political conflict has influenced the growing literature on the gendering of violence and war (Stiglmayer 1994; Jacobs *et al.* 2000). Central to this literature is a critical concern with the reification of the bodies of women in the reproduction of power relations, both across social structures and within institutional organizations. The claim is not being made here that there is a critical consensus amongst feminists on the convergence of gender, violence and political power, nor that these complex relations are believed to be reducible to each other. However, it is suggested that the occurrence of strip searching and the meanings of sexual violation that were articulated by prisoners were not divorced from the psychological, emotional, physical and other violences that are legitimized by assumptions about access to the bodies of women in confinement. Neither could the normalization of these practices, nor their gendered meanings, be separated from institutionalized State violence during the political conflict in Northern Ireland.

Notes

1 Armed with batons and shields and in full protective clothing.
2 The 'Kesh or the 'Blocks were vernacular names for Long Kesh and the H-Blocks/Maze prison respectively.

Chapter 10

'Working within the system': resistance in the context of 'normalization', 1986–98

The mission statement is to maintain a prison system of a high standard, with an appropriate balance being struck between the needs of security and control and the desirability of forward-looking regimes which give prisoners the opportunity to prepare themselves to resettle successfully in the outside world. At the same time there is an obligation on the authorities to increase the efficiency and effectiveness with which the Prison Service meets its objectives (NIPS 1987: 1).

The new strategy of empowerment softens disciplinary power while reinforcing it (Hannah-Moffat 2001: 176).

The final phase of prison administration during the 'Troubles', between the 1980s and the Belfast Agreement (1998), saw the development of policies that were intended to normalize relations between the prison authorities and political prisoners. As we have seen, this was advanced by four interconnecting developments: the management of the abnormal conditions of political imprisonment through the application of managerial and technocratic solutions; a programme of prison building and reforms (HMP Maghaberry opened during this time); placing a greater emphasis on public accountability and transparency, including greater operational efficiency and cost consciousness; and encouraging inmate participation. Yet, whilst these initiatives were officially represented as a framework for achieving the 'end of conflict' in the prisons, they were far from being politically neutral or lacking in administrative intrigue. Rather, the implementation of prison reforms came to reflect a different paradigm in which 'strategic plans, aims, and objectives became expressions of the battleground upon which the prison authorities *chose either to resist or engage constructively with prisoners* ... they did not remove the underlying struggles' (McEvoy 2001: 280, emphasis added). Nevertheless, McEvoy's point is that the managerialist approach to 'normalization' was not devoid of progressive changes that contributed to the relatively bloodless resolution of conflict in prison in the 1990s. However, very few of these new initiatives brought a significant material improvement to women's prison regimes. Furthermore, it is clear from the very terms of these objectives that women prisoners did not feature in the grand design of prison policy as meriting specific arrangements that would make issues such as pre-release training, compassionate leave, parole and other conditions relevant to their needs. Neither were they imagined to be active participants in the processes of direct or constructive engagement between prisoners and the administration.

Instead, 'normalization', in so far as it altered the conditions of women's imprisonment, saw the reconfiguration of prison relations around three newly articulated tenets of managerialism, which were *responsibility*, *resources* and *rights*. 'Responsibility' referred to the strategy of channelling prisoners' energies into personal development and engaging them in the enterprise of successfully managing their confinement and preparing for their eventual release. This objective was connected to processes of individualization in holding out to political prisoners the objectionable option, as far as they saw it, of participating in a rehabilitative relationship which required them to submit to professional and official evaluation, accept criminal culpability and distance themselves from their affiliates in prison. But if the shift in emphasis on to the personalized consequences of imprisonment reinforced the lot of women prisoners in narrowly defined, pastoral terms, it also displaced them from the realities of politics and gender which were integral to their lives inside and beyond prison. Few, if any, of the new programmes addressed women's specific custodial needs and problems, their roles as mothers and partners (although still imprisoned), or appropriately prepared them to become workers, citizens or activists in the communities to which they were to return.

The second pretext for conflict centred on women prisoners' secondary position in accessing resources and practical supports for achieving the developmental goals which had been presented as part of the new settlement. Whereas the marginality of women prisoners in planning and provision had been the basis of previous confrontations, it was reinforced by the priorities of cost-effectiveness which were consistent with the new ethos of managerial efficiency. The issue of resources established the conditions for prisoners to exploit contradictions in managerialist aspirations at two levels. First, the issue revealed a clash in the respective interpretations of officials and prisoners as to what self-development should amount to and achieve. Secondly, it reflected an official determination to minimize the opportunities for prisoners to exploit any new arrangements for 'political' purposes.

The inferior facilities and resources available to women prisoners prompted the Republicans to sue the prison service for entitlements in line with men prisoners. Paradoxically, the litigation strategy reflected the kind of self-interested entrepreneurialism that ought to have been endorsed within the neoliberal framework of prison governance in the 1990s. However, this ideal type of prisoner became less palatable to the authorities when prisoners exercised these rights 'inappropriately' and to the detriment of 'fairness' and discipline. Moreover, the negative reactions to the prisoners' goals of pursuing their 'rights' revealed a further contradiction in official penal discourse as prison administrators reacted to their claims as the tactics of vexatious, self-seeking and subversive women. However, the conflictual implications of the new penal governance must first be set in its theoretical context.

Governmentality and new managerialism in the Northern Ireland prison system

Contemporary theories of governance are concerned with the expansive character of social controls and the opportunities they present for deepening the regulation of individuals. These formations are thought to occur through matrices of State and non-State modes of governing, and centre on the governed subject as a complex social agent, bound within a multitude of economic, social, legal and personal freedoms and constraints (Miller and Rose 1990). Alongside this development, largely influenced by Foucault's theory of governmentality, has been an emphasis on government as the production of prolific networks of power and knowledge which may be directly or tangentially connected with the activities of State agencies. In this context, 'government' has come to describe the 'conduct of conduct' or the 'practices, techniques and rationalities involved in the calculated shaping of human capabilities and structuring the field of possible actions' (Dean 1996: 47).

Critical governance, or 'governmentality', theory has emerged alongside, and contested, the rise of neoliberal ideals of the market state, individual entrepreneurialism, personal responsibility and 'the free exercise of personal choice amongst a variety of options' (Miller and Rose 1990: 24). These rationalities have extensively influenced the field of penology. First, they refer to the primacy of risk-management and the reduction of 'criminogenic' contamination in the prison system, or other criminal justice fields, and involve 'techniques for identifying, classifying, and managing groups according to dangerousness' (Feeley and Simon 1994: 173). Secondly, organizational, resourcing and administrative relations within criminal justice agencies have been subordinated to a free-market paradigm (Garland 1997). This has been significantly aligned, post-Woolf (1991), to a reductive emphasis on fiscal discipline, resource management and performance targets as measures of competent penal governance. Thirdly, contemporary social policy has been concerned with replacing 'passive' and dependent relations between individuals and social providers with consumerist and clientilist bonds. In prisons, this has been reflected in a departure from therapeutic or welfarist models to regimes which encourage prisoners to 'actualise their own reform' (Garland 1997: 191). Such methods direct prisoners towards 'sentence management' programmes and techniques for 'empowering' them to examine their past criminal behaviour and attitudes towards authority, and motivating them to exercise 'responsible' life-choices and learn to govern themselves as preparation for release. The ultimate goal of this enterprise is to produce 'the self-confining, prudent individual whose behaviour is aligned with the goals of the prison authorities' (*ibid.*: 192).

Without minimizing the significance of governmentality theory to penal analysis, it is important to note that it has largely been used to identify a denser meshing, if not a near-totalizing paradigm of regulation and discipline. However, government is also characterized by the irregularities and limits which its very complexity produces, as the practical implementation of policy is often informed by unintentional and unexpected outcomes, financial constraints and sectional conflicts of interest (Dean 1996: 65). In this context, political programmes are 'rarely implanted unscathed, and are seldom judged to have achieved what they set out to do. Whilst "governmentality" is eternally optimistic, "government" is a congenitally failing operation' (Miller and Rose 1990: 10). Some further caveats are also relevant. A central tenet of governmentality theory involves the assumption that disciplinary power has been refined from the raw and immediate enforcement of rule or ideological inculcation to extenuated and indirect practices, or what Garland (1996) called 'government at a distance'. Not only has this been disproved by the persistence of institutional coercion in prisons, but as Garland (2001) later argued, the sovereign role of the State has not receded in the realms of law enforcement and punishment but produced and sustained new regimes of rule. The approach also largely assumes the uncontested expansion of governing discourses without reference to the role of resistance or other 'adverse' or 'negative' responses from prisoners as constituent elements in the development of new initiatives in the first place. Thus, the importance of prisoner resistance to the development of new governing strategies, as well as the penological understanding of imprisonment (political or otherwise) as a site of contested legitimacy, needs to be foregrounded.

Feminist criminological theory adds some additional nuances to this scenario. In an environment which allocates a privileged place to the values of close regulation, self-management and 'responsibilization' (Garland 1996), women are, or are expected to be, exemplary self-governing citizens and highly self-surveilling with respect to various norms of 'femininity'. Arguably, too, the innovation of subjective techniques and imperatives in the service of inducing personal responsibility reflects a continuation of the forms of close governance which theorists of women's imprisonment have observed since the inception of the penitentiary. As Hannah-Moffat (2001: 163) comments:

> changes in contemporary penality cannot be viewed in isolation from past strategies of governing. We can combine past analyses of penal discipline with the more recent accounts of neo-liberal strategies of governing to demonstrate changes in penality, and to enhance our understanding of the interrelatedness and interdependence of various strategies and logics of punishments.

A further point highlights the implications of these developments for women political prisoners. Because of the nature of their convictions and their construction as exceptional to criminal and gendered norms, female political prisoners were not readily identifiable as the passive, needy or socially harmed women of penal discourse who usually represent the most eligible subjects for penal intervention and rehabilitation. This is not to say that women political prisoners were beyond the reach of 'mainstream' correctional imperatives, nor that their political organization immunized them from their influence. Instead, their self-exclusion and insistence on their political standing were key factors in labelling them as impediments to the viability of prison reform in Northern Ireland more generally. In this context, the official objectives became focused on removing the obstructions which had been put in place, either by the prison system or by prisoners themselves, which prevented individuals from embracing 'consensual' and 'voluntaristic' forms of engagement with the prison regime.

Responsibilizing women political prisoners: Mourne House, HMP Maghaberry

The precise timing of the introduction of 'normalization' is subject to some debate when women prisoners are brought into the framework. Whereas the official claim to a new direction in penal policy was announced as early as 1982, the implementation of 'normalizing' policies was contested by prisoners up to and beyond the early 1990s. McKeown (2001: 155–9) argued that its effectiveness in the Maze prison was also reliant on the strategy of 'constructive engagement' adopted by Republican prisoners after 1987. With the exception of enhanced security, none of the 'progressive' elements of the new policy were implemented with regard to women until the move to Mourne House in 1986, at the earliest.

A turning point for fostering 'participation' was reached in 1988, following the introduction of a series of pre-release and home leave schemes for prisoners in their last year of sentence. These were increasingly taken up by political prisoners (NIPS 1992: 2), who had boycotted similar programmes since the 1970s. Working-out schemes were also introduced in the same year for life-sentence prisoners on the last nine months of their sentence. Prisoners had to 'progress through' programmes with the prison education department and probation service before their licence was granted (NIPS 1988: 26). 'Sentence planning' was introduced in 1994. Under the scheme prisoners 'agreed with the Prison Service a programme of activity with built in milestones and targets' (NIPS 1996: 24). The transfer of prisoners from Britain to Northern Ireland was resumed in November 1992, and the two remaining Republican women prisoners in Britain, Martina Anderson and Ella O'Dwyer, were transferred from HMP Durham to Mourne House on 27 July 1994.

The increased number of Republican prisoners applying for release and parole licences was informed by the larger political implications of Sinn Féin's departure from its historical policy of abstention in 1986.[1] The practical import of ending abstentionism was that Republican prisoners were able to adopt a new tactic of 'pragmatic' or 'strategic' engagement with the administration, by seeking to improve their conditions whilst limiting any apparent compromise to their fundamental political objectives. In 1987, IRA prisoners in the Maze and Maghaberry prisons ended their boycott of life-sentence review procedures on the grounds that non-participation had kept their members in prison for their full term, weakened morale and placed additional strains on prisoners' families and communities. Individuals were also given leave to participate to a partial degree in some prison programmes, and to co-operate with welfare or probation personnel if it furthered the objectives of obtaining parole or release. Participation in life-sentence review boards presented a different set of problems because of the wider implications of committing to the probationary approach, which entailed participating in psychiatric and personal development assessments, and involved a tacit commitment to the criteria of criminalization. In effect, this required prisoners to produce evidence of having become a 'depoliticized, repentant and remorseful individual, most unlikely to commit a scheduled offence again' (Rolston and Tomlinson 1988: 184). Elizabeth argued, however, that the new climate of mutual engagement reflected an instrumental adaptation on both sides to broader political realities:

> From the administration point of view, they wanted to defuse the jail struggle. They didn't want to give anybody a weapon as such for attacking the system. Again, you have to see it in context of what was happening on the outside. They saw that to be a little more progressive with the prison system worked in their favour in terms of it kept the smooth running of the place, because let's face it, without the prisoners' consent, the prisoners' co-operation, you've chaos. It's not a matter of telling a prisoner what to do, because of course the prisoners weren't going to do it, and they knew that (Elizabeth, commanding officer, Maghaberry).

Nevertheless, few of these initiatives directly benefited women prisoners, as only a handful of women in the 1990s were serving sentences for life or over ten years. Moreover, there were few substantive regime changes with respect to association, or relaxing internal security procedures in Mourne House. The official attitude to women political prisoners was that they were still 'dangerously' well organized, prone to subverting the system and intent on pursuing their objectives by mobilizing external protests and focusing unwelcome media attention on the prisons (NIPS 1988: 1). Furthermore, the prison authorities insisted that new programmes for prisoners could only be supported in a more security-conscious and technologically enhanced prison environment (*ibid.*: 10). A strong element of mutual antagonism between staff and prisoners also persisted as a result of the years of conflict at Armagh. According to a former member of staff, given the lack of specialist training, the attitudes that had been fostered during the years of prison conflict, and the lack of senior female personnel within the prison service at the time, there was a sense that some officers sought to retrieve some of the authority they had 'conceded' in the aftermath of the 1981 hunger strike (former officer, Armagh and Maghaberry). There was a corresponding view that the promotion of prison order through mechanisms of 'rights' and 'choice', 'empowered' prisoners at the expense of staff, and could only be rectified through stringent application of the rules (*ibid.*). Instead, the more efficient regulatory and surveillant environment at Mourne House led to extended forms of personalized and group control:

When we first went to Maghaberry they isolated us in small wings. There were seven cells to a wing, wee tiny corridors, very narrow, and the cells with the low ceilings. You're living on top of people. Everything is designed for isolation in it. [They] split us up into these wings. We had no contact with the women at the other section of the corridor. There was only about 28 Republicans left. We had quite a few releases, long-term releases. At one stage there was only three of us on the ground floor. There were other Republican prisoners who were on a different wing – but they were integrated.[2] It's unbelievable, because these were women that we were sharing cells with in Armagh, and when we went to Maghaberry, we had no contact with them except in the yard. The only reason we had contact with them in the yard was because they hadn't the staff to staff two yards. They actually tried to implement a really rigorous regime in terms of small, petty things, like, if you didn't go to the yard, you got locked in your cell, which never operated before. There were only so many allowed to move at the one time. [We were] escorted down to the yard, and so many were allowed in the yard at the one time – things like that. We had to break that all down again. You were constantly coming up against different things all the time that you had to break down (Elizabeth, commanding officer, Maghaberry).

All our movements were noted. If you went to take a bath that was noted. They had a bath book and all that type of stuff. You were supposed to say, 'excuse me officer, I've just had a bath.' We'd go, 'fuck that.' Obviously we weren't going along with that. The cameras were all over the yards but they didn't actually get them on to our wings. Prisoners would have just wrecked them ... The red book system was in use but they didn't invoke it; they didn't call you a red book prisoner but they done everything else. This was quite cunning, if you think of it, because as soon as you're a red book prisoner your solicitor is on the case quite strongly. The case with us was that we were just shipped about that often. We could come back from a visit and find our clothes would be packed, and we'd be getting moved (Kathleen, sentenced prisoner, Maghaberry).

An additional dimension to introducing 'normalized' social relations involved posting male officers at Mourne House in the early 1990s. Opposite-sex postings arose out of the Fresh Start (1986) initiative, which introduced equal access for male and female officers to a range of postings and grades. The benefits of the policy to staff were also thought to be transmitted to prisoners as it facilitated the idea of a 'humane regime', in which social relations outside the prison were reflected as far as possible within prisons. Moreover, opposite-sex posting was deemed to be beneficial for good order. As a female governor in Maghaberry commented: 'mixing works very well. It lowers tensions. The mixture of female staff with male staff is felt to be beneficial because prisoners, as with anyone, will meet people from the different sexes as both figures of authority and as caring figures. It is unhealthy and artificial to have same-sex persons in prisons as authority and caring figures.'

Whilst these claims can only be borne out by a more extensive study, criminologists have suggested some grounds for viewing opposite-sex postings as inappropriate for prisoners already coping with separation from their families, because they do not generate 'gender-sensitive' practices, and because the presence of male officers adds to stresses over the invasion of a woman's dignity or privacy that are already inherent in prison. In addition, the policy has contributed to increased conflict and institutional violence when male special support officers have been deployed in the event of disturbances in women's prisons (Arbour 1996). Responses from the prisoners, moreover, suggest that the existing barriers to establishing 'positive' interpersonal relations between the political prisoners and male uniformed officers at Mourne House were compounded by the prisoners' belief that the NIO was introducing a novel approach to maintaining an additional security presence. These apprehensions became clearer, as the following section explains, in the context of staff violence during a wing search at Mourne House in 1992.

'Humane regimes' and the resilience of penal coercion

On 2 March 1992, the 21 political prisoners and 13 women in the 'ordinary' regime were subjected to an enforced mass strip search by female officers, supported by male special support officers, after a period in which strip searching had resumed to the level of entry to and exit from parole or work release programmes:[3]

It was terrible because that started it at about half [past] nine or quarter to ten that morning and it went on until ten o'clock that night. And we had to listen, each of us, to each woman getting brutalized and beat and abused. They [women officers] literally came in, trailed the woman off the bars or whatever, took all her clothes. There were male screws outside with Alsatian dogs, and I could hear every single detail. Everyone was in riot gear, with visors, helmets, shades, gloves, black boiler suits, and it was all done in a military fashion, like eight fall in, right arm up the back, lock left, turn right, you know it was all very strategic. That went on from ten in the morning 'til last thing at night and it was horrific. So what we did was, when they took our clothes off, we would say, 'right you took them off you can put them back on again'. So we made them put our clothes back on again and it was equally as bad. We refused to walk from our cell up to [the] Association [Room], so we got trailed up. They literally trailed us up by our arms. They're trailing us up, and your clothes are around your neck, your whole breasts and chest is exposed, your bra and whatever. And there's a whole gauntlet of male screws, there must have been about twenty of them on a small wing, and they had Alsatian dogs. And when they were trailing us up, it was really horrific because the dogs were barking, you thought you were going to get beat [sic], you thought you were going to get attacked. So when we were locked into Association we just wrecked it. We broke windows, TVs, broke furniture and all that. Anything at all we broke it. And that went on all day and that total aggression lasted for the whole week (Kathleen: sentenced prisoner, Maghaberry).

With the 'return' of random strip searching, the prisoners:

realised that there was going to be a new policy here. And in a way you can see why, not that you can justify it, but the numbers of the women had risen to twenty-odd. You had a lot of women on the wing, and a lot of strong political women who would have had profiles, according to the RUC. And they [the prison administration] saw that as a kind of strengthening of our hand. It was embarrassing them, because a group of women went into the jail who were actually dictating the terms. You had hundreds of men on the other end who were conforming prisoners, who were going along with this notion that Maghaberry was the ideal jail. They had spent thirty and a half million [pounds] on the jail and security, and it was the model prison and we were the disruptive element. And the politics of disruption just didn't suit the authorities at that stage so we were going to get punished for having our political structure. What better way to punish women than to humiliate them (*ibid.*).

The Prison Service later defended the action on the basis that an officer had overheard a conversation during a visit in which a child mentioned that a gun had been taken into the prison. The number of wing searches had also increased during the previous year because of the discovery of drugs on the male side of the prison. All the political prisoners, who had refused to comply with the order to co-operate with full cell and body searches, were subsequently punished for breaching the prison rules. According to former prisoners, the incident confirmed the coercive basis of the 'progressive' impetus of the humane regime. Similarly, in her analysis of penal reforms in the Canadian correctional system, Kelly Hannah-Moffat has perceptively linked the re-emergence of penal coercion to the failure of the responsibilizing project. This punitive relationship, she argues, converges on a new stratum of the punishable women, the 'high-risk and high-need' female prisoner, whose continued resistance to 'pastoral power' and 'empowering programmes' serves to authorize and legitimize special methods of punishment:. 'The construction of this group of women as "disruptive", "risky", "mentally ill" and "potential escapees" is used to justify the use of force, searches, involuntary transfers, and prolonged solitary confinement, as well as the transfer of women to segregated units in men's maximum security penitentiaries' (Hannah-Moffat 2001: 176).

Furthermore, she continues, there is 'no contradiction' between enhanced security practices and the expansion of 'freedoms' within reformed regimes, as the refusal by prisoners to be voluntarily reinscribed into novel governing strategies promotes new logics of 'risk management' and penal enforcement:

> Risk management is constructed as the responsibility of the prisoners and the authorities ... The status of 'maximum' security, or 'high-risk', which results in punitive treatment, can be altered if and *when the prisoner chooses to comply with the carceral regime* by engaging in risk-minimising conducts such as participating in programmes, refraining from self-injury and from injuring others, and complying in the institution's regulations (*ibid.*: 186, emphasis added).

The continued primacy of security in Mourne House in the 1990s was a consequence both of the failure to engage women political prisoners within the terms of 'constructive engagement', and the continuing dearth of legitimacy which prison reforms were claimed to address. In addition, the fact that the objectives of 'secure confinement' frequently won out over those of 'rehabilitating' political prisoners reflected the fact that these questions had been left unresolved in the Murray Commission (1975) into the modernization of women's imprisonment in Northern Ireland. The regime that Mourne House was meant to foster was embedded in a correctional model which anticipated that the political prisoner population would either have considerably diminished, or become one whose claims to differential status would have been resolved, politically or otherwise (*ibid.*: 74–5). The optimistic assurances of the Murray Commission that 'liberal' regimes and 'flexible' security systems would automatically emerge following occupation of the new prison were not borne out in practice.

The recurrence of conflict was not, contrary to official claims, simply rooted in the refusal by political prisoners to engage constructively with the regime. Rather, it was reinforced by structural deficiencies in policies and practices for directly addressing the specific issue of women's imprisonment for all categories, and the persistent official evasiveness as to how a 'rehabilitative' ethos could be consistent with the realities of political imprisonment. Whilst prison reform in the England and Wales and Canadian prison systems has at least sought to address 'gender-sensitive' (Shaw 1992), 'gender-tested' (Carlen 1998: 156) or 'women-centred' (Task Force on Federally Sentenced Women 1990) policies and programmes, there has been no comparable evaluation of women's imprisonment in Northern Ireland. Although feminist and critical analyses of the contemporary layering of new forms of control over a grid of benevolent discipline have in part been levelled at past or current misdirections in applying penal reforms, prison regimes for women in Northern Ireland continued to be defined by their neglect as a specific policy issue, and by the primacy of securitization defined largely in relation to male political prisoners.[4]

The litigation strategy: converting penal privileges into political 'rights'

In 1993, the Republican women prisoners at Maghaberry filed a series of lawsuits against the prison administration of Northern Ireland on the grounds of sexual discrimination with respect to equal access to educational, recreational, visiting and association facilities (Memorandum, Sinn Féin POW Department 1993). They cited the adverse effects on maintaining contact with their families, especially their children, because of the inadequate visiting facilities, the lack of crèche facilities in the women's prison (although one was provided in the male prison) and the lack of privacy on visits. They also sought legal redress for the interruptions to their education arising out of regular closures of the training facilities and the withdrawal of evening classes. The prisoners also contended that the 'mental stimulation necessary for long term-imprisonment' (*ibid.*) was curtailed because of restricted inter-wing association, and because there were only seven women on each wing. In addition, they maintained that women prisoners had access to the exercise yard for two and a quarter hours daily, compared to the six hours allowed to men prisoners. Finally, they alleged that the delays in checking and forwarding 'political and feminist material, books of poetry, magazines and newspapers and family photographs' effectively subjected their correspondence to undue censorship (*ibid.*). Furthermore, the Republican prisoners contended that the NIO operated 'a policy of dual political and gendered discrimination', on the grounds that they were not allowed full access to resources and facilities because, as non-conforming prisoners, they were not deemed to benefit from such incentives:

> For protesting about conditions ... women have been heavily penalized individually by losing remission, spending periods in solitary confinement and having visits taken off them ... and penalized collectively by the continual denial of both inter-wing association and exercise facilities. The women feel that they must continue to raise these issues, because no-one should have to change their political ideology in order to live in a safe and humane environment, and no woman should ever be expected to accept anything less than is offered to a man in a similar position (*ibid.*).

The recourse to judicial review was prompted by their decision to clarify entitlements that were within the remit of the NIO, but which were applied in practice according to discretionary and security assessments, and considerations of cost. The principles of institutional triage and economy of scale, however, tended to reproduce long-standing discrepancies in provision in the Northern Ireland prison system, because they rendered additional expenditure on women's prisons to be the least cost-effective and administratively viable. Moreover, as Young (1990: 53–8) argues, the drive for economic discipline in the contemporary political economy establishes a new 'welfarist authoritarianism' which centres on the altered meaning of the 'responsible' citizen as a moderate consumer of social goods. In practice, the downward fiscal drive which is connected with rationalizing targets and identifying best-value approaches to evaluating needs is connected to the lowering of expectations amongst prisoners, and cumulatively reinforces existing assumptions that women demand, and therefore receive, less from the distributive culture in prison:

> We always have dealt in very, very small numbers of [women] prisoners in Northern Ireland. This had two effects. One is the lack of programmes because it is very difficult to employ teachers or employ specialists on contracts when you may have two today of a particular class of prisoner, and one tomorrow. You never could maintain continuity. So, female prisoners have never been an issue in Northern Ireland, as such. They've never been affected by any of the vagaries of the system, or any changes in the system (male governor, Maghaberry).

Their reason for pursuing on the basis of unequal treatment with non-politically affiliated men in the same prison was that their case was only legally viable on the grounds of sex discrimination. However, any success in formalizing parity of treatment and provision would have effectively obliged the prison administration to dispense with differential conditions between those prisoners who were conforming to the integration policy, and those who were not. In this sense, as Kathleen argued, the litigation strategy was also about gaining judicial backing for conditions which they might then claim were commensurate with political status:

> We decided to do judicial reviews, but we also knew we weren't going to win them. The judicial reviews were just a matter of asserting legal rights because we knew ourselves that if there was ever an opportunity to set precedents, we had a responsibility to do it. We were never recognised by anyone as being political

prisoners, women and men. So that was a fundamental thing for us all. Unofficially they knew we had the structures, but unofficial [is] no good to you when you're taking them to court (Kathleen, sentenced prisoner, Maghaberry).

The litigation strategy has to be placed in the context of structural and distributive pressures which influenced the uneven provision of resources. Access to educational and workshop facilities were curtailed because the high level of staff absenteeism, averaging about 20 per cent annually in the 1990s, meant that there was insufficient staff to escort prisoners to facilities. Breaches of security on the men's side of Maghaberry meant that access to workshops was occasionally suspended for all prisoners. The administrative concern with public accountability and the effectiveness of the prison service were also allied to the commitment to justifying public expenditure through controlling staffing costs, minimizing wastage and optimizing the use of resources and facilities. Prisoner costs rose from £70,000 per prisoner annually at the beginning of the 1990s (NIPS 1993: 1) to £75,297 by 1998, 'of which pay and directly related staff costs constitute[d] around 80 per cent of total expenditure' (NIPS 1998: 23).[5] These objectives were deemed to be frustrated by the refusal of the Republican women to use facilities with Loyalist and non-political prisoners, thereby raising the cost of running and staffing facilities more than once. Furthermore, whilst improved psychiatric and medical facilities were introduced at Maghaberry, women prisoners experienced problems in getting access to services such as breast examinations, regular cervical smears or confidential services provided by women medical staff:

We were in the most secure jail in Western Europe and we were responsible for all these heinous crimes. So, obviously, you're not allowed to travel. They'd only bring you to an outside hospital if, for example, you were haemorrhaging, or having a baby. If you discovered a lump in your breast, even then it wouldn't be an immediate thing, they'd wait a week or two before they'd bring you out (Kathleen, sentenced prisoner, Maghaberry).

The litigation strategy as a disciplinary problem

Beneath the administrative resistance to the prisoners' strategy of advocacy were concerns about their motives. Adams (1992: 88) has noted that the trend of litigation in prisons has been viewed as 'an

201

excess, a crisis or simply a sign that prisoners were wasting time with "frivolous suits"'. From the perspective of senior prison administrators and the NIO, the legal strategy was also connected with the more sinister politicized dimensions of organized opposition and disruption. The NIO robustly contested the prisoners' cases on the grounds that rulings in their favour would lead to the disproportionate allocation of resources to the political group at the expense of the 'ordinaries'. The insistence by Republican prisoners in Mourne House on separate access to the gym, sports facilities and workshops supported the official view that the litigation strategy was fundamentally about seeking more favourable treatment than that available to other prisoners. This was viewed with irony by senior staff, in whose opinion the politicals' drive for segregated facilities established a form of hierarchical privilege over 'more vulnerable' prisoners, and demonstrated a telling lack of solidarity with them. Whilst none of the former prisoners claimed that their recourse to litigation was inseparable from the objective of formalizing their political status, Elizabeth argued that the longer term effects of their actions was to gain improved conditions 'for all prisoners. We were doing our best to upgrade everything ... to get a better quality of life for people in jail' (Elizabeth, commanding officer, Maghaberry).

Nevertheless, these justifications supported the view of staff that there did not appear to be a reasonable basis for the prisoners' case. Because they were already perceived to be beneficiaries of better welfare and resourcing, their motives could only be attributed to a disruptive and subversive attitude, born out of having too much time on their hands, their liking 'for a spoiler ... if it wasn't one thing, it would be another' (officer, Maghaberry). 'Prisoners are very quick to turn privileges into rights and this is part of the difficulty of the prison service in Northern Ireland, that there are a number of very bad practices which have almost become part of the institutional attitude' (official visitor, Maghaberry). Furthermore, prison officers viewed it as detrimental to discipline:

> The position could have been avoided by the management ... When they're going to grant and enhance a regime, they should sit down and look, before they do anything, and say, 'the applications are this, have we got the resources?', rather than saying to the prisoners, 'you can have it', and then ignoring the cost. This is actually how management manipulate prison officers, saying to prisoners, 'you can have it', knowing full well they don't have the resources, knowing full well that prisoners will put pressure on the staff. Then they'll have to take resources from somewhere

else, to give them, before the staff will take the abuse (Prison Officers' Association spokesman).

Even relatively benign challenges by women to penal norms are constructed as potential disciplinary problems. Bosworth (1999: 144–52) found that women prisoners' requests for minor changes in the regulations have to be couched in 'acceptable' terms. Similar problems arose in Mourne House when the Republican prisoners requested that personal toiletries could be sent in to them or made available in the 'tuck shop'. The toiletries were initially highly restricted by their contents and volume, and because of the risk of importing illicit or potentially poisonous or explosive substances. A number of specified brands were delivered, after they had been screened by security. According to former prisoners and a former official visitor, this concession provided another reason for staff to conduct cell searches for 'suspect items'. Furthermore, even these minor forms of interaction were likely to be perceived as a symptom of more extensive and opportunistic forms of subversion in the service of their broader political campaign:

> Like down at Maghaberry, I remember the chief, who I was quite friendly with. She seemed an awfully reasonable woman who would bend the rules a bit. I mean, she really did see the women as women. Prisoners were only allowed to have so much money but she knew that hair colourants cost more than that, and was perfectly prepared for them to have more so that they could do their hair. [She] really did see them as individuals and as women and did a mothering role. The old [attitude] that women in prison have lost their femininity, she didn't have that. She said that sometimes strip searching was a major issue of the month and would be brought up umpteen times that month, and then maybe for two or three months it wouldn't be, and [then] it was about food or it was about work opportunities, or library facilities, and then strip searching would come up again, and she felt that there was a certain pattern. I think it was part of a plan to keep pushing at the system, you know, the group said to themselves, 'now we'll take that out up there, but we'll try that here' (official visitor, Maghaberry).

A former IRA commanding officer in Mourne House indicated that access to governors was contingent on adopting an attitude that established credibility and authority, whilst refraining from 'aggression' (Elizabeth, commanding officer, Maghaberry). Similarly, because their requests were often concerned with improving day-to-day resourcing and conditions, the very issues that they approached staff about were perceived as trivial, vexatious and marginal to the larger concerns of the prison administration:

> I had a session with the girl who runs the Provos. She's not a bad girl, actually. She came to talk to me because the visits were about half an hour late in starting. She'd heard the workshop might not have opened the other day. I had to say, 'I'm sorry, you're lucky the other day you got the visits, because with a hundred and eighteen staff on sick leave, nothing is guaranteed.' So it depends where you start from. In terms of fear of your life, in terms of fear of being beaten, in terms of fear of being starved, in terms of fear of living in manky, grotty sheets and blankets and whatever else, Maghaberry is a little heaven, but no doubt the girls in Maghaberry would say there are things going wrong … I think Maghaberry female [prison] is a place where there is no fear, where there's dignity, where there's self-respect, a sense of worth, and so on (governor, Maghaberry).

The crucial context to this response is that senior prison staff felt themselves to be faced with an unmanageable series of conflicting demands from prisoners, public opinion and political partisanship on law and order and security, as well as holding the view that their difficulties were often disregarded by the political Executive and at prison service headquarters. Moreover, whilst governing staff in other prison systems have been critical of an ever-expanding managerialist and bureaucratic emphasis in prison administration (Quinn 1995), an additional dimension in Northern Ireland was that initiatives on performance targets and efficiency were regarded as abstracted procedural and administrative 'dogma', which were far distant from the complex realities of managing political prisoners. Aligned to this criticism of bureaucratic 'interference' was a sense of themselves as a new breed of tough, pragmatic administrators who had transferred from the prison systems in England and Wales and Scotland, or risen through the ranks on fast-track promotion programmes, and were neither swayed by sectional or sectarian loyalties nor dazzled by technocratic agendas. Similarly, many contrasted their direct and straight-talking dealings with prisoners with the machinations of prison service officials at the NIO:

> It's all to do with performance indicators, lean structures – buy a book on management! I run Maghaberry prison, which I'm told

is the most complex prison in the British Isles, and is such largely because it has long-term sentenced prisoners, female prisoners, female young offender prisoners, it has a psychiatric prison, it has a special unit for prisoners under special protection like the supergrasses, and so on. It's quite a complex operation, and thirteen per cent of my staff are on sick leave. My work is cut out every day to open the prison, not cancel visits, the workshops are closed more often than they're open, education at night has gone (senior staff, Maghaberry).

The alienation of the middle and upper strata of 'hands on' prison managers was compounded by a resentment at the initiatives that were produced by external factors, and in particular by the political commitments to modify elements of the regime or conditions in the context of ongoing negotiations connected with the political process.[6] Governors also deflected the criticisms of the usual sources of administrative ire – political supporters of the prisoners, 'the media' and prison reform groups – as the 'preserve of the spectators, it is not the preserve of the participants' (governor, Maghaberry). Whilst most senior staff claimed they were not opposed in principle to altering correctional objectives or changing their relationships with prisoners, most of those interviewed made the observation that the 'politicization' of prison policy constantly interfered with consistency of treatment of prisoners, to the detriment of maintaining order and implementing reforms across all the regimes:

We've given as much as we can give. There's not a great deal left to give. The arguments these days are things like compassionate home leave, that used to be 24 hours, we've pushed it to 48. We were criticised for not going to 48, so we went to 48, and we were criticised for not going to 72. I mean in Northern Ireland, the number of occasions a prisoner can be out on home leave is astonishing, it really is. But you've got to draw the line somewhere. Nowhere else in the world could you get a multi-murderer and the day after sentence, his mother would die and we would give him 48 hours on leave, unescorted. So, I think that's why the Provos are no longer pushing for a great deal. The only thing the Provo girls push for with me, and they're quite right to, is consistency. Because we are so short of staff, you can never guarantee that the newspaper will arrive at nine in the morning or ten in the morning, the world's not going to come to an end. They would always tell me if they were going to go public on this to the press. Last week, their OC said to me, 'well, we just want to tell you we're going to go public', and I said, 'fine', and she looked at me and she said, 'would you not want to stop us?', and I said, 'No. Your going public's not going to add to the situation, it's not going to take away from the situation, in fact you want to write to the press, just make sure it's accurate' (governor, Maghaberry).

Penal governance and the punishment of 'entrepreneurial' resistance

Since Mathiesen (1965) identified prisoners' use of judicial review and grievance procedures as an expression of 'censoriousness', litigation has been viewed as a critical domain in which penal power and legitimacy are contested. Rights-based advocacy has played an important role in establishing the values of formal equality and proceduralism against arbitrary and personalized forms of authority, or the more coercive forms of inducing co-operation that arise in prison (Livingstone and Owen 1993). However, whilst legal defence or penal rights advocacy are formally admissible and available, these strategies are shaped by discursive and structural qualifications and constraints. The obstacles to accessing legal assistance must be seen in the context of deterrents such as the lack of financial and personal resources, the high levels of personal confidence, articulation and education that are infrequently found amongst prisoners and the protracted processes of judicial review which deter the majority of prisoners who are serving short-term sentences.

In addition, feminist legal theory has been concerned with the normative basis of the dominant construction of 'rights' and 'equality', which have conventionally omitted women from the social contractarian tradition of legal discourse (Pateman 1988). Administrative guidelines for equal treatment or provision remain imbued with (and undermined by) normative, 'gender-neutral' criteria which obscure the very differences in women's penality that they are meant to address. Discrimination cannot be remedied simply by assuming that different groups can utilize the same means to access resources and services. Carlen (1998: 73) further argues that the problem is infrastructural in that women have been continuously negated by conventional standards of 'difference' and 'equality' which alternately 'invoke either an infantilising paternalism ("women prisoners are different to men, they need treatment rather than punishment"), or a formal – but unsubstantiated – equality ("women and men are equal – [and] therefore ... should be subject to the same rules")'. In this context, even the most committed programme of short-term prison reforms, which may in principle be radical, 'often lend[s] a spurious appearance of legitimacy to prison regimes without diminishing their fundamentally debilitating effects' (*ibid*.: 166).

Moreover, further opportunities for punishment arise out of the ideological shift in penal governance towards 'distributive justice', with its efforts to produce the 'depoliticized client-consumer' characteristic of late welfare capitalism, and 'reinforce ... the one-dimensionality of contemporary policy discourse and the containment function it serves' (Young 1990: 75). Recent critical feminist penology has observed that the assertion of rights by women prisoners leads to a new cycle of redisciplining (Hannah-Moffat 2001), as well as the elaboration of punitive logics against those prisoners who represent the 'flawed consumers' of neoliberal, penal governance (Snider 2002: 370). Thus, whilst the 'entrepreneurial, self-interested' individual exerts extensive political purchase in penal reform discourse, in practice such prisoners are constrained within prescribed correctional imperatives, reinforced by multilateral regulatory and punitive mechanisms.

The question remains whether penal reforms in Northern Ireland can be straightforwardly described in terms of neoliberal governance, or whether, as McEvoy (2001) argues, they were extensions of a transparently political strategy for managing conflict within the prisons as part of the larger objective of containing violence. This chapter has suggested that the contradictory core of neoliberal penal governance, between 'choice' and 'responsibility' and a reauthorized, augmented punitive domain, acquired a particular configuration in the context of 'normalizing' political imprisonment in Northern Ireland. It has explored the limitations of 'resource based' indices of penal 'progress' as adequate responses to prison conflict, and their role in investing penal reform with an obvious political utility. In this context, 'normalization' was consistent with previous hegemonic stratagems for containing terrorism within the prisons. Furthermore, the language of redistributive 'rights', the formation of new clientilist–consumer relations and an emphasis on the 'entrepreneurial self' were harnessed to underlying anxieties and obstructions when prisoners utilized these very discourses to resist and challenge the regime. Women political prisoners in Northern Ireland continued to be negatively constructed, not just in terms of their deviation from behavioural norms and correctional objectives, but also in managerialist terms as vexatious, opportunistic litigants, political agitators whose rhetoric of rights obscured their 'selfish' sectional demands, and as disruptive, subversive and violent female prisoners.

Notes

1 The abstention policy, which had stood since 1925, had prohibited members of Sinn Féin and the IRA from taking their seats if elected to the 'illegitimate' parliaments of Westminster and the Dáil in Dublin.
2 These had previously 'resigned' from the Republican group in Armagh to facilitate their parole applications.
3 The background and aftermath to this incident are discussed in Chapter 2.
4 This observation was true both at the time these events took place and afterwards. The first review of the conditions of women's imprisonment in Northern Ireland did not occur until 2002 following an inspection of Mourne House by the Prison Inspectorate (Her Majesty's Chief Inspector of Prisons 2002). Subsequently, a series of highly critical reports condemned the violation of women prisoners' rights in Mourne House and the poorly planned transfer of women to the refurbished young offenders centre at Hydebank (Northern Ireland Human Rights Commission 2004). A follow-up inspection in 2004 reported that 'virtually none of our recommendations, including those fundamental ones, were put into effect. Indeed, the treatment of, and conditions for women at Mourne House became worse' (Her Majesty's Chief Inspector of Prisons/Chief Inspector of Criminal Justice in Northern Ireland 2004: 5).
5 This compared with an average of £47,000 per prisoner in England and Wales in the late 1990s.
6 Interviews with staff were conducted in early 1998.

Chapter 11

'Turning this place inside out': extending the constituency of prison struggle

The thing about when you go on protest is this feeling of family. You're with your own, and as long as you're with your own, nothing can touch you (Winnie, Republican sentenced prisoner, Armagh).

All families suffer horrendously, but each would be a separate case in determining the hardship and what exactly was sufferable for men and women. For families on the outside and dependants it's insecurity, it's loss. It's equivalent to a death ... and for the person inside, they're suffering as well. They have the same fears there (Louie, Loyalist former prisoner/community worker).

This chapter takes the analysis of political imprisonment beyond the parameters of institutional resistance to consider the parallel struggles inside and beyond the prison walls. It explores the material, emotional and ultimately politicized relationships between prisoners and community that were brought about by the extended experience of political imprisonment. A key theme in the social survival of prisoners and their families centred on the reconstruction of the 'family' as source of social continuity. The meaning of the 'family' as articulated by the prisoners is rooted in the heterosexual, nuclear unit and constructed through socio-religious and gendered norms. However, the allocation of roles amongst working-class families in Northern Ireland has also

209

been profoundly shaped by deep socio-historical stresses, including male absenteeism due to imprisonment (although nothing has been written about the absence of women in this circumstance), the impact of sectarianism on jobs, housing and incomes, and the immense burdens that were placed on women to ensure family survival in the context of poverty and violence. The concept of 'family' thus acquired a dual meaning as prisoners applied analogies of kinship to their prison community and to the politicization of family life. The chapter initially explores the political meanings of the coping strategies that prisoners and their families employed as they developed an awareness and practice of shared resistance. However, the subsequent analysis of political imprisonment and mothering explores the institutionalized contradictions in penal discourses of 'familiness', which both reinforce an ideal of 'good mothering', whilst at the same time magnifying the institutional barriers to achieving this end practically. The final section examines the ideological reorientation of Republican prisoners as a consequence of the 'prison debates' in the late 1980s, and links it with the maturation of concepts and strategies of collective resistance within and outside the prisons. In accounting for prison resistance in these terms, this chapter makes the consciously feminist point that the definition of 'the prison campaign' in Northern Ireland incorporated various tributaries of struggle which redefined prison resistance in gendered and collective terms.

Political imprisonment and family survival

Imprisonment is a form of social death which is not only caused by the severance of individuals from familial supports and emotional relations, but also by the considerable stresses and hardships which their absence causes to their families outside. The loss of contact with partners and children resembles an extended web of punishment: '[w]hen … legally sanctioned punishment takes the form of incarceration, the concept of individual punishment for individual law-breaking collapses' (Shaw cited in Coulter 1991: 21). Political imprisonment had far wider consequences for women than the loss of a prisoner. From the early 1970s, women in working-class Republican and Loyalist communities took on roles as supports for the welfare of prisoners, and organizing against institutional abuses and better conditions for prisoners (McGuffin 1973: 75; Coulter 1991; Hughes 1992; Clarke 1995). But whereas Loyalist women relatives shared the same deprivations and stresses as Republicans, their efforts to articulate these problems and find support were largely curbed by the greater stigma attached to imprisonment in their community, the fact that 'prison matters' were largely appropriated by male spokespersons and representatives, and socially conservative values which consigned most problems with isolation and hardship to the private, domestic realm. Women were more conspicuous in Republican organizations such as the Irish Republican Prisoners' Welfare Organization and the Green Cross Fund, which organized welfare for the families of prisoners, transport to and from prisons, and acted as mediators between prisoners and the outside. The Relatives' Action Committee, which gained international exposure for the Republican prisoners in the Maze and Armagh prisons in the late 1970s, was largely organized by female relatives of prisoners. Its successor, the National H-Block/Armagh Committee, skilfully mobilized electoral support for political status among a wide range of political and humanitarian constituencies during the hunger strikes. These activities allowed the entry of working class women with little previous experience of formal political organization into the public sphere. Women relatives also campaigned against the institutional abuse of prisoners, whilst being themselves susceptible to obstruction and body searches whilst on prison visits. They endured social marginalization, political harassment and impoverishment, and encountered official discrimination and humiliating treatment when making costly, infrequent and stressful visits to prisoners in Britain (Clarke 1995).

Politicizing alienation, loss and coping

Prisoners experience separation as a double jeopardy; as personal isolation from their communities, and as anxiety and stress about the welfare of their families outside. Whilst women prisoners reported many of the predicaments of being 'cut off' from their families that generally arise in prison, they also referred to constant feelings of guilt and stress about the violence that their families outside were exposed to, whilst considering themselves to be relatively 'safe' or more insulated from random sectarian attacks. These stresses were also connected with ongoing concerns about relatives' sickness, problems with their children, financial worries and sexual jealousy or feelings of being abandoned by partners. The financial and emotional 'burden' of supporting a prisoner also induced feelings of guilt. Jennie and Eilís described the drain on the resources that their families, often on social welfare or low incomes, incurred from visiting one or more relatives in prison a week. Jennie (sentenced prisoner, Armagh) commented: 'we crippled our families, got them in debt and danger, having to get food parcels, clothes and stuff, so we weren't too bad, you know. We were very well off, in fact. Our families had nothing, we were still okay.' Eilís (internee, Armagh) added:

We actually restricted our own visits. For example, because we were interned, we were entitled to three visits a week. Some of us were actually taking those three visits a week. And then it dawned on you, that your mother's not just your mother anymore. Your mother is getting pulled out three days a week, to travel to Armagh and to get back. And at that time they did not have any money, plus the time, when you came from big families as well. So we stopped the visits, we stopped the parcels because we didn't need so much in parcels. They put a terrible strain on the family, so we stopped them.

Their concerns were also related to more practical problems, such as the safety of their families whilst travelling to and from prisons, the late arrival or non-arrival of visitors, the strip searching of relatives or the confiscation of items left for prisoners. The obstruction or harassment of visitors was a frequent cause of confrontation with staff. Mary, Anna's sister, also described the mutual concealment and emotional masking that occurred between prisoners and their families:

even outside for families, we were worried about how you were reacting inside, and you were worrying about how we reacted outside. The golden rule if you were on the outside was, 'keep your prisoner protected'. Keep their morale up if they were inside. The family thing was to keep the best side out. If something was life and death it had to be told. Part of the whole thing from the start of the Troubles was to break you. Break you inside or outside, whatever way [they could]. Families had to be strong.

As Goffman (1991) and Sykes (1958) have observed with men in prison and Bosworth (1999: 111) with women, prisoners cope with the emotional stresses of imprisonment through masking or 'putting up a front' to family, staff and other inmates. A recurring theme in the interviews refers to the elaborate systems which prisoners adopted for burying their feelings by 'getting on with it', keeping worries and fears to themselves and not 'dragging people down', concealing their anxieties from relatives and guarding against betraying 'weaknesses' to staff. Consequently, prisoners established alternative, informal supports for dealing with problems of stress and depression and encouraging women to express their problems within the group:

You got to keep that drive or everybody went down ... There was a real mixture of activities that people constantly did, association on the corridor, visit each other in cells. We used to be very conscious if there was somebody who was too much on their own. Whenever that actually happened, if somebody was doing her time a bit hard, we tried to have support mechanisms all the time, from whatever source. If the support mechanisms didn't work, it'd be woman to woman. Somebody would work with that person through her bad patch, or whatever. I remember one prisoner's brother being shot. Everybody was devastated. The whole support mechanisms automatically went into gear (Eilís, internee, Armagh).

Another source of disruption to family relations derived from the official harassment of prisoners' families, either as a consequence of their own political activities, the fact that certain households were 'known' to the authorities as sympathizers or because family members were on the run. Many of the prisoners had at least one sibling or relative in prison. One prisoner spoke of the constellation of loss, separation and anxiety that arose from the criminalization of her family:

My mother died when I was in. She dropped dead. So I got out for a few hours. That kind of thing, really, added to the strain. I was the eldest of ten. My sister got lifted six months later. My father was very conservative, went to Mass every day, Gaelic speaker, didn't drink and all that. I hadn't seen him for over a year, he'd been on the run. I remember the day, it was Easter Monday, and the screw came to my cell early in the morning. I knew there was something wrong. I thought it was my Da, because I hadn't seen him. My mother, she'd been up to see me a few days before, and she'd been down to Dublin to see my Da, and she dropped dead. So you'd all that kind of stuff to contend with. I remember making a conscious decision not to cry, taking the attitude, 'life goes on'. Some of the women thought about me, 'she's an absolute hard bastard', because of the attitude I adopted. It was my way of grieving, to become more disciplined, more determined that this regime was not going to break me. Because, you know, you're basically on your own in there, you had to get through your time as easy as possible, whatever way you could (sentenced prisoner, Armagh).

The pervasiveness of 'familiness' in women's prisons has been extensively discussed in penology as an overwhelmingly pernicious

213

influence. Women's relationships in prison are intensively mediated through normative expectations of gender, family and 'domesticity'. Women political prisoners negotiated certain aspects of family and domestic structures in prison within these prescribed contexts. Whilst the notion of 'family' remains historically specific and critically contested, the prisoners' usage of analogies of 'family' to describe an alternative 'private' sphere which referenced emotional, interpersonal and friendship ties reflected the social, penal and political conditions in which they sustained a sense of community. Although feminist analysis has rightly been concerned with the deployment of discourses of the 'family' as a reactionary rather than progressive tactic, black feminists, for example, have argued that hostile external forces such as racism have recast the black family as a sphere of social reinforcement and affirmation (Collins 1990: 44–48; Yuval-Davis 1998). The penalization of prisoners' communities and the shared experiences of political conflict and resistance were similarly significant factors in shaping and reshaping family relations in Northern Ireland. The activism of prisoners' relatives also challenged the institutional public/private dichotomy by asserting that the treatment and welfare of prisoners were not strictly 'internal' prison concerns, but related to the broader conflict. Moreover, the class and cultural homogeneity of the women in the Republican group contributed to their internal cohesion by providing a shared base of political values and enabling them to maintain communal identity:

> Because in situations like that, two things stand for you. One is your beliefs, and the second is the discipline that you have around you. That keeps you going. Plus, you've that feeling of family, that you're all in it together, and when one gets battered you feel it the same way. There's a lot of comradeship there. For the years I was in Armagh jail, they were my family. My family outside were the people who came up to visit me, but inside, the women in Armagh were my family. That kept me going. But if your beliefs were ricky you were snookered (Winnie, sentenced prisoner, Armagh).

Political imprisonment and the struggle to be a mother

The obligations that are laid upon women to continue to mother and act as the principal carer whilst in prison are upheld by extensive social norms and expectations. Furthermore, as Carlen (1998: 41) points out, the imperative to be a 'good mother', 'is a distinct feature of women's imprisonment, despite the considerable institutional obstacles to allowing women to do so.' The factors that prevented women from having a 'normal' labour or keeping their very young children derived from the familiar intersection of security priorities, the denial of appropriate medical support and an inadequate environment in prison.

A very small number of women mothered children in prison whilst serving sentences for political offences, despite extensive obstacles. In Armagh, women with children experienced isolation on the mother and baby unit on 'C' wing, and faced strip searching themselves, and the 'checking' of 'the baby's pram and clothes' if they left the wing for visits (IIP 1985: 2). Two sentenced women gave birth to children whilst on the Republican protest in Armagh. They were initially denied extra dietary supplements and antenatal care until these 'privileges' were restored in the seventh month of their pregnancy (Women Against Imperialism 1980: 19). Moreover, women on the non-cooperation protest were effectively denied the right to remain with their children until they were six months old, despite official policy, because they could not be kept in 'reasonable conditions' in the prison (*ibid.*). The starkest choice for these women was either to keep their child in 'C' wing under an 'ordinary' regime, or to give up their children for care outside the prison if they wished to remain on the protest. On returning from the hospital in which they had given birth, for example, the two sentenced prisoners were told that they would have to be locked in their cells full time with their children if they insisted on returning to the Republican wing at Armagh. Both women sent their children out to relatives, and rejoined the protest.

May gave birth to a girl two weeks before her imprisonment in Armagh, and mothered her daughter there until she was one year old. As a remand prisoner, May was not allowed under the prison rules to join the sentenced Republican prisoner group.[1] She was told that the poor state of the sentenced wings, which were in the oldest part of the prison, meant that she could not transfer there with her baby:

I had to go in every morning to speak to the governor about getting on the other wing to be with the rest of the girls. I was kept on a totally different wing because I had the child and they wouldn't allow me on to the main wing. So I had to propose this to him every morning, and he would say to me [that] they had to [ensure] the health and safety of the child, because of the steps. Which you can't fight with, because they have so many fire regulations and other things where a child is concerned (May, remand prisoner, Armagh).

She described her emotional dilemma when she had to give her child up for care by relatives in order to join her Republican peers on the sentenced wing as:

> like a death, that was the only way I could ever have described it, because the pain, it went so deep. Leaving your child for years. You were always thinking, putting in your mind that the one minute she's with you, and the next she's not. Not so much worrying about me, but worrying about the child. Thinking, 'how is she going to get on? How difficult is it going to be for her?' Because she was with me in the cells continuously, she'd never been away from me once. I suppose with dealing with all of that you couldn't be weak, and you couldn't be seen to be weak, because if that was the case, they'd put one up on you. You couldn't allow them to trample you down or get to you so much. So then you thought, 'I'll get over this, I'll get through it and I'll get on.' And you did get through it, get over it and get on. But it was difficult (May, remand prisoner, Armagh/sentenced prisoner, Maghaberry).

Themes of death, bereavement and loss were also woven through other prisoners' accounts of their relationships with their children. Kathleen's husband and two young children had moved to the Republic of Ireland when she was sentenced. She described the trauma of cutting off from her family as a necessary aspect of the emotional discipline required to cope with imprisonment:

> I think the separation from the family, from my kids, was particularly hard. They were living in the South, and they travelled up every week to come up to see me. I knew they were frightened and that. Knowing all that made it very hard. And I'll be honest, with the screws and all the stuff they dished out, it didn't annoy me in a sense. The more they gave out the stronger you got. It was a sense of empowerment and a sense of character that we all felt, and we all said, 'OK, you've been cut off from each other. You haven't seen your family – well fuck them'. That was the attitude. You definitely divorced it. I remember even when I got out and was sitting talking with my sisters. One asked me, 'what do you reckon about the kids?' I said, 'I'm going to say something that sounds really terrible, but I deliberately didn't think about the kids.' If I had thought about the kids I would have been broke, I would have broke like a plate. So I didn't. How could you? (Kathleen, sentenced prisoner, Maghaberry).

Narratives of mothering were also dominated by a sense of fractured relationships with their children. Women spoke of their abiding guilt about 'abandoning' their children, or being torn between their choices as political Volunteers and motherhood, between 'looking after themselves' and their desire to provide stability and continuity for them. Some women said that they retrospectively tried to make up to their children after release, but continued to be alienated from them, as well as from their sense of selves as 'good mothers'. Whilst the network of support provided by female relatives in caring for their children outside was pivotal to sustaining their families whilst they were in prison, many women referred to their isolation on being reinscribed in the role of 'a mother' after release, in comparison with the 'independence', equality and affirmation which they experienced in prison:

> My family expected me to be this mother. I didn't feel like a mother. I just saw myself as a single woman. I had to look after number one. Sometimes it's selfish, when I look back, but that's the way it was in prison. People say, 'did you not miss your kids?', and I say, 'No', and [they are] disgusted with me. But I say, 'how can you miss something that you haven't got?' What you haven't got, you can't miss. Why sit in your cell and depress yourself with, 'I could be doing this for my child, I could be doing that?' That goes out the window. Once I went into jail I put that all aside. I said, 'I'm going to look after number one', because I knew my family was looking after my kids. I had nothing to worry about … Even when I got out I pushed them away. At first it was great to see them on a visit. But they were on the outside. It's a different kettle of fish. You were sort of backing off, and I spent so much time away from them. I could not accept I was a mother. I had my own independence in jail, looked after number one, or else the girls [other prisoners]. Then all of a sudden, sitting there with two children, 'what am I supposed to do here?' And the kids were all over me as usual. Then, until I had a child a year ago, that's when I felt like a mother again. Maybe because I went through the whole thing again. But I'm still settling, still to this day after two years (Hannah, sentenced prisoner, Maghaberry).

Even in the 1990s, the stated official commitments in *Serving the Community* to 'maintain … prisoners' family bonds' (NIPS 1991a: 12) appeared particularly hollow in the light of the need for women prisoners to resort to judicial review to get appropriate facilities and childcare support during visits. As Carlen (1998: 80) cogently noted, the 'official concern about "families" in the women's prisons is at best nothing more than an empathic collusion in the still-dominant ideological illusion of "happy family-ness". At its worst, it is either muddle-headedness or institutionalized hypocrisy.' Moreover, as discussed in Chapter 2, the continuous subordination of most prison reforms and conditions to the larger concerns of the political process up to and beyond the Belfast Agreement meant that the specific problems and needs of women prisoners (political or ordinary) remained as marginal to the prisoner release programme after 1998 as they had been during their imprisonment.

The mutual politicization of Republican prisoners and their community

The aftermath of the 1981 hunger strike witnessed a slow, but discernible broadening of the Republican political agenda from its previously narrow emphasis on national reunification and the 'armed struggle', the redirection of the movement towards electoral politics, and the closer alignment between the prisoners and community activists in broadening the terms of the prison campaign. Crucially, these developments were reflected in the maturation of the prisoners' thinking and organization. In 1986, in what Republicans subsequently referred to as the 'prison debates', prisoners embarked on 'the dual task [of] internal politicization [and] external mass mobilization' ('Morrigan', *Iris Bheag* 1987: 2: 5–7). The previous years of resistance, and especially the no-wash/Blanket and hunger strikes, had conferred considerable authority on the prisoners with their communities, and enabled them to emerge as a significant bloc in the formation of political strategy and ideology. Furthermore, events in the prisons had played a significant role in the internationalization of the prisoners' (if not necessarily the Republican) cause with various left, feminist and anti-colonial movements.

This period also saw the 'democratization' of the Republican internal structures in the prisons, with the development in the 1990s of prisoner collectives called 'coistí', or wing committees, which were responsible for collective welfare and the strategic development of relations with officialdom. A second development entailed a searching critique of the direction of Republican strategy in the light of the containment of PIRA's armed campaign by the British Army by the mid-1980s, and the implications of adopting an electoral strategy after 1986, with its additional resonances for the enlarged role for Sinn Féin's political strategy *vis-à-vis* the PIRA's military one (McKeown 2001: 160–70).

A third factor involved the influence of prisoners in engaging the Republican agenda with a social and political programme for pursuing its new electoral objectives, and for establishing frameworks for a future settlement to the conflict. These developments were allied to ideological and political advancements in the prisons. Influenced by Paulo Freire's *Pedagogy of the Oppressed* (1972) which had sought to radicalize the Latin American rural and urban underclasses, prisoners developed educational collectives (the 'coistí') wherein they engaged Republican ideology with Marxist, feminist and anti-imperialist political thinking. Their developing ideas were outlined in a series of publications which were distributed in the prisons and across Republican political organizations.

Prison writing was a significant aspect of the resistant culture, which generated a body of articles, creative writing and political theory that appeared in the Republican prisoners' 'house journals', *An Glór Gafa* (*The Captive Voice*) and *Iris Bheag* (*Little Journal*). The importance of this output was its articulation of wide-ranging analyses and strategies for breaking down 'the self imposed isolation' and 'deep-seated fear of reformism' in the Republican movement (*Iris Bheag* 1987: 3: 6). Furthermore, women prisoners used them as a forum for confronting the Republican movement with the inescapable issues of the subordination of women in articles on domestic violence, rape, abortion and reproductive rights, economic and social inequality and costs of imprisonment to women within and outside the prisons. In one collective article, the 'women POWs, Maghaberry' condemned the social sanctions to which female partners of men prisoners were exposed if they were suspected of 'disloyalty'. 'Some husbands would prefer that their partners sat in the house and do the confinement with them', they wrote (*Iris Bheag* 1987: 13: 9). 'This is selfish, but may not be a conscious feeling. Every man is scared about losing his partner, especially a wife, when he is in gaol and will do anything to keep that partnership together, including making the demand that his partner stop at home, and uses emotional pressure such as "if you loved me, you'd do this".' Moreover, they challenged the double standards by which Republicans may have begun to come to terms with the fact that 'the woman [outside] can be the forgotten prisoner', but failed to recognize the predicaments of women prisoners. The article continued: 'the period of remand when a woman finds herself in that position, then the trial, which will eventually end in sentencing in most cases can be a very trying time, especially when children are involved ... the problems that are experienced by women in this position is something that needs much debate and/or discussion' (*ibid.*: 8). Yet, the irony remained that women prisoners instigated these debates and their general thrust was with educating men. As Kathleen wryly remarked: 'part of the political growing up process was getting the Republican leadership to talk about vaginas' (sentenced prisoner, Maghaberry).

The significance of prisons as 'universities of revolution' (MacStiofáin 1975: 57) has been widely noted (Jackson 1970; Davis 1988; Seale 1991; Churchill and Vander Wall 1992; McConville 2003). McKeown (2001) has extensively examined this autodidactic influence on the emergence of a radical intellectual leadership in the PIRA, whose willingness to depart from traditional Republican thinking was significant in directing it towards political engagement and negotiation in the 1990s. Whilst the relationships between political developments in the prisons and the route to the peace talks were more complex and multilateral (McEvoy 2001), it is plausible to suggest that the educational movement expressed a transitional point between the insularity and isolation of the Blanket/no-wash and hunger strikes, and the broader ideological shifts and mutual politicization which arose from direct engagement between prisoners and their communities. For former political prisoners, this strategy was also directed towards the longer-term, practical goals of social reconstruction and community development after their release. Jennie, Kathleen and Louie work in prisoners' support organizations. Eilís and Annie are employed in community-based projects for women. Anna and Winnie are active in promoting cultural programmes, whilst Áine was involved in a community campaign to gain public funding for an Irish language school in West Belfast. However, the familiar problems with high unemployment, poverty, poor housing, low access to health and education and political, economic and social marginality continue to blight communities and to persist as burdens borne by women in Northern Ireland, 'post-conflict'. As Kathleen commented, the contradictions of women's political struggle were, and remain, 'huge'.

Note

1 After her trial and sentencing, May was allowed to join the Republican group in Armagh and transferred with them to Maghaberry in 1986.

Chapter 12

Conclusion: 'doing your time right' – penal pain, resistance and survival

Through my whole experience in jail, if you were willing just to sit back and take it all, they'd have been willing to delve it out. The only reason that people have got today what they've got is through the jail struggle … The protests were stepping stones towards that, and I think we made a bigger impact on the outside as well. It's something you never forget, that it came from that struggle and sacrifice (Elizabeth, commanding officer, Maghaberry).

You have vulnerability, you have free will, your bodily functions made you vulnerable while you were there. You're sexless in jail. Psychologically you're sexless, because if you look at yourself as being a woman, the first thing that's associated with being a woman is being vulnerable, and you can't afford to be vulnerable when you're in that situation. So you literally become sexless. The vulnerabilities that would have made you female no longer exist. You push them out of the road as quick as humanly possible to survive, literally just to survive. It's as if there's all these wee doors in my head and I can close them or open them at will. Jail did that to me. It strips you of your femaleness, it really does (Winnie, sentenced prisoner, Armagh).

In the course of interviews, former prisoners frequently talked about doing their time 'right' to reference different and contradictory aspects of their self-awareness. 'Doing your time right' encapsulated, on the one hand, a unifying narrative of collective solidarity in the face of penal atomization and alienation. On other occasions, the phrase described an ethic of conduct arising from their disciplinary fortitude in surviving imprisonment. In this context, doing your time 'right' embraced elements of subjective self-affirmation, as well as ideological rectitude and solidarity in struggle. Finally, the broader frame of reference for doing your time 'right' connected their deployment of strategic and political skills in altering their conditions with achieving some of their wider political objectives.

On the other hand, the values of doing your time well, or at least avoiding doing your time 'hard', were not divorced from withstanding the pains of imprisonment and maintaining personal integrity against surveillance, correction and bodily intrusion. Rather, the infusion of these values into narratives of survival illustrated the fact that few regarded themselves as having emerged from prison unscathed or unchanged. Neither was the concept separable from the necessity of making difficult choices between conflicting positions, in dealing with problems as 'women' or 'as political Volunteers', or relinquishing those emotional attachments or aspects of the self which were connected with their penal victimization.

'Doing your time right', then, expresses a consciousness of the contradictory nature of their experiences and actions. Their narratives of resistance alternated between their positions as penal subjects and resisting agents, as perpetrators of violence or intimidation and as victims, as agents of collective transformation and as individual survivors, whilst also understanding them as a complex whole.

Furthermore, not only did they consciously understand the contradictions of alternating between a series of 'gendered' and 'political' penal positions, but their prison struggle secured a transformation of these categories. Their campaign brought about *the gendering of political imprisonment* and ensured the disruption of various academic, managerial and political traditions of conceiving of prison conflict. In this context, rather than treating the dialectics of prison conflict solely in terms of the struggle over political legitimacy, this study stresses its multiple meanings over a range of objectives – political ideology, gendered autonomy, agency and subjective integrity – and across a range of institutions – the State, the gender system and the penal system.

Secondly, their struggle adds another dimension to *the politicization of women's imprisonment*, which has been central to the feminist, critical penological project. Just as 'State punishment' cannot be a primary or discrete explanatory framework for accounting for women's political imprisonment, neither can 'gender' solely account for the discursive and material organization of penal subordination that they experienced. These tensions between political and gendered difference resurface as separate, although interconnected, themes across different chapters. Thus, whilst Chapter 3 closely examined the epistemological stresses between 'women's' and 'political' subjectivities, this 'anomaly' informed the disjunctures between penal securitization and 'care', the shortcomings in policy and in penal reforms, the jeopardies of marginalization within the prison system as well as within their own political structures, and their problematic configuration within both feminist thinking and the wider politics of conflict management in Northern Ireland.

'Resistance' as a question of penal power

In analysing agency and resistance in repressive institutions, penologists confront a classic duality. Either one assigns incontrovertible explanatory power to the coherence of penal punishment and the recuperative powers of penality, or alternatively, one can attribute significant transformations to everyday acts of appropriation and self-legitimation. The former position risks reducing subjectivity and agency to, at best, interstitial 'freedoms', and at worst, to a discourse of endless subjection to domination. The latter position is open to charges of eluding the facts of penal pain and understating the coerciveness of prison.

In this context, one can position Carlen's (2002a) emphasis on the abiding punitive weight and destructive effects of the prison, and its ability to sustain its repressive logic and legitimacy, alongside Hannah-Moffat's (2001) analysis of the appropriative capacity of penal governance, which negatively converts internal challenges or 'humanizing' reforms into more elaborated constraints. Thus, the transformative alternatives that might be available within existing penal discourses are always and already subject to mutating and versatile processes of 'carceral clawback' (Carlen 2002a). These perspectives contrast with the possibilities of resistant agency and identity which Bosworth (1999: 156) argues 'reveal the relationship between power and punishment ... by demonstrating the grounded nature of all configurations of power', and which illuminate 'how the legitimacy of the prison is constantly being negotiated by the prison population'.

It would be mistaken to reduce the complexity of these respective positions to a new polarity in which either 'structure' or 'agency' emerge as privileged, foundational explanations. Whilst Carlen and

Hannah-Moffat rightly focus on the hegemonic and repressive processes of penal subjugation, Bosworth dignifies the knowledge claims of prisoners in confronting their disempowerment, whilst also reflecting their own consciousness of the extensive constraints on achieving personal or institutional transformation. Indeed, Bosworth's analysis concludes with an implicitly 'pragmatic' affirmation of resistance as already constrained within a paradigm of 'surviving', 'managing' and getting through their imprisonment.

Similar differences in emphasis between structural power and penal resistance emerge in the analysis of political imprisonment in Northern Ireland. McEvoy's (2001) analysis of the 'progressive' formations of penality gives an account of the State's management of political imprisonment as it extricated itself from explicit coercion, to the use of 'exceptional' measures, and finally to a negotiated political settlement. He delineates the forces and techniques available to the liberal-democratic State for managing political dissent and violence, and in the process reinforcing its own legitimacy. If McEvoy leans towards the primacy of the State as the principal agent of penal change, McKeown (2001), in contrast, proceeds from post-colonial theories of 'resistance of the oppressed' to stress the importance of political will and consciousness on the part of prisoners. McKeown's consciously positioned analysis, as a former PIRA commanding officer and hunger-striker in the Maze, grants agency to prisoners as self-reflexive and self-authorizing subjects whose experience of prison struggle enabled them to emerge as positively changed individuals.

The centrality granted to the State and political prisoners, respectively, forces each theorist to relinquish a degree of complexity. If McEvoy has 'erred' towards a teleological account which sometimes obscures the importance of subaltern struggle, in McKeown there is an occasional lack of contradiction in accounting for unavoidable areas of 'collusion', as well as the self-justifications and evasions on the part of political prisoners as well as penal administrators.

In this book, I have tried to argue for a dialectical relationship which acknowledges the violence, hegemonic power and repression of the prison, whilst arguing for the effectiveness of multilateral and innovative resistance. This argument relies on the mutuality of the conditions of power and resistance and the contingency of penal domination, without laying claim to resistance as an escape from structures of punishment. Nevertheless, whilst prison power appears to be a unitary entity which enforces its own coherence, its mechanisms were vulnerable to fragmentation and some of its constituent elements – resources, disciplinary programmes, categorization systems and even violence – were partly reappropriated through resistance. In this context, a more fluid and complex pattern of prison rule emerged as it was confronted and negotiated on various structural and ideological levels.

It is also acknowledged that the longitudinal scope of this study, which covers 26 years, has made the task of tracing the shifting patterns of punishment and resistance less difficult than that for students of short-term or occasional incidents of resistance in prison. Moreover, this emphasis on the continuity of internal prison struggles cannot exclude the significance of external developments such as political violence and mobilization, State responses and national and international political influences in exacting changes in the penal apparatus in Northern Ireland.

The contradictions of 'resistance'

If the patterns of resistance by women political prisoners maintained their own internal contradictions, they also elucidate larger penological dilemmas about structure and agency. By offering an analysis of a continuum of penal rule and resistance, this book suggested that the relationship between structural power and localized resistance is not contradictory. Rather, an analysis of situated struggle at the microsphere is viable without relinquishing a sense of the material influences of penal structures. In addition, the model of a continuum of various 'fields of resistance' relates preconceived, organized political resistance to spontaneous acts of subversion, sabotage and exploitation of the contradictions in prison rule.

But in attempting to loosen the false dichotomies of 'structure' and 'agency', or 'power' and 'resistance', I have unavoidably established a new set of binary relationships. This has relied on a notion of punishment which, as noted above, is based on a particular alignment of the repressive State, gendered domination and the punitive apparatus of prison. However, it has also argued that prison rule is contested and contingent, and that resistance occurs across the penal terrain, taking place neither in one form nor on one front. Theories of prison punishment and resistance can thus legitimately commence from situated, embodied analyses of power.

Mindful that 'resistance' is a contested and elusive concept, this book also addressed the ways in which different sociological traditions disqualify everyday resistance for 'failing' to achieve either the material transformation of conditions, or for showing 'insufficient' evidence of consciousness or intentionality. Classical Marxism, for example, insists that 'resistance' is about the historical attainment of revolution in which the vestiges of the bourgeois State (and its punitive apparatus) 'wither away'. The liberal tradition centres on a notion of power vested in the (paternalistic) State and attaining a balance of interests between government and citizens through the consensual social contract. Both paradigms privilege 'rational' social action, either in terms of revolutionary 'class consciousness' or self-interested citizenship, as the defining characteristic of social transformation. These explanatory frameworks either tend to render as inconsequential, or find it difficult to explain away, the accidents, errors, fatal flaws and unconscious reflexes which contribute to the sometimes inconclusive and unforeseen aspects of resistance. In one sense, the struggle by women political prisoners is closer to the Marxist transition in consciousness wherein groups move from acting 'of themselves' whilst embedded in common subordination, to acting 'for themselves' in transforming their suppressive conditions. But this book has also explored the varying textures of lived resistance which created prolific opportunities out of the conditions of subordination.

Appendix I

Researching women political prisoners

Prison research is inevitably a political process because it confronts the limits of State accountability and institutional transparency. Attempting research on the internal administration of the prison system in Northern Ireland magnified these concerns, so that conducting interviews acquired complications over and above the usual quandaries of gaining approved admission from the Northern Ireland Office to prisons and staff, establishing links and trust with gatekeepers and respondents, and corroborating contested events.

The role of the State as the primary, exclusionary 'gatekeeper' in Northern Ireland, especially where prisons, policing and 'national security' are involved, has been well documented by those who have previously experienced it. The prison system, in particular, was sealed from the research gaze during the conflict for interlocking practical, political and ideological reasons. This included the practical necessity of protecting employees from exposure to harm and to prevent breaches of security, and the criminalization of research activity which 'aids terrorism' under both the regular official secrecy provisions and emergency legislation (Hogan and Walker 1989: 155–62). Additionally, there have been 'informal' prohibitions on overly 'theoretical', politically sensitive or contentious research which does not meet official criteria of ideologically 'neutral', policy-oriented and practice-relevant work (Taylor 1988), and the exclusion of research which is deemed to be 'hostile' (critical) or to offer 'propaganda' value to paramilitaries.

Indeed, this issue of legitimacy pervaded the research process. In societies in conflict, the question of whose perspectives are sought becomes a radically polarizing one, where the selection of one set of perspectives is likely to exclude another. In this sense, the question of 'access' to respondents is ineluctably politically determined, and whereas the likelihood of establishing the plausibility of a research project with antagonistic groups was not completely foreclosed, my options were narrowed and the 'choices' were starker. Like McEvoy (2001: 371) and McKeown (2001: 4), I conducted interviews with prisoners in the community after their release because my efforts to secure access to the prisons to conduct research were, predictably, unsuccessful. Furthermore, I was already aware that officially sanctioned access would have invariably alienated serving prisoners, prisoners in the community, and Loyalist and Republican prisoners' organizations. This had been made clear to me in a letter from the Republican commanding officer in Mourne House in October 1996, which also stated that the Republican group declined interviews because they had previously co-operated with an unnamed research project and were 'angry' and 'disappointed' with the misrepresentation of themselves and their perspectives. However, they supported my decision to contact the Republican prisoners' organizations.

I eventually contacted individual administrators within the prison service directly, and was given clearance for an escorted visit to Maghaberry prison, where I interviewed some officers and arranged to interview others outside the prison. The problem of accessing staff in the security forces in Northern Ireland by 'getting around' institutionalized obstacles has been similarly resolved by others who recruited sympathetic internal respondents, or conducted research with personnel outside the workplace (Brewer and Magee 1991). The rest of the interviews were gained through gatekeepers from Loyalist and Republican prison welfare and community development organizations which are run by former prisoners. Thereafter, I met other respondents through personal introductions from women who had been interviewed.

The fieldwork for this study was conducted between February 1997 and August 1998, around the period preceding and just after the signing of the Belfast Agreement on 10 April 1998. For this study, I interviewed the following sources:

- Fourteen women former prisoners, of whom twelve were Republican, one Loyalist and a non-political prisoner who had made links with the Republican group in Mourne House to resolve some problems of alleged bullying by staff. The periods in which they served their sentences, their roles in the prison protests and their alibis are outlined in Appendix II. In accordance with the ethical conventions for preserving the anonymity of respondents in prison ethnography, and because all interviews were conducted in 1997 and 1998, whilst the conflict was ongoing, interviewees are not identified by their own names. Former prisoners are referred to by the names of women who were interned or imprisoned for their activities in labour, Republican and feminist struggles in Ireland in the late nineteenth and twentieth centuries.

- Nine people from the voluntary sector who worked closely with women prisoners including former and current members of Boards of Visitors, a doctor, a welfare worker from a non-governmental organization and three prison chaplains. Pastoral workers such as these played a significant mediating role throughout the prison conflict. Moreover, political prisoners refused to work with the statutory probation or welfare sector on the basis that the requirement to acknowledge their 'crimes' was antithetical to their political status.

- Three members of the political prisoners' support community including a lawyer, and a prisoners' relative and a community worker who were both active in community-based prisoners' welfare groups.

- Eleven former and serving staff were interviewed, from uniformed officers to senior governors and prison administrators.

Interviewing women in a conflict 'zone' is fraught with intersecting power relations, divisions and prohibitions, not least of which are the threat or actuality of violence against 'informers' (Corcoran 2005). The influence of paramilitary 'discipline' in the community is manifest in the codes and values of non-disclosure which were endorsed and practised within Loyalist and Republican areas. Furthermore, as feminist analysts of war have pointed out, paramilitary and State violence interacts with, and sustains, a multitude of violences and social oppressions against women, children and 'non-combatants'. Thus, the element of risk in participating in research was borne by respondents. Access to Loyalist women presented a different range of problems, as I had no obvious social or political points of entry to Loyalist communities. Indeed, my otherness was established by the 'Catholic' inferences that could be drawn from my name and my Southern Irish accent. Three Loyalist women initially agreed to be interviewed, but then decided to select one to represent their views in an interview.

It was necessary for me to defer, then, to the complex realities of sectarian division and political alienation, routine self-surveillance and 'research fatigue' on the part of communities and respondents. Apart from personal safety, other pressing material constraints, including limited time and money and the demands of childcare and work, made it imperative that respondents should not incur any further costs by participating in the research. Interviews were conducted in respondents' homes, my home or local community facilities.

The decision to privilege the narratives of women former prisoners in this book consciously addressed both the 'insurrection of subjugated knowledges' (Foucault 1980: 82) and the concrete risks taken by the researched in challenging the many conventions of silence they were subjected to.

Appendix II

Prisoners interviewed

Prisoners interviewed
</>

Alias	Administrative phase	Prison	Role in protests	Other remarks
Nora Connolly	Reactive containment	Armagh	Campaign for political status	Internee with political status. Mother
Meg Connery	Reactive containment	Armagh	Campaign for political status	Internee, later sentenced. Escapee
Anna Parnell	Reactive containment	Armagh	Campaign for political status	Sentenced with political status
Eilís Ní Riain	Reactive containment	Armagh	Campaign for political status	Interned with political status. Escapee
Jennie Wyse-Power	Reactive containment	Armagh	Campaign for political status	Sentenced with political status
Aine Ceannt	Reactive containment/ criminalization	Armagh	Non-cooperation/ no-work campaign	Sentenced with political status
Annie Cooney	Reactive containment/ criminalization	Armagh	Non-cooperation/ no-work campaign	Interned. Later sentenced without political status
Winnie Carney	Criminalization	Armagh	Non-cooperation/ no-wash protest. Strip-search campaign	Sentenced without political status
May Gibney	Criminalization/ normalization	Armagh/ Maghaberry	Segregation Strip-search campaign	Remand/sentenced without political status. Mothered child in prison
Elizabeth O'Farrell	Criminalization/ normalization	Armagh/ Maghaberry	Segregation. Strip-search campaigns	Remand/sentenced commanding officer (PIRA), Maghaberry

Hanna Sheehy-Skeffington	Criminalization/ normalization	Maghaberry	Strip-search campaign. Litigation	Sentenced. Mother
Louie Bennett	Normalization	Armagh/ Maghaberry	Loyalist segregation campaign	Remand/sentenced
Kathleen Clarke	Normalization	Maghaberry	Strip-search campaign. Litigation	Sentenced. Mother. Education officer (PIRA), Maghaberry
Maud Gonne MacBride	Normalization	Maghaberry	Non-political prisoner	Sentenced. Mother

References

Adams, G. (1996) *Before the Dawn: an Autobiography.* London: Heinemann/ Dingle: Brandon.

Adams, R. (1992) *Prison Riots in Britain and the USA.* Basingstoke: Macmillan.

Adler, F. (1975) *Sisters in Crime: The Rise of the New Female Criminal.* New York, NY: McGraw-Hill.

Alexander, Y. and O'Day, A. (eds) (1984) *Terrorism in Ireland.* London: Croom Helm.

Alexander, Y. and O'Day, A. (1986) *Ireland's Terrorist Dilemma.* Dordrecht: Martinus Nijhoff.

Allen, H. (1998) 'Rendering them harmless: the professional portrayal of women charged with serious violent crimes', in K. Daly and L. Maher (eds) *Criminology at the Crossroads: Feminist Readings in Crime and Justice.* Oxford: Oxford University Press, pp. 55–67.

Amnesty International (1973) 'Memorandum submitted by Amnesty International to the Parker Committee on Interrogation Procedures', in J. McGuffin (ed.) *Internment.* Tralee: Anvil, pp. 197–210.

Amnesty International (1978) *Report of an Amnesty International Mission to Northern Ireland.* London: Amnesty International.

Anderson, B. (1991) *Imagined Communities: Reflections on the Origins and Spread of Nationalism.* London: Verso.

Anderson, M. and O'Dwyer, E. (1997) 'Let's talk', *Journal of Prisoners on Prisons. Special Issue: Republican Prisoners of War*, 7: 40–1.

Arbour, L. (1996) *Commission of Inquiry into Certain Events at the Prison for Women in Kingston.* Ottawa: Office of Public Works and Government Services (JS42-73 1996E).

Aretxaga, B. (1995) 'Dirty protest: symbolic overdetermination and gender in Northern Ireland ethnic violence', *Ethos*, 23: 123—48.

Aretxaga, B. (1997) *Shattering Silence: Women, Nationalism and Political Subjectivity in Northern Ireland.* Princeton, NJ: Princeton University Press.

Ballinger, A. (2000) *Dead Women Walking: Executed Women in England and Wales 1900–1955.* Dartmouth: Ashgate.

Becker, J. (1977) *Hitler's Children: The Story of the Baader-Meinhof Gang.* London: Michael Joseph.

Beresford, D. (1987) *Ten Men Dead: The Story of the 1981 Hunger Strike.* London: Grafton.

Bordo, S. (1993) *Unbearable Weight: Feminist, Western Culture and the Body.* London: University of California Press.

Bosworth, M. (1998) 'Resisting identities: the paradox of femininity.' Unpublished paper, New York, NY: Fordham University at Lincoln.

Bosworth, M. (1999) *Engendering Resistance: Agency and Power in Women's Prisons.* Dartmouth: Ashgate.

Bottoms, A.E. (1983) 'Neglected features of contemporary penal systems', in D. Garland and P. Young (eds) *The Power to Punish: Contemporary Penality and Social Analysis.* London: Heinemann, pp. 166–202.

Bottoms, A.E. and Sparks, J.R. (1995) 'Legitimacy and order in prisons', *British Journal of Sociology*, 46: 45–62.

Bowker, L.H. (1977) *Prisoner Subcultures.* Massachusetts: Lexington Books.

Boyle, K., Hadden, T. and Hillyard, P. (1980) *Ten Years on in Northern Ireland: The Legal Control of Political Violence.* London: Cobden Trust.

Brewer, J.D. and Magee, K. (1991) *Inside the RUC.* Oxford: Clarendon Press.

British/Irish Rights Watch and Committee on the Administration of Justice and Irish Commission for Prisoners Overseas (1997) *Report to the European Committee for the Prevention of Torture and Inhuman or Degrading Treatment or Punishment: The Situation of Irish Republican Prisoners in the United Kingdom.* London: British/Irish Rights Watch.

Brown, M. (2002) 'The politics of penal excess and the echo of colonial penality', *Punishment and Society*, 4: 403–23.

Brown, W. (1995) *States of Injury: Power and Freedom in Late Modernity.* New York, NY: Princeton University Press.

Brownmiller, S. (1974) *Against Our Will: Men, Women and Rape.* London: Secker & Warburg.

de Brun, B. (1988) 'Women and imperialism in Ireland', *Women's Studies International Forum*, 2: 323–8.

Buckley, S. and Lonergan, P. (1984) 'Women and the troubles', in Y. Alexander and A. O'Day (eds) *Terrorism in Ireland.* London: Croom Helm, pp. 75–87.

Burton, J. (1979) *Deviance, Terrorism and War.* Oxford: Martin Robertson.

Cain, M. (1994) 'The symbol traders', in M. Cain and C.B. Harrington (eds) *Lawyers in a Postmodern World.* Buckingham: Open University Press, pp. 15-48.

Cameron, Lord (1969) *Disturbances in Northern Ireland* (Cmnd 532). Belfast: HMSO.

Campbell, B., McKeown, L. and O'Hagan, F. (eds) (1994) *Nor Meekly Serve My Time: The H-block Struggle, 1976–1981.* Belfast: Beyond the Pale.

Carlen, P. (1983) *Women's Imprisonment: A Study in Social Control.* London: Routledge & Kegan Paul.

Carlen, P. (1988) *Women, Crime and Poverty.* Milton Keynes: Open University Press.

Carlen, P. (1994) 'Why study women's imprisonment? Or anyone else's?', *British Journal of Criminology*, 34: 131–9.

Carlen, P. (1998) *Sledgehammer: Women's Imprisonment at the Millennium.* Basingstoke: Macmillan.

Carlen, P. (2002a) 'Carceral clawback: the case of women's imprisonment in Canada', *Punishment and Society*, 4: 115–21.

Carlen, P. (2002b) 'Controlling measures: the repackaging of common-sense opposition to women's imprisonment in England and Canada', *Criminal Justice*, 2: 155–72.

Carlen, P. and Tchaikovsky, C. (1996) 'Women's imprisonment in England and Wales at the end of the twentieth century: legitimacy, realities and utopias', in R. Matthews (ed) *Prisons 2000.* London: Macmillan, pp. 201–218.

Carlen, P., Hicks, J., O'Dwyer, J., Christina, D. and Tchaikovsky, C. (1985) *Criminal Women.* Cambridge: Polity Press.

Carroll, B. and Welling Hall, B. (1993) 'Feminist perspectives on women and the use of force', in M.R. Stevenson and R.H. Howes (eds) *Women and the Use of Military Force.* London: Lynne Rienner, pp. 11–22.

Carroll, W.K. (ed.) (1992) *Organizing Dissent: Contemporary Social Movements in Theory and Practice.* Canada: Garamond Press.

Christian Response to Strip Searching (CRSS) (1986) *A Christian Response to Evaluate the Practice of Strip-searching in Northern Ireland Prisons.* Belfast: CRSS.

Christian Response to Strip Searching (CRSS) (1993) *The General Strip Search in Maghaberry Women's Prison, Monday March 2, 1992.* Belfast: CRSS.

Churchill, W. and Vander Wall, J.J. (1992) *Cages of Steel – the Politics of Imprisonment in the United States.* Washington, DC: Maisonneuve Press.

Clarke, S. (1995) *No Faith in the System.* Dublin: Mercier.

Clemmer, D. (1965) *The Prison Community.* New York, NY: Rinehart.

Cohen, S. (1985) *Visions of Social Control.* Cambridge: Polity Press.

Cohen, S. and Taylor, L. (1981) *Psychological Survival: The Experience of Long-term Imprisonment* (1st edn. 1972). Harmondsworth: Penguin Books.

Collins, P.H. (1990) *Black Feminist Thought: Knowledge, Consciousness and the Politics of Empowerment.* Boston, MA: Unwin Hyman.

Colville, M. (1992) *Report of an Inquiry into the Operational Policy in Belfast Prison for the Management of Paramilitary Prisoners from Opposing Factions* (Cmnd 1860). London: HMSO.

Committee on the Administration of Justice (CAJ) (1987) *Strip Searching and the Irish Community and Strip Searching in Prison*: *Briefing Paper.* Belfast: CAJ.

Connolly, C. (1994) 'Ourselves alone: Clár na mBan conference report', *Feminist Review*, 50: 118–26.

Coogan, T.P. (1980) *On the Blanket: The H-Block Story*. Dublin: Ward River Press.

Cooper, D. (1995) *Power in Struggle*. Buckingham: Open University Press.

Cooper, H. H. A. (1979) 'Woman as terrorist', in F. Adler and R. Simon (eds) *The Criminality of Deviant Women*. Boston, MA: Houghton Mifflin, pp. 150–7.

Corcoran, M.S. (1999) 'Mapping carceral space: territorialisation, resistance and control in Northern Ireland's women's prisons', in S. Brewster, *et al.* (eds) *Ireland in Proximity: History, Gender, Space*. London: Routledge, pp. 157–72.

Corcoran, M.S. (2005) 'Researching women political prisoners in Northern Ireland: ethnographic problems and negotiations', in T. Skinner *et al.* (eds) *Researching Gender Violence: Feminist Methodology in Action*. Cullompton: Willan Publishing, pp. 125–45.

Corrado, R.R. (1979) 'Ethnic and student terrorism in western Europe', in M. Stohl (ed.) *The Politics of Terrorism*. New York, NY: Marcel Dekker, pp. 191–257.

Coulter, C. (1991) *Web of Punishment: An Investigation*. Dublin: Attic Press.

Crawford, C. (1999) *Defenders or Criminals? Loyalist Prisoners and Criminalisation*. Belfast: Blackstaff Press.

Crawley, H. (2000) 'Engendering the State in refugee women's claims for asylum', in S. Jacobs *et al.* (eds) *States of Conflict: Gender, Violence and Resistance*. London: Zed Books, pp. 87–104.

Daly, K. and Maher, L. (eds) (1998) *Criminology at the Crossroads: Feminist Readings in Crime and Justice*. Oxford: Oxford University Press.

Darby, J. (ed.) (1983) *Northern Ireland: The Background to the Conflict*. New York, NY: Appletree/Syracuse University Press.

D'arcy, M. (1981) *Tell Them Everything*. London: Pluto.

Davis, A. (1971) *If They Come in the Morning*. London: Orbach & Chambers.

Davis, A. (1988) *Angela Davis: An Autobiography*. (1st edn. 1976). London: Women's Press.

Dean, M. (1996) 'Putting the technological into government', *History of the Human Sciences*, 9: 47–68.

Diplock, Lord (1972) *Report of the Commission to Consider Legal Procedures to Deal with Terrorist Activities in Northern Ireland* (Cmnd 5185). London: HMSO.

Dobash, R.E., Dobash, R.P. and Gutteridge, S. (1986) *The Imprisonment of Women*. Oxford: Blackwell.

Dodge, L.M. (1999) 'One female prisoner is of more trouble than twenty males: women convicts in Illinois prisons, 1835–1896', *Journal of Social History*, 32: 907–30.

Douglas, M. (1984) *Purity and Danger*. New York, NY: Ark.

Drake, C.J.M. (1996) 'The phenomenon of conservative terrorism', *Terrorism and Political Violence*, 8: 29–46.

Duff, R.A. and Garland, D. (eds) (1994) *A Reader on Punishment*. Oxford: Oxford University Press.

Edgerton, L. (1986) 'Public protest, domestic acquiescence: women in Northern Ireland', in R. Ridd and Callaway (eds) *Caught up in Conflict: Women's Responses to Political Strife*. London: Macmillan, pp. 61–83.

Elshtain, J.B. (1995) *Women and War*. Chicago, IL: University of Chicago Press.

Enloe, C. (1983) 'Women in liberation armies', in C. Enloe (ed) *Does Khaki Become You? The Militarisation of Women's Lives*. London: Pluto, pp. 160–9.

Evelegh, R. (1978) *Peace Keeping in a Democratic Society: The Lessons of Northern Ireland*. London: C. Hurst.

Fairweather, E., MacDonough, R. and McFadyean, M. (1984) *Only the Rivers Run Free. Northern Ireland: The Women's War*. London: Pluto.

Faith, K. (1993) *Unruly Women: The Politics of Confinement and Resistance*. Toronto: Press Gang.

Farrell, M. (1980) *Northern Ireland: The Orange State*. London: Pluto.

Farrell, M. (1983) *Arming the Protestants*. London: Pluto.

Farrell, M. (1986) *The Apparatus of Repression. Field Day Pamphlet* 11. Derry: Field Day Publications.

Faul, D. (1978) *Women in Jail in Northern Ireland*. Dungannon: D. Faul.

Faul, D. (1983) *The Stripping Naked of Women Prisoners in Armagh Prison, 1982–1983*. Armagh: D. Faul.

Faul, D. and Murray, R. (1975) *The RUC: The Black and Blue Book*. Dungannon: D. Faul.

Faul, D. and Murray, R (1978a) *H Blocks British Jails for Irish Political Prisoners*. Dungannon: D. Faul.

Faul, D. and Murray, R. (1978b) *The Castlereagh File: Allegations of RUC Brutality 1976–1977*. Dungannon: D. Faul.

Faul, D., Murray, R. and Brady, B.J. (1975) *Internment 1971–1975*. Dungannon: D. Faul.

Feeley, M. and Simon, J. (1994) 'Actuarial justice: the emerging new criminal law', in D. Nelken (ed) *The Futures of Criminology*. London: Sage, pp. 173–201.

Feldman, A. (1991) *Formations of Violence: The Narrative of the Body and Political Terror in Northern Ireland*. Chicago, IL: University of Chicago Press.

Foucault, M. (1979) 'On governmentality', *Ideology and Consciousness*, 6: 5–22.

Foucault, M. (1980) *Power/Knowledge: Selected Interviews and Other Writings 1972-1977*, (ed. C. Gordan) Brighton: Harvester Wheatsheaf.

Foucault, M. (1990) *The History of Sexuality. Vol. 1. An Introduction*. Harmondsworth: Penguin Books.

Foucault, M. (1991) *Discipline and Punish: The Birth of the Prison*. Harmondsworth: Penguin Books.

Franco, J. (1992) 'Gender, death and resistance: facing the ethical vacuum' in J.E. Corradi *et al.* (eds) *Fear at the Edge: State Terror and Resistance in Latin America*. Oxford: University of California Press, pp. 104–18.

Fraser, N. (1989) *Unruly Practices: Power, Discourse and Gender in Contemporary Social Theory*. Minneapolis, MN: University of Minnesota Press.

Freire, P. (1972) *Pedagogy of the Oppressed*. Harmondsworth: Penguin Books.

Gardiner, Lord (1975) *Report of a Committee to Consider, in the Context of Civil Liberties and Human Rights, Measures to Deal with Terrorism in Northern Ireland* (Cmnd 5847). London: HMSO.

Garland, D. (1996) 'The limits of the sovereign state: strategies of crime control in contemporary society', *British Journal of Criminology*, 36: 445–71.

Garland, D. (1997) 'Governmentality and the problem of crime: Foucault, criminology, sociology', *Theoretical Criminology*, 1: 173–214.

Garland, D. (2001) *The Culture of Control: Crime and Social Order in Contemporary Society*. Oxford: Oxford University Press.

Genders, E. and Player, E. (1988) 'Women lifers: assessing the experience' in A. Morris and C.Wilkinson (eds) *Women and the Penal System. 19th Cropwood Conference Series*. Cambridge: University of Cambridge Press.

Georges-Abeyie, D.E. (1983) 'Women as terrorists', in L.Z. Freedman and Y. Alexander (eds) *Perspectives on Terrorism*. Delaware: Scholarly Resources, pp. 71–84.

Giallombardo, R. (1966) *Society of Women: A Study of a Women's Prison*. London: Wiley.

di Giovanni, C. (ed.) (1990) *Light from behind the Bars*. Slough: St Paul Publications.

Goffman, E. (1991) *Asylums* (1st edn. 1961). Harmondsworth: Penguin Books.

Gormally, B. and McEvoy, K. (1995) 'Politics and prison management: the Northern Ireland experience', in L. Noaks *et al.* (eds) *Contemporary Issues in Criminology*. Cardiff: University of Wales Press, pp. 276–313.

Gormally, B., McEvoy, K. and Wall, D. (1993) 'Criminal Justice in a divided society: Northern Ireland prisons', in M. Tonry (ed.) *Crime and Justice: A Review of Research. Vol. 17*. Chicago, IL: University of Chicago Press, pp. 51–135.

Gramsci, A. (1971) *Selection from the Prison Notebooks* (ed. Q. Hoare trans. G. Nowell Smith). New York, NY: International Publishers.

Hahn-Rafter, N. and Gibson, M. (eds) (2004) *Criminal Woman, the Prostitute and the Normal Woman: Cesare Lombroso and Guglielmo Ferrero*. Durham, NY: Duke University Press.

Hannah-Moffat, K. (2000) 'Empower: neo-liberal governance in Canadian women's prisons', *British Journal of Criminology*, 40: 510–31.

Hannah-Moffat, K. (2001) *Punishment in Disguise: Penal Governance and Federal Imprisonment of Women in Canada*. Toronto: Toronto University Press.

Heffernan, E. (1972) *Making it in Prisons*. New York, NY: Wiley.

Heidensohn, F. (1985) *Women and Crime*. Basingstoke: Macmillan.

Hennessey, J. (1984) *Report of an Inquiry by HM Chief Inspector of Prisons into the Security Arrangements at HM Prison, Maze* (Cmnd 203). London: HMSO.

Her Majesty's Chief Inspector of Prisons and the Chief Inspector of Criminal Justice in Northern Ireland (2004) *Imprisonment of Women in Northern Ireland: Ash House, Hydebank Wood Prison. Report on an Unannounced Inspection, 28–30 November*. Belfast.

Her Majesty's Chief Inspectorate of Prisons (2002) *Report on a Full Announced Inspection of HM Prison Maghaberry, 13–17 May*. London: HMSO.

Her Majesty's Inspectorate of Prisons (2004) *HM Prison Durham (Females): Report on an Unannounced Inspection, 5–9 January.* London: HMIP.

Hillyard, P. (1978) 'Police and penal services', in J. Darby and A. Williamson (eds) *Violence and the Social Services in Northern Ireland.* London: Heinemann, pp. 117–39.

Hillyard, P. (1983) 'Law and order', in J. Darby (ed.) *Northern Ireland: The Background to the Conflict.* New York, NY: Appletree/Syracuse University Press, pp. 32–60.

Hillyard, P. (1987) 'The normalisation of special powers from Northern Ireland to Britain', in P. Scraton (ed.) *Law, Order and the Authoritarian State.* Milton Keynes: Open University Press, pp. 279–312.

Hirst, J. (1995) 'The Australia experience: the convict colony', in N. Morris and D.J. Rothman (eds) *The Oxford History of the Prison.* Oxford: Oxford University Press, pp. 235–65.

Hogan, G. and Walker, C. (1989) *Political Violence and the Law in Ireland.* Manchester: Manchester University Press.

Home Office (1995) *Statistics of Offences against Prison Discipline and Punishments in England and Wales* (Cmnd 3316). London: HMSO.

Home Office (1979) *Inquiry into the United Kingdom Prison Service: Evidence of the Home Office, the Scottish Home and Health Department and the Northern Ireland Office, Volume One*, London: HMSO.

Howard League for Penal Reform (1999) *Life in the Shadows: Women Lifers.* London: Howard League.

Howe, A. (1994) *Punish and Critique: Towards a Feminist Analysis of Penality.* London: Routledge.

Howes, R.H. and Stevenson, M.R. (eds) (1993) *Women and the Use of Military Force.* Boulder, CO: Lynne Rienner.

Hoy, S. (1996) *Chasing Dirt: The American Pursuit of Cleanliness.* Oxford: Oxford University Press.

Hughes, W.J. (1992) 'The Northern Ireland troubles: long-term prisoners and their children', in R. Shaw (ed.) *Prisoners' Children: What Are the Issues?* London: Routledge, pp. 147–60.

Ignatieff, M. (1978) *A Just Measure of Pain: The Penitentiary in the Industrial Revolution 1750–1850.* Basingstoke: Macmillan.

Irish Council of Churches (ICC) and Irish Commission for Justice and Peace (ICJP) (1990) *Study of the Northern Ireland Prison System.* Dublin and Belfast: ICC/ICJP.

Irish Information Partnership (IIP) (1985) *Strip Searches at Her Majesty's Prison for Women, Armagh, Northern Ireland.* Gondregnies: Irish Information Partnership.

Jackson, G. (1970) *Soledad Brother: The Prison Letters of George Jackson.* Harmondsworth: Penguin Books.

Jacobs, S., Jacobson, R. and Marchbank, J. (2000) *States of Conflict: Gender, Violence and Resistance.* London: Zed Books.

Jamieson, R. (1998) 'Towards a criminology of war in Europe', in V. Ruggiero, *et al.* (eds) *The New European Criminology: Crime and Social Order in Europe.* London: Routledge, pp. 480–506.

Jamieson, R. and Grounds, A. (2002) *No Sense of an Ending: The Effects of Long-term Imprisonment amongst Republican Prisoners and the Families.* Monaghan: EXPAC.

Jessop, B. (1990) *State Theory: Putting the Capitalist State Back in its Place.* Cambridge: Polity Press.

Jones, A. (1991) *Women Who Kill.* London: Victor Gollancz.

Kelly, L. (1988) *Surviving Sexual Violence.* Cambridge: Polity Press.

Kennally, D. and Preston, E. (1971) *Belfast, August 1971: A Case to be Answered.* London: Independent Labour Party.

Kitson, F. (1977) *Bunch of Five.* London: Faber & Faber.

Klein, D. (1979) 'The etiology of female crime', in F. Adler and R. Simon (eds) *The Criminality of Deviant Women.* Boston, MA: Houghton Mifflin, pp. 58–81.

Krause, K. and Williams, M.C. (1997) *Critical Security Studies: Concepts and Cases.* London: UCL Press.

Learmont, J. (1995) *Review of Prison Service Security in England and Wales and the Escape from Parkhurst Prison on Tuesday, January 3, 1995* (Cmnd 3020). London: HMSO.

Lee, J.J. (1993) *Ireland 1912–1985: Politics and Society.* Cambridge: Cambridge University Press.

Leibling, A. (1992) *Suicides in Prison.* London: Routledge.

Lester, A. and Taylor, P. (1989) *'H' Wing, HM Prison, Durham.* London: Women in Prison.

Liddington, J. (1989) *The Long Road to Greenham: Feminism and Anti-militarism in Britain since 1820.* London: Virago.

Livingstone, S. and Owen, T. (1993) *Prison Law.* Oxford: Clarendon Press.

Lloyd, A. (1995) *Doubly Deviant, Doubly Damned: Society's Treatment of Violent Women.* Harmondsworth: Penguin Books.

Lombroso, C. and Ferrero, W. (1895) *The Female Offender* (1st English edn). London: T. Fisher Unwin.

Lombroso-Ferrero, G. (1972) *Criminal Man according to the Classification of Cesare Lombroso, with an Introduction by Cesare Lombroso.* (1st edn. 1911). New Jersey: Montclair.

London Strategic Policy Unit (1988) *Working Together to End Strip Searching: Report of a Conference, December 5 1987.* London: London Strategic Policy Unit.

Lord, E. (1995) 'A prison superintendent's perspective on women in prison', *Prison Journal,* 75: 257–69.

Loughran, C. (1983) 'Armagh and feminist strategy', in T. Lovell (ed.) *British Feminist Thought.* London: Blackwell, pp. 170–83.

Lowry, D. (1976) 'Internment in Northern Ireland', *Toledo Law Review*, 8: 169–208.

Ludwig, G.A. (1981) 'Hunger-striking: freedom of choice or the State's best interest?', *New England Journal of Criminal and Civil Confinement*, 10: 169–92.

MacDonald, E. (1991) *Shoot the Women First*. London: Arrow.

MacKinnon, C.A. (1989) *Towards a Feminist Theory of the State*. Cambridge, MA: Harvard University Press.

MacStiofáin, S. (1975) *Memoirs of a Revolutionary*. Edinburgh: R. & R. Clarke.

Mandaraka-Sheppard, A. (1986) *The Dynamics of Aggression in Women's Prisons in England*. Aldershot: Gower.

Marquart, J.W. (1986) 'Prison guards and the use of physical coercion as a mechanism of prisoner control', *Criminology*, 24: 347–65.

Martin, E. (1989) *The Woman in the Body: A Cultural Analysis of Reproduction*. Milton Keynes: Open University Press.

Mathiesen, T. (1965) *The Defences of the Weak: A Sociological Study of a Norwegian Correctional Institution*. London: Tavistock.

Mathiesen, T. (1997) 'The viewer society: Michel Foucault's "panopticon" revisited', *Theoretical Criminology*, 1: 215–34.

May, Lord Justice (1979) *Report of the Committee of Inquiry into the United Kingdom Prison Services* (Cmnd 7673). London: HMSO.

McCafferty, N. (1981) *The Armagh Women*. Dublin: Co-op Books.

McConville, S. (2003) *Irish Political Prisoners, 1848–1922: Theatres of War*. London: Routledge.

McEvoy, K. (2001) *Paramilitary Imprisonment in Northern Ireland: Resistance, Management and Release*. Oxford: Oxford University Press.

McGuffin, J. (1973) *Internment*. Tralee: Anvil.

McKeown, L. (1996) 'Jailtacht/Gaeltacht', *Cascando: The National Student Literary Magazine. Irish Double Issue*, 5/6: 43–9.

McKeown, L. (1998) ' "Unrepentant Fenian bastards": the social construction of an Irish Republican prison community.' PhD dissertation, Queen's University Belfast.

McKeown, L. (2001) *Out of Time: Irish Republican Prisoners, Long Kesh, 1972–2000*. Belfast: Beyond the Pale Press.

McKittrick, D., Kelters, S., Feeney, B. and Thornton, C. (1999) *Lost Lives: The Stories of the Men, Women and Children who Died as a Result of the Northern Ireland Troubles*. London: Mainstream.

McNay, L. (1992) *Foucault and Feminism*. Cambridge: Polity Press.

Miller, P. and Rose, N. (1990) 'Governing economic life', *Economy and Society*, 19: 1–31.

Moen, D. (1999) 'The criminalisation of political prisoners in Northern Ireland.' Unpublished paper presented at the Annual conference of the British Society of Criminology, 13–16 July, Liverpool.

Murray, D. (1975) *Report on a Local Inquiry Held to Consider a Proposal by the Department of Finance to Acquire Compulsorily under the above order Certain Land at Maghaberry, County Antrim for the Purpose of Providing Prison*

Accommodation and Facilities on that Land. Land Acquisition and Compensation (Northern Ireland) Order 1973. Belfast: HMSO.

Narey, M. (1998) *Report of an Inquiry into the Escape of a Prisoner from HMP Maze on the 10th of December, 1997, and the Shooting of a Prisoner on 27th December, 1997* (Cmnd 658). London: HMSO.

National Council for Civil Liberties (NCCL) (1986) *Strip Searching: An Inquiry into the Strip Searching of Women Remand Prisoners at Armagh Prison between 1982 and 1985.* London: NCCL.

National Labour Women's Committee (1985) *Stop the Strip Searching in Armagh: Report of a Delegation to Armagh, 1984.* London: Labour Party.

Newton, C. (1994) 'Gender theory and prison sociology: using theories of masculinities to interpret the sociology of prisons for men', *Howard Journal*, 33: 193–202.

Northern Ireland Human Rights Commission (2004) *Report on the Transfer of Women from Mourne House Unit, Maghaberry Prison to Hydebank Wood Young Offenders Centre.* Belfast.

Northern Ireland Office (1981) *Day to Day Life in Northern Ireland Prisons.* Belfast: HMSO.

Northern Ireland Office (1982) *The Prison Rules (Northern Ireland).* Belfast: HMSO.

Northern Ireland Office (1985) *Armagh Prison Strip Searching: The Facts.* Belfast: HMSO.

Northern Ireland Prison Service (1977) *Report on the Administration of the Prison Service for 1972–1976* (Cmnd 40). Belfast: HMSO.

Northern Ireland Prison Service (1978) *Report on the Administration of the Prison Service for 1977* (Cmnd 9). Belfast: HMSO.

Northern Ireland Prison Service (1979) *Report on the Administration of the Prison Service for 1978* (Cmnd 250). Belfast: HMSO.

Northern Ireland Prison Service (1980) *Report on the Administration of the Prison Service for 1979* (Cmnd 800). Belfast: HMSO.

Northern Ireland Prison Service (1981) *Report on the Administration of the Prison Service for 1980* (Cmnd 6). Belfast: HMSO.

Northern Ireland Prison Service (1982) *Report on the Administration of the Prison Service for 1981* (Cmnd 5). Belfast: HMSO.

Northern Ireland Prison Service (1983) *Report on the Administration of the Prison Service for 1982* (Cmnd 63). Belfast: HMSO.

Northern Ireland Prison Service (1984) *Report on the Administration of the Prison Service for 1983* (Cmnd 608). Belfast: HMSO.

Northern Ireland Prison Service (1985) *Report on the Administration of the Prison Service for 1984* (Cmnd 3). Belfast: HMSO.

Northern Ireland Prison Service (1987) *Annual Report on the Work of the Prison Service for 1986/87* (Cmnd 125). Belfast: HMSO.

Northern Ireland Prison Service (1988) *Annual Report on the Work of the Prison Service for 1987/88* (Cmnd 42). Belfast: HMSO.

Northern Ireland Prison Service (1989) *Annual Report on the Work of the Prison Service for 1988/89* (Cmnd 1). Belfast: HMSO.

Northern Ireland Prison Service (1990) *Annual Report of the Prison Service for 1989/90* (Cmnd 2). Belfast: HMSO.

Northern Ireland Prison Service (1991a) *Serving the Community: The Northern Ireland Prison Service in the 1990s.* Belfast: HMSO.

Northern Ireland Prison Service (1991b) *Annual Report on the Work of the Prison Service for 1990/91* (Cmnd 46). Belfast: HMSO.

Northern Ireland Prison Service (1992) *Annual Report for 1992* (Cmnd 331). Belfast: HMSO.

Northern Ireland Prison Service (1993) *Annual Report for 1992/93* (Cmnd 29). Belfast: HMSO.

Northern Ireland Prison Service (1995) *Annual Report for 1994/95* (Cmnd 65). Belfast: HMSO.

Northern Ireland Prison Service (1996) *Annual Report for 1995/96* (Cmnd 536). Belfast: HMSO.

Northern Ireland Prison Service (1998) *Annual Report for 1997/98* (Cmnd 999). Belfast: HMSO.

O'Brien, B. (1995) *The Long War: The IRA and Sinn Fein from Armed Struggle to Peace Talks.* Dublin: O'Brien Press.

O'Dowd, L., Rolston, B. and Tomlinson, M. (1980) *Northern Ireland between Civil Rights and Civil War.* London: CSE Books.

O'Dwyer, E. (1986a) *Letter from HMP Durham, England. 25 September 1986* (addressee unknown).

O'Dwyer, E. (1986b) *Letter from HMP Durham, England. 10 October 1986* (addressee unknown).

O'Dwyer, E. (1986c) *Letter from HMP Durham, England. 18 August 1986* (addressee unknown).

Oliverio, A. (1997) 'The state of injustice: the politics of terrorism and the production of order', *International Journal of Comparative Sociology*, 68: 48–63.

O'Malley, P. (1990) *Biting at the Grave: The Irish Hunger Strikes and the Politics of Despair.* Belfast: Blackstaff Press.

Opsahl, T., O'Malley, P., Gallagher, E., Elliott, M., Faulkner, L., Lister R. and Gallagher, E. (1993) *A Citizen's Inquiry: The Opsahl Report on Northern Ireland.* Dublin: The Lilliput Press/Initiative 1992.

Pateman, C. (1988) *The Sexual Contract.* Cambridge: Polity Press.

Pateman, C. (1989) *The Disorder of Women.* Cambridge: Polity Press.

Phoenix, J. (1998) *Making Sense of Prostitution.* London: Macmillan.

Pickering, S. (2001) 'Undermining the sanitised account: violence and emotionality in the field in Northern Ireland', *British Journal of Criminology*, 41: 485–501.

Pollak, O. (1979) 'The masked character of female crime', in F. Adler and R. Simon (eds) *The Criminality of Deviant Women.* Boston, MA: Houghton Mifflin, pp. 37–44.

Pollock, J. (1978) 'Early theories of female criminality', in L.H. Bowker (ed.) *Women, Crime and the Criminal Justice System.* Lexington, MA: Lexington Books, pp. 25–50.

Porter, R. (1990) *Mind-forg'd Manacles: A History of Madness in England from the Restoration to the Regency.* London: Penguin Books.

Poulantzas, N. (1980) *State, Power, Socialism.* London: Verso.

Prison Reform Trust (2000) *Justice for Women: The Need for Reform.* London: Prison Reform Trust.

PROP (1976) *Don't Mark his Face: Account of the Hull Prison Riot, 1976, by the Prisoners Themselves.* London: National Prisoners' Movement.

Quinn, P.M. (1995) '"Reflexivity run riot": the survival of the prison catch-all', *Howard Journal,* 34: 354–62.

Radzinowicz, L. and Hood, R. (1979) 'The status of political prisoner in England: the struggle for recognition' [*sic*], *Virginia Law Review,* 65: 1421–81.

Ramazanoglu, C. (ed.) (1993) *Up against Foucault.* London: Routledge.

Rees, M. (1985) *Northern Ireland: A Personal Perspective.* London: Methuen.

Rock, P. (1996) *Reconstructing a Women's Prison: The Holloway Redevelopment Project, 1968–1988.* Oxford: Clarendon Press.

Rolston, B. and Tomlinson, M. (1988) ' "The challenge within": prisons and propaganda in Northern Ireland', in M. Tomlinson *et al.* (eds) *Whose Law and Order?* Belfast: Sociological Association of Ireland, pp. 167–91.

Roseneil, S. (1995) *Disarming Patriarchy: Feminism and Political Action at Greenham.* Milton Keynes: Open University Press.

Russell, D. (1995) *Women, Madness and Medicine.* Cambridge: Polity Press.

Sawicki, J. (1991) *Disciplining Foucault: Feminism, Power and the Body.* London: Routledge.

Schafer, S. (1974) *The Political Criminal: The Problem of Morality and Crime.* New York, NY: Free Press/Macmillan.

Schmid, A.P. and Jongman, J.J. (1988) *Political Terrorism: A New Guide to Actors, Authors, Concepts, Data Bases, Theories and Literature.* Amsterdam: North Holland Publishing.

Scraton, P., Sim, J. and Skidmore, P. (1991) *Prisons under Protest.* Milton Keynes: Open University Press.

Seale, B. (1991) *Seize the Time: The Story of the Black Panther Party and Huey P. Newton* (1st edn 1970). Baltimore, MD: Black Classic Press.

Seifert, R. (1994) 'War and rape: a preliminary analysis', in A. Stiglmayer (ed) *Mass Rape: The War against Women in Bosnia-Herzegovina.* London: University of Nebraska Press, pp. 54–72.

Shannon, E. (1989) *I am of Ireland: Women of the North Speak Out.* Boston, MA: Little, Brown & Co.

Shaw, M. (1992) 'Issues of power and control: women in prison and their defenders', *British Journal of Criminology,* 32: 438–52.

Shaw, M. (1995) 'Conceptualising violence by women', in R.E. Dobash *et al.* (eds) *Gender and Crime.* Cardiff: University of Wales Press, pp. 115–31.

Shaw, M. (2000) 'Women, violence and disorder in prisons. In an ideal prison?', in K. Hannah-Moffat and M. Shaw (eds.) *Critical Essays on Women's Imprisonment in Canada.* Halifax, NS: Fernwood Publishing, pp. 61–70.

Shilling, C. (1993) *The Body and Social Theory.* London: Sage.

Sim, J. (1990) *Medical Power in Prisons: The Prison Medical Service in England, 1774–1988.* Milton Keynes: Open University Press.

Sinn Féin Prisoner of War Department (SFPOW) (1993) *Memorandum on Discrimination against Women Prisoners in Mourne House, HMP Maghaberry.* Belfast: Sinn Féin.

Sinn Féin Women's Department (1981) *Women in the New Ireland.* Dublin: Sinn Féin.

Smart, C. (1989) *Feminism and the Power of Law.* London: Routledge.

Smart, C. (1992) 'The woman of legal discourse', *Social and Legal Studies*, 1: 29–44.

Smart, C. (1995) *Law, Crime and Sexuality: Essays in Feminism.* London: Sage.

Snider, L. (2002) 'Constituting the punishable woman: atavistic man incarcerates postmodern woman', *British Journal of Criminology*, 43: 354–78.

Sparks, R., Bottoms, A.E. and Hay, W. (1996) *Prisons and the Problem of Order.* Oxford: Clarendon.

Spjut, R.J. (1986) 'Internment and detention without trial in Northern Ireland 1971–1975: ministerial policy and practice', *Modern Law Review*, 49: 712–40.

Standing Advisory Commission on Human Rights (SACHRE) (1986) *Strip Searching of Women Prisoners.* Belfast: SACHRE.

Stanko, E.A. (1996) 'Safety talk: conceptualizing women's risk assessment as a "technology of the soul" ', *Theoretical Criminology*, 1: 479–99.

Stenson, K. (1998) 'Beyond histories of the present', *Economy and Society*, 27: 333–52.

Stevenson, J. (1996) *'We Wrecked the Place': Contemplating an End to the Northern Irish Troubles.* New York, NY: Free Press.

Stiglmayer, A. (ed.) (1994) *Mass Rape: The War against Women in Bosnia-Herzegovina.* London: University of Nebraska Press.

Sykes, G.M. (1958) *The Society of Captives: A Study of a Maximum Security Prison.* Princeton, NJ: Princeton University Press.

Task Force on Federally Sentenced Women (TFFSW) (1990) *Creating Choices: Report of the Task Force on Federally Sentenced Women.* Ottawa: Correctional Services Canada.

Taylor, P. (1997) *The IRA and Sinn Féin.* London: Bloomsbury.

Taylor, R. (1988) 'Social scientific research on the "Troubles" in Northern Ireland: the problem of objectivity', *Economic and Social Review*, 19: 123–45.

Theweleit, K. (1996) *Male Fantasies. Volume 1. Women, Floods, Bodies, History* (2nd edn). Cambridge: Polity Press.

Thompson, E.P. (1991) *Customs in Common.* London: Merlin Press.

Tomlinson, M. (1995) 'Imprisoned Ireland', in V. Ruggiero *et al.* (eds), *Western European Prison Systems: A Critical Anatomy*. London: Sage, pp. 194–227.

Urban, M. (1992) *Big Boys' Rules: The Secret Struggle against the IRA.* London: Faber & Faber.

United Campaign against Strip Searching (UCASS) (1989) *Strip-searching Personal Testimonials – An Enquiry in the Psychological Effects of Strip Searching.* London: ALA/UCASS.

Vetter, H.J. and Perlstein, G.R. (1991) *Perspectives on Terrorism.* Monterey, CA: Brooks/Cole Publishing.

Walker, S. and Worrall, A. (2000) 'Life as a woman: the gendered pains of indeterminate imprisonment', *Prison Service Journal*, 132: 27–36.

Walsh, D.P.J. (1983) *The Use and Abuse of Emergency Legislation in Northern Ireland.* London: Cobden Trust.

Ward, D.A., Jackson, M. and Ward, R.E. (1979) 'Crimes of violence by women', in F. Adler and R. Simon (eds) *The Criminality of Deviant Women.* Boston, MA: Houghton Mifflin, pp. 115–38.

Ward, D.A. and Kassebaum, G.E. (1966) *Women's Prison Sex and Social Structure.* London: Weidenfeld & Nicholson.

Ward, J. (1993) *Ambushed: My Story.* London: Vermilion.

Ward, M. (ed.) (1986) *A Difficult, Dangerous Honesty: Ten Years of Feminism in Northern Ireland – a Discussion.* Belfast.

Ward, R. (2002) 'Invisible women: the political roles of Unionist and Loyalist women in contemporary Northern Ireland', *Parliamentary Affairs*, 55: 167–78.

Widom, C.S. (1981) 'Perspectives of female criminality: a critical examination of assumptions', in A. Morris and L. Gelsthorpe (eds) *Women and Crime. Cropwood Conference Series.* Cambridge: University of Cambridge Press, pp. 33–48.

Wilkinson, P. (1977) *Terrorism and the Liberal State.* London: Macmillan.

Wilkinson, P. (2001) *Terrorism versus Democracy: The Liberal State Response.* London: Frank Cass.

Women against Imperialism (WAI) (1980) *Women Protest for Political Status in Armagh Gaol.* Belfast: WAI.

Woodcock, J. (1994) *The Escape from Whitemoor Prison on Friday, September 9, 1994* (Cmnd 2741). London: HMSO.

Woolf, Lord (1991) *Prison Disturbances, April 1990: Report of an Inquiry* Cmnd 1456). London: HMSO.

Worrall, A. (1995) *Offending Women: Female Lawbreakers and the Criminal Justice System* (2nd edn). London: Routledge.

Young, I.M. (1990) *Justice and the Politics of Difference.* Princeton, NJ: Princeton University Press.

Young, I.M. (1997) *Intersecting Voices: Dilemmas of Gender, Political Philosophy, and Policy.* Princeton, NJ: Princeton University Press.

Yuval Davis, A. (1998) 'Race and criminalisation: black Americans and the punishment industry', in J. James (ed.) *The Angela Y. Davis Reader.* Oxford: Blackwell, pp. 61–73.

Zedner, L. (1998) 'Wayward sisters: the prison for women', in N. Morris and D.J. Rothman (eds) *The Oxford History of the Prison.* Oxford: Oxford University Press, pp. 295–324.

Zimmer, L. (1997) 'How women reshape the prison guard role', in D. Dunn (ed.) *Workplace/Women's Place: An Anthology.* Los Angeles, CA: Roxbury, pp. 288–99.

Zwerman, G. (1988) 'Special incapacitation: the emergence of a new correctional facility for women political prisoners', *Social Justice*, 15: 31–47.

Newspapers/journals

An Phoblacht/Republican News (*APRN*)
Armagh Observer
[Belfast] *Newsletter*
Belfast Telegraph
Craigavon Times
Daily Express
Daily Mirror
Daily Telegraph
Derry Journal
Glor Gafa
Guardian
Iris Bheag
Iris: The Republican Magazine
Irish Independent
Irish News
Irish Press
Irish Times
Lurgan Examiner
Magill
Mail
Observer
Sunday Independent
Sunday News
Sunday Press
Sunday World
The Sunday Times
The Times

Index